# EUROPE

 **BY BIKE**

## 18 TOURS GEARED FOR DISCOVERY

Second Edition

Karen & Terry Whitehill

THE MOUNTAINEERS

5 4 3 2
5 4 3 2 1

Published by The Mountaineers

1011 SW Klickitat Way, Seattle, Washington 98134

Published simultaneously in Canada by Douglas & McIntyre, Ltd., 1615 Venables Street, Vancouver, B.C. V5L 2H1

Published simultaneously in Great Britain by Cordee, 3a DeMontfort Street, Leicester, England, LE1 7HD

Manufactured in the United States of America

Edited by Meredith Waring

Maps by Newell Cartographics
All photographs by the authors
Cover design by Watson Graphics
Book design by Bridget Culligan Design
Typesetting by The Mountaineers Books
Computer layout by Michelle Taverniti

Cover photograph: *The authors cycle the hillside lane above the Château Gaillard in northern France.*

Library of Congress Cataloging in Publication Data
Whitehill, Karen, 1957–
    Europe by bike : 18 tours geared for discovery / Karen & Terry Whitehill. -- 2nd ed.
        p.   cm.
    Includes index.
    ISBN 0-89886-317-1
    1. Bicycling touring--Europe--Guidebooks.  2. Europe--Guidebooks.
I. Whitehill, Terry, 1954–   . II. Title.
GV1046.E85W55   1993
796.6'4'094--dc20                                          92-39524
                                                              CIP

# CONTENTS

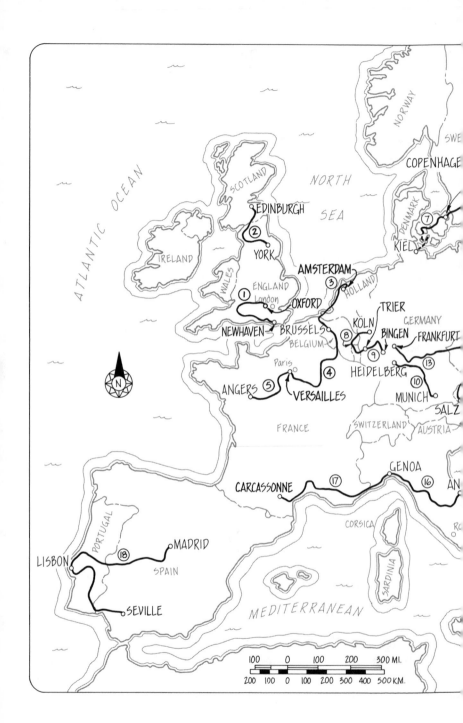

## MAP LEGEND

- - - - FERRY

——— TOUR

○ CITY or TOWN

— · — COUNTRY BOUNDARY

# PREFACE

In some ways, it seemed like we had never left. In some ways, it seemed like we had been gone forever. When we returned to Brussels International Airport in April, 1991, seven years after our first trip to Europe, we were still the same flight-weary American couple we were before, once again shoving a pair of overloaded bicycles out into a chilly Belgian afternoon. We were exhausted, frightened, nervous, and a little nauseated from too much airline food and too many hours without sleep. We were eager to see old friends, excited to visit favorite places, ready to retrace much of the 11,000-mile cycle journey that had kindled our love for bicycle touring in the first place. But something was very different on this April day. We were also parents.

Sierra was asleep in her bicycle trailer before we made it out of the airport lobby, her two-year-old body worn out from a journey that had begun 20 hours earlier in Portland, Oregon. The other travelers in the drafty hallway stared at her as we rolled past, smiling at her peaceful pose inside the bright neon of her "chariot." We paused as the automatic doors popped open and the cool April air poured in. *Do we really want to do this?* I wondered for what seemed like the millionth time. *Do we really want to drag this precious child thousands of miles over European roads?* Cold fear gripped my stomach.

Then I thought of "Grandma" Berta, awaiting our arrival at her home near Munich; of Georges, who had snapped our picture and greeted us with hugs as we came through Belgian customs; of Sylvie, a French woman who planned to cycle with us from southern Germany to Budapest in Hungary; of Tom and Jan in England and Heinz and Yetty in northern Germany, couples who had already scheduled their summer vacations around our visit. These were all dear friends we had met on our first two trips to Europe. These were all special people I wanted my daughter to know, too.

Yes, there was fear and weariness and doubt when we began our new adventure—there always is. But there was anticipation, too—anticipation of eight months together filled with quiet roads and starry ceilings, anticipation of thousands of miles lined with farmers' smiles and French bakeries, of castles and cathedrals, of vineyards and olive groves, and anticipation of the best of all—anticipation of all the new people who were about to become our friends.

## A NOTE ABOUT SAFETY

The authors have provided important tips on bicycle safety in the introduction to this book. In addition, they and the publisher have taken all reasonable measures to ensure the accuracy of the route descriptions contained herein. Even so, bicycling entails certain unavoidable risks, and routes may have changed after this book was written. Current political conditions also may add to the risks of travel in Europe in ways that this book cannot predict. For these reasons, the descriptions in this book are not guarantees that a particular trip will be safe for you or your party. When you take a trip, you assume responsibility for your own safety. Keeping informed about current road conditions, weather changes, and political developments, and utilizing your common sense, are keys to a safe, enjoyable tour.

# PART I

# EUROPE BY BIKE

*Bouncing down a cobblestone street in Beilstein, Germany*

# WHY BY BICYCLE?

We sat drinking coffee in our favorite travel bookstore a few days ago, poring over new European maps as we worked on the second edition of this book. Two women sat beside us at another table, planning their summer trip to Europe. We couldn't help but eavesdrop. The names were too familiar. "Let's allow at least two days in Amsterdam," one said. "OK, then we take the train to Paris," agreed the other. "We'll head for Rome from there ..." We glanced at each other and smiled, shook our heads slightly, and went back to our task.

Is this what European travel is all about—an endless succession of big cities and overnight trains? Two days in Amsterdam, a night on the train, three days in Paris, another train, finish in Rome, a train, a plane, and home. Is this Europe? Not if you choose to see Europe by bike. If you see Europe by bike, you see a French farmer shouting at his cows as they cross a mud-splattered lane in Normandy. You see an Italian olive picker gathering fruit in a beaten wicker basket. You see a gray-haired English couple sipping tea inside their auto, pulled off on the shoulder of the road. And you see a Greek fisherman mending his nets beside a sparkling harbor on the Peloponnese Peninsula.

Sure, you might still see Amsterdam and Paris if you travel by bicycle. Maybe you'll even see Rome. But in between the growling cities, you'll have time to breathe, you'll have time to listen, and you'll have time to mold your memories. And, perhaps the best of all, you'll have time to watch that French farmer as he works his cows, to call out *"buon giorno"* to that Italian olive picker as he moves his basket from tree to tree, to stop and share a "cuppa" with the English couple, and perhaps even to meet that Greek fisherman's family when he invites you home for dinner.

No, you won't "see it all" if you travel by bicycle (and despite what many train and bus travelers think, they don't either). Instead, you'll see the best. And you'll see it well.

# PLANNING YOUR TRIP

Begin with a good general book on European travel. *Let's Go: Europe* by Harvard Student Agencies and *Europe Through the Back Door* by Rick Steves are two of the books we studied, but there are a host of excellent choices available. These books will provide you with more of the information pertinent to general European travel than this book has room for. Just to get you started, though, here's a brief summary of the most important things to do.

**PASSPORTS AND VISAS.** If you don't have a passport for international travel, you should apply for one two or three months in advance of your departure date. At peak times, the application process can take several weeks. Go to a passport agency or U.S. post office. Once you get your passport, xerox the pages that show the date and place of issue, passport number, and your name. Leave one xerox copy at home with someone you can contact from Europe, and take one with you, stored separately from your passport. This will help ensure a quick replacement if the passport is lost or stolen.

You'll also need to apply in advance for visas to certain Eastern European countries. Check with the passport office or with your travel agent to be sure. None of the countries covered in this book require an advance visa at the present time.

**OTHER DOCUMENTS.** If you're a full-time student, be sure to check into obtaining an International Student Identification Card (ISIC) for your trip. This card could entitle you to major savings on your plane flight to Europe, as well as discounts on museum admissions, transportation, and many other things on which you'll be spending money once you're there. You'll need to show proof of nationality, student status, and age to get the card, and you'll be asked to provide a passport-type photo and a small fee. Check at a Council Travel office or write to the Council on International Educational Exchange, 205 East 42nd Street, New York, New York 10017.

Another document that will come in handy as you're traveling in Europe is an International Camping Carnet. If you're planning to camp as you cycle, this is a necessary document in Sweden and Denmark (although you can purchase camping passes in the respective countries, too). The International Camping Carnet is also good for discounts in some campgrounds in other European nations.

We found our carnet to be an excellent piece of identification to hand over at camping offices or hotels when we didn't want to part with our passports—for instance, when we needed them for banking or mail pickup during the day. (Tourist registration practices vary from country to country. Some managers will require that you turn over your passport until they can complete endless paperwork; others will settle for the carnet, and others will ask only for your first name.)

If you want to buy the carnet before you go, you'll need to purchase it through the National Campers and Hikers Association, 4804 Transit Road, Building No. 2, Depew, New York 14043. The cost of about $25 includes membership in the NCHA, with associated privileges (organization magazine and equipment discounts).

**HEALTH INSURANCE.** If you're taking a brief vacation from work or school to travel, you'll probably have health insurance already. But if you're giving up "normal" life (as we did on our first time over), with goodbyes to job, apartment, car, and related insurance policies, you may want to give serious thought to investing in special medical insurance for travelers.

Ask your travel agent about a policy that covers medical and hospi-

*Greeting the morning with a toothbrush in a Greek olive grove*

tal expenses, medical evacuations, repatriation of remains, baggage, and trip cancellation. He or she may be able to clue you in to a good deal.

Also, write to the International Association for Medical Assistance to Travelers, 417 Center Street, Lewiston, New York 14092, or 40 Regal Road, Guelph, Ontario, Canada N1K 1B5. A free membership (donations are eagerly accepted) in this nonprofit organization will provide you with the names of English-speaking physicians in more than 400 cities throughout the world. Associated doctors have agreed to serve English-speaking patients at fair prices.

**HOSTELS.** If you're thinking of using hostels as one of your accommodation options along the way, you'll need to get an International Youth Hostel Federation card. Nonmembers can stay, but must pay more, in hostels in Sweden and Yugoslavia. (Many Greek hostels don't require cards at all.) As a married couple, we did our best to avoid the segregated lodgings and noisy surroundings common to European hostels, but there were a few times when, stuck without a campground or an affordable hotel, we wished we'd had a card. Even if you plan to spend most of your time camping, many hostels allow members to set up tents outside.

Check your city telephone directory under "American Youth Hostels" to find a local office where you can purchase your card, or write to American Youth Hostels, P.O. Box 37613, Washington, D.C. 20013-7613, or the Canadian Hostelling Association, 1600 James Naismith Drive, #608, Gloucester, Ontario, Canada K1B 5N4. Ask for information and an application form. You may want to purchase a handbook with a complete listing of international hostels, too.

**RESEARCH.** Before you begin your trip, contact the national tourist offices of the European countries you're planning to visit. We wrote to each country's U.S. office, telling them of our trip and requesting free maps and general information. Any good city maps you can obtain in advance will be a blessing later, as there's nothing worse than riding into a large city without an adequate map. We also asked for specific information on cycling and camping. With the growing popularity of cycle tourism and the increase in long-distance cycle routes, many European countries have special publications available on the subject.

We've included tourist-office addresses with the tours in Part II. After you've written your letters and sent them off, it will be exciting to discover what the mailbox holds for you each day, and you can spend your evenings dreaming over brochures and maps and planning your sightseeing itinerary.

We used tourist-office literature, along with travel books checked out from the library, to help us make our choices about where to go and what to see, composing our cycling routes in a connect-the-dots game that was both challenging and exciting. The tours in Part II reflect our hours of research, and you'll find that each of the 18 routes includes a number of major tourist destinations.

Undoubtedly, you'll want to learn more about the history and specific features of the countries you'll visit than this book can tell you, so get to know the travel shelves of your local bookstore or library before you go. Every minute you spend familiarizing yourself with the places you'll be visiting will enhance your appreciation for and understanding of the things you see.

You may want to carry a favorite travel guide with you on your trip. We waited to buy our guides until we arrived in each new country, thus cutting down on weight and expense, but if you're visiting only one or two countries on your ride, it will be easier to make your purchases at home. We've noted the titles of pertinent guidebooks with each tour route in Part II.

**MAPS.** Rather than spend an incredible amount of money buying detailed maps of each country at home, we used the free maps provided by the tourist offices to do our rough figuring of routes, times, and distances, then bought 1:200,000 or 1:300,000 maps within each country when we arrived. Maps are considerably less expensive in Europe than in bookstores at home. If you want to take advantage of the increasing number of specialized cycling maps available for specific European regions, you will find yourself spending more, though.

Again, if you'll be covering only a small area on your trip, you may want to go ahead and buy your maps in advance. It will save you shopping time and "now where is that bookstore?" hassles. Be sure to take along a good map of the area you'll be arriving in. That way, you'll at least be able to get out of the airport and on your way without difficulty. Also, if you'll be crossing borders at some point in your journey, you'll want to plan ahead to be sure you have the proper map (or know where to find a town with a bookstore within a few kilometers).

**MAIL.** We completed one more task during our pretrip planning that brought us a day of excitement and joy every three weeks throughout our ride. As we worked out our cycling routes, we compiled a list of cities, addresses, and tentative dates, choosing the best times and places to pick up mail from home. We distributed this list to families and friends, instructing them how to address the letters correctly and warning them to mail at least two weeks in advance of our pickup dates (three weeks in Greece and Hungary—forget it in Czechoslovakia).

For pickup at post offices, use the following address style: WHITEHILL, Terry, c/o Poste Restante, Main Post Office, Brussels, Belgium. *Poste Restante* (general delivery) mail should be picked up at the central post office in cities with more than one post office. In some countries (France, for example) you will be asked to pay a slight per-letter fee.

For American Express pickups (free if you have their travelers' checks), use this address style: WHITEHILL, Terry, Client Letter Service, American Express, 2 Place Louise, Brussels, Belgium. Ask for a list of American Express office addresses when you buy your checks. Note: some offices are only affiliates and do not accept mail.

**CONDITIONING.** One more thing you should begin working on well in advance of your departure date is you! Too many cyclists spend the first weeks of their already short vacations wishing they had replacement sets of muscles and backup cardiovascular systems. Start working on your physical conditioning several months before your trip if you want to get the most enjoyment from those early weeks in the saddle.

If winter weather won't allow you to do much preparatory riding for a spring tour, any strenuous physical activity will help. Try jogging, racquetball, swimming, or rapid walking—anything that gets your heart rate up and your muscles pumping. Of course, cycling is the best way to toughen up the muscles you'll use the most. Try making friends with a stationary bicycle at the local gym. The fact that you haven't been "sitting around" before your trip will help you toughen up the beginning tourer's constant foe—the tender rear end.

If you haven't done cycle touring before, go out on at least one realistic trial run before your trip. If you'll be camping in Europe, it's a good idea to ride and camp at home first. If you're going to stay in hotels or hostels, then simply go out with loaded packs, preferably overnight, to get a feel for handling your suddenly heavy bicycle and to find out what a daily riding regimen is like.

Despite all your efforts to prepare, if this trip is your first, it'll feel like it. Expect to be nervous on the flight, terrified when you roll out of the airport, and absolutely exhausted for the first week. We had 15,000 miles of European roads already behind us when we made our most recent trek to Europe. Yet all that "experience" didn't eliminate our jitters *or* our aching muscles. It will take your body time to adjust—ease up and give your tired legs the rest they need. And instead of concentrating on mileage totals or accomplishing preset goals, simply let yourself enjoy.

# BUYING AND OUTFITTING A BIKE

If you'll be buying a new bicycle for your trip, and your knowledge of what to look for is limited, do what we did. Find two or three bike shops with a good selection of touring equipment, acquaint yourself with some knowledgeable employees, and begin asking questions. You'll probably get different opinions on which brand is best from every person you talk to, but if you keep listening, eventually you'll be able to make a good decision based on your specific needs and the information you've collected.

Another good way to find out more about touring bicycles, equipment, and maintenance is to read a general book on the sport of bicycle touring. *The Bicycle Touring Book* by Tim and Glenda Wilhelm and *Living on Two Wheels* by Dennis Coello are both good resources. And take advantage of cycling seminars at your local bicycle or outdoor equipment shop, if you have the opportunity.

Important things to look for in touring bikes are the following:

- A sturdy frame, strong enough to carry heavy loads.
- Correct fit for the rider. It's too big if you can't straddle the frame with both feet flat on the ground and have an inch of clearance between you and the bar.
- Superior-quality wheels and touring tires (we recommend "clinchers" with Kevlar reinforcing) to provide you with a stable and durable ride. Choose from $1\frac{1}{8}$-inch width to $1\frac{3}{8}$-inch width, depending on how much rough-road cycling you intend to do.
- A high-quality, dependable braking system. If you haven't toured before, you'll be surprised at how much longer it takes to stop a loaded bicycle than an unloaded one.
- Gearing that provides from 10 to 21 speeds, with the most important factor being the low-range capability. If you're new to touring, ask a bike shop employee to explain the complexities of gears and sprockets to you. Hills seem much steeper with a loaded bicycle, and you'll need the "granny" gears that a good touring bike offers more often than you might expect.

Mountain bikes have enjoyed increasing popularity in the past decade. There is no absolute rule that says you must use a touring bike for your trip. In fact, we used a "city-type" bicycle on our most recent European journey, and it performed well enough to pull a toddler and a trailer more than 6,000 miles. However, if you do choose to ride a mountain or "city" bike, be sure to use a street tire rather than a "knobby." And plan to work harder and cover less distance than you would on a special touring bike.

If you're like most people, price is an important factor when making your purchase, too. On our first trip, we went for middle-of-the-line touring bikes and equipped them with low-riding front racks and with rear racks. Because we knew we would be traveling together, we selected identical bikes (except for frame size) for ease of maintenance. Although one of those bicycles was "retired" and replaced by a city bike on our last outing, the other now has almost 20,000 miles on it—and it's still going!

"Extras" we consider to be touring essentials include a frame-mounted water bottle (if you use it for juice or pop, expect mold), front and rear fenders, a rearview mirror, and a bell. European cyclists live and die by their bells, and in some countries they're required by law. Other extras you'll need for your bike are toe clips, padded handlebars (or padded riding gloves), and a light source. We avoided night cycling at all costs, so we chose not to mount lights on our bicycles. Instead, we each carried a strong flashlight that could be attached to the handlebars in case of a dire emergency (or an unlit tunnel).

One more item you won't want to neglect is a comfortable bike seat. Get to know your bike seat before you go. Some hard-core cyclists might tell you that discomfort is just one of the penalties of the sport, that the seat must be rock hard to ensure freedom of movement, or some other crazy thing. Don't listen to them. You and your bike are going to be spending a lot of hours together. Before you go, make sure you're not incompatible. If you just can't get comfortable on any seat, invest in a "cushy" gel cover to put some padding between you and your foe.

You'll also need to choose touring bags for your bike. If you'll be staying in hotels or hostels and you're a light packer, you might be able to get along with a handlebar bag and two rear saddlebags. If you're camping out, carrying cooking equipment, or going for the long haul, you'll probably need the works—two front bags, two rear bags, and a handlebar bag.

Important things to look for in touring bags are color (bright and visible are best), quality of construction (i.e., durability), ease and security of attachment to racks, and efficiency of closure system (zippers, drawstrings, etc.). You'll be amazed at how many times you dig into your bags in a single touring day. It's very important to have panniers that are both easy to use and durable. Shop around—bike bag prices range from reasonable to sky high. You'll have to match your budget to your needs when making a personal selection.

We talked to lots of other cyclists who had spent twice as much on their touring bags as we did, and we all agreed on one thing. No matter how expensive the bags, they didn't keep their contents dry. All of us relied on plastic grocery sacks or giant plastic garbage bags to keep our belongings dry in the rain. Check on the latest developments before you make your purchase. Perhaps some innovative manufacturer

*A beaten bike bag tells a tale of many miles.*

has finally mastered the trick of keeping water out of bags that are repeatedly subjected to driving rainstorms, gallons of road spray, and occasional tidal waves from passing trucks. We'll believe it when we see it!

Select your bags with their purposes in mind—a handlebar bag for valuables, delicate items, and things you want quick access to (camera, sunglasses, chocolate bars); two back bags to carry heavy or bulky items; and low-riding front bags to catch the extras. You'll need to do some experimenting with loading to minimize the wobble and weave. It's particularly important to load the front bags evenly. We were surprised to discover what seemingly insignificant things affected our wobble rates. As a result, we became positively superstitious about packing, driving each other crazy with our quirks and arguing about who got the bottle of vitamins or where an extra package of dry soup should go.

One trick for a pair of riders with identical bags (or for a single rider who has trouble staying organized) is to number bike bags or differentiate them in some way and try to pack the same items in the same bag each day. Our packs started out with numbers, then they gained identities from the cloth souvenir patches we sewed on them. These patches, showing cities or tourist sights, also make excellent conversation starters with the local citizens.

Finally, you'll need to put together a maintenance kit for your bicycle, including such items as the following:

- Adjustable wrench—6-inch
- Allen wrenches
- Brake pads (long-term trip only)
- Cables—one replacement each for gears and brakes (long-term trip only)
- Chain link removal tool (long-term trip only)
- Foldup tire (long-term trip only)
- Freewheel tool (long-term trip only)
- Helmet
- Locks—we carried both a metal shackle and a cable lock
- Locks for seat and hubs (optional)
- Lubricant
- Phillips and/or regular screwdriver
- Pliers
- Pump and pressure gauge
- Spokes—at least three or four
- Spoke wrench
- Tire irons
- Tubes—one or two for irreparable punctures or quick changes

If you're fortunate enough to tour Europe at several-thousand-mile whacks, as we are, you may want to mail additional replacement parts (e.g., tires, tubes, brake pads) to a European friend. Although bike shops in the north are rich in excellent touring gear, you'll still have difficulty finding touring equipment in Spain, Greece, and parts of Eastern Europe.

# WHAT TO TAKE

The items you'll require as a "normal" European traveler are listed in most general travel books—passport, camping carnet, hostel card, student identity card, and money. We've already dealt with most of them, but here are some things you should know about money, security, and equipment.

**MONEY.** Travelers' checks are one of the safest and most convenient ways to go. Purchasing travelers' checks usually involves paying a commission charge, but members of certain organizations and holders of special types of bank accounts can avoid these extra fees. Even if you do have to pay a commission charge, the security of knowing your travelers' checks will be replaced if lost or stolen is well worth the effort and cost of getting them. Be sure to keep a copy of your check numbers separate from your checks, and leave a list at home with someone you can contact.

If you'll be staying in Europe for several months, you may want to consider having some of your funds sent over later, but this can be quite an inconvenience—and expense. We chose to live with plump money pouches for a few months instead. Be sure to keep at least some American dollars (we carried about $100 in bills) in reserve for emergencies, especially if you'll be traveling in Eastern Europe. Some Eastern countries still require that international tickets (bus, train, plane, boat) be paid for in Western currency.

If you already have (or can easily obtain) a major American credit card, such as American Express, Visa, or MasterCard, bring it along. These cards are becoming increasingly handy in Europe, and you'll be glad you have one if you lose your travelers' checks or need to pay an unexpected medical bill. Check with your agency to discover how your card can be used in Europe.

**SECURITY.** Three essential things you'll want to take along on your trip are an under-clothing money pouch, a sturdy bicycle lock, and common sense.

Money pouches come in many styles (shoulder, neck, or belt), but their purpose is always the same—to help you avoid the pickpockets and purse snatchers who prowl the streets of tourist areas looking for anyone foolish enough to carry an exposed wallet or handbag. For comfort, we stowed our pouches inside our handlebar bags when we were cycling, but we always put them on as soon as we entered a large city or when we left our bikes for even a moment. Don't make the mistake of one California cyclist we talked to. He put down his handlebar bag "just for a minute" while waiting for a train in Rome. The next time he looked, the bag was gone, along with passport, travelers' checks, and his visa for a trip to India.

Simple good fortune and the efforts of the guardian angel who has ridden more than 17,000 bumpy miles on our handlebars may be responsible for the fact that we have never had a single item stolen during nearly three full years of European travel. Certainly, we have been forced into vulnerable positions often, simply because of the nature of our transportation and accommodations. But, throughout our travels, we have unfailingly followed some commonsense rules that have helped us to emerge unscathed while those around us have fallen prey to thieves and pickpockets.

- We always wear our money pouches inside our clothing when we are in a large city or mingling in a crowd.
- We always remove our valuables from our bicycles when we leave them unattended.
- We always lock our bikes securely in a high-visibility area if we leave them for even a moment in a large city, or for several minutes in a small one.

Much of the crime that victimizes tourists in Europe takes place in big cities or high-density tourist areas, so be especially careful there. Vigilance is also a necessary survival tool if you'll be using trains or frequenting train stations on your trip. The great thing about bicycle touring is that you'll be in between these places more than you'll be in them. We were continually delighted by the honesty of the Europeans we met. Despite our disadvantage as linguistically ignorant foreigners and (initially) inexperienced travelers, we encountered very few attempts to overcharge us or to steal from us. Still, it never hurts to be careful.

**PLANE TICKETS.** You'll want to shop around for a plane ticket that's best for you. Because we were planning to stay in Europe for several months but didn't have a specific return date set on our first trip over, we bought an "open-ended" ticket. This allowed us to select our return date any time within one year after our departure. However, it limited the cities we could choose for our arrival and departure, eventually forcing us into a snowy ride to Brussels to catch a late-March plane flight home.

You'll have more freedom if you buy a one-way ticket to Europe and purchase your return flight there, but this option is usually more expensive, and it requires responsible money management on your part. Tickets that allow you to arrive in one city and depart from another

*Use a sturdy box from a bike shop to pack your bicycle for the airplane or a long train journey.*

are often excellent options for cyclists. Probably the cheapest ticket setup is to fly in and out of the same city within a six-month time period. Find a travel agent you trust. Discuss your needs and budget, and decide on an itinerary that's best for you.

Keep in mind your arrival time in Europe when you buy your plane ticket. A midday or morning landing time will help you avoid the frustrations we faced our first time over—a frenzied assembly and loading job in the airport lobby and a twilight sortie into an unfamiliar city on arrival day.

**BICYCLES AND RELATED GEAR.** What about your bicycle? Can you bring it with you? Yes. Getting it to Europe can be a bit of a headache, but it's well worth it. Although many European train stations rent bicycles to tourists, you won't find the quality you want for long-distance cycling in a train station lineup. Buying a bicycle once you're over involves a heap of hassle and expense. In the northern countries where excellent touring gear is now available, you'll pay 50 to 100 percent more for cycling equipment than you do at home.

If you already have a touring-quality bicycle, bring it with you. If you're thinking of buying one for the trip, do it at home. Most major airlines will accept your bike at no extra charge as one of your two allotted pieces of checked luggage. Charter flights may be more stingy. Again, check with your travel agent or carrier.

Regulations will also vary as to whether your bike must be boxed, bagged, or simply wheeled aboard. The majority of carriers will require you to at least turn the handlebars sideways and remove the pedals so that the bike takes up less space. We recommend a full boxing job to help ensure your bicycle makes it safely to your destination. We carefully dismantled our bikes, removing handlebars, pedals, and front wheels. Then we put them inside sturdy bike cartons provided by a local bike shop, padding them with excess baggage such as sleeping bags and clothing. We closed the boxes securely with a strong filament tape, and we wrote names, flight numbers, and destinations on the boxes and all other pieces of luggage.

You'll probably sweat and squirm when you relinquish your bike to a burly baggage handler, and you'll undoubtedly worry about it during the entire flight. We did! But if you're careful in your packing job, the odds are good that you and your bicycle will roll happily out of the airport and onto European soil several hours later.

**CLOTHING.** What are you going to carry? This will vary, depending upon the length of your trip. Don't overdo it on clothes, as you'll certainly want to buy souvenirs, and you can put some of them to use right away if you leave an extra T-shirt or pair of shorts behind.

A good rain jacket is crucial, unless you're only cycling Greece in August. Rain pants are limited in their effectiveness for the cyclist, however. They tend to get you wet from the inside if the rain doesn't get you from without. We opted for polypropylene long underwear instead, wearing this under gym shorts when the weather was wet or cold. Polypro provided needed warmth, and it dried quickly when the rain finally stopped (or when we did). Also, a pair of sweat pants is useful for sightseeing or looking for a room in a city, or for when you're setting up your tent in a campground and don't want to freeze before you have a place to change.

We don't use cycling shoes when touring in Europe, mainly because we do so much walking when we're not pedaling. However, if you're accustomed to riding in biking shoes, bring your favorite pair along. Toss in a pair of lightweight sandals, too. They're great for airing out fragrant bikers' toes, and they come in handy for the often less-than-hygienic European campground showers.

If you'll be doing some cool-weather cycling, invest in a pair of rubberized biking booties to avoid the discomfort of cold and soggy feet. The booties are light and compact, and they help prevent frozen toes when you get off your bike after a cold day. Warm, waterproof gloves are also a necessity in nasty weather.

**CAMPING GEAR.** The European campground system is extensive, well organized, and inexpensive, so take advantage of the campgrounds here whenever possible. You'll meet the Europeans at their best—when they're on vacation, having fun, and eager to talk to others. Camping outside of organized campgrounds is acceptable in many countries, provided you obtain the landowner's permission. We met a host of fascinating people this way—from dairy farmers to auto salesmen to olive growers. Sweden also allows freelance camping on unfenced land (Tour No. 6), but most other European countries frown on the practice. Make it a policy to get an OK before you stay.

If you're camping, your baggage weight will increase markedly, but we found the extra pounds to be worth the payoff in campground friendships and reduced costs. In fact, after several months on the road, we still preferred the familiar walls of our tent to the constantly changing and often drab surroundings of hotel rooms.

If you'll be camping in Europe, you're probably an experienced camper at home. You'll need the same equipment—tent and rainfly, sleeping bag, a lightweight tarp for covering your bike, stove and fuel, matches, cookset, and an all-purpose rope to use as a clothesline. As mentioned earlier, we also carried two flashlights that doubled as emergency bike lights.

Choose your tent carefully. Make sure it's roomy enough for your baggage, tough enough to withstand European downpours, and light enough to allow you to navigate the hills without hiring a sag wagon to carry your gear. European campgrounds are usually set up for car and trailer use, and this often means less-than-ideal surfaces for sleeping. A good lightweight sleeping pad is a welcome comfort for tired muscles at the end of a tough riding day.

You won't be able to build fires in European campgrounds, and you shouldn't plan on any freelance wiener roasts either. We carried a Gaz cookstove that has done morning coffee duty and evening dinner duty for almost three years without giving us a problem. Unlike white gas, the small blue fuel cartridges the stove uses are easy to obtain in Europe (make sure you bring a model that uses full-size canisters). They grace the shelves of grocery stores and gas stations, are often sold at campgrounds, and are almost always available in hardware stores. Watch for the small blue Camping Gaz signs in store windows as you pedal through towns.

Water is always a concern when you're on the road and exercising hard. Carry enough containers to hold the water you'll need on hot and hilly days. Although bottled water is widely available (and widely consumed) in Europe, we have swallowed the tap water in every European country we've cycled through—without dire results. Let budget, convenience, and individual constitution dictate your choice. If you're camping, you'll need additional containers for cooking, washing, etc. We found 2-liter pop bottles to be wonderfully handy for a variety of needs.

You'll also need to be thinking ahead about food shopping if you're camping and cooking. Regardless of our day's destination, we tried to always carry one night's emergency rations (a couple of packages of dry soup or something similar) so that if we stumbled on a lovely campspot or got caught between towns, we could sleep and eat without having to ride to a restaurant or store.

**MISCELLANEOUS GEAR.** Here's an alphabetical list of other general items we took along:

- Address book—for sending postcards home and recording addresses of new friends
- Aspirin
- Camera and film; also a photo log
- Compass—for route finding and for locating sun-bathed tent spots
- First-aid kit
- Foreign-language dictionary
- Gifts for European friends—souvenir pins are popular, or carry music cassettes, T-shirts, etc.
- Glasses or contacts—second pair for emergency replacement
- Guidebooks—the more the merrier
- Journal—for recording those memories you don't want to forget
- Maps—for arrival and any good city maps
- Mirror
- Needle and thread
- Pictures—family snapshots to share with friends
- Playing cards
- Prescriptions
- Shampoo and soap
- Sunglasses and sunscreen
- Toilet paper—a must if you're camping, as European campgrounds often neglect this item
- Towel
- Vitamins
- Watch

# SURVIVAL SKILLS

At last, after all the planning, the preparation, the purchases, and the planes, you'll arrive. You'll watch as your bike carton comes tumbling down the baggage chute, and you'll claim it with trembling hands. You'll unpack, assemble, repack, and load, then make your way through customs to officially set foot on European soil. Now what? Enjoy!

All the preparation you've done should ensure a pleasurable trip, but here are a few additional tips, gathered from our years of "learning by doing," that will help you avoid the potholes and find the smoother roads ahead.

**SECURITY AGAIN.** We've already mentioned the importance of keeping your valuables in an under-clothing money pouch and of locking your bicycle when you leave it unattended. Security is always a concern when you leave your bags and bike to enter the tourist flow on foot—for example, when you're visiting a large city while staying in a hotel or campground. When we stayed in rooms, we always asked the proprietors to provide us with a place to lock our bicycles (off the street) and they generally complied quite graciously. If a hotel manager won't accommodate your bicycle and there are other rooms available, try someplace else.

Our bikes claimed the other bed in a tiny room in Vienna where we celebrated our fourth wedding anniversary; they spent Christmas with us in our room above Las Ramblas in Barcelona; they shared a

*Even the best lock can't protect against poor locking techniques.*

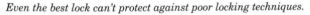

restaurant/hotel storage room with several bags of pigs' legs in southern Spain; and they hid behind a table in a hotel dining room in Carcassonne.

In campgrounds, we used a tree or post to lean and lock our bikes, then covered them with a lightweight tarp (which doubled as a groundsheet for picnics) to protect them from the weather. We zipped our bags and gear into the tent when we left to sightsee, and we took our cameras and other valuables with us. A zipper and a bit of fabric won't do much to deter a thief, so strike up conversations with your campground neighbors before you leave. That way, those around you know what body goes with what tent, and they'll be more likely to keep an eye on things while you're away. (We usually positioned our bag of dirty clothes next to the tent doorway, as an added discouragement for would-be thieves.)

**SAFETY AND HEALTH.** Besides taking care of your passport, money, and possessions, what are some ways you can take care of yourself while you're traveling?

For riding safety, keep to secondary roads whenever possible. If you follow the tour routes we've described, you'll be on quiet roads most of the time. Whenever we had to decide between main road "straight shots" and circuitous secondary routes, we chose the longer route, and we've tried to provide you with small-road options when our routes do stray onto busy thoroughfares. If you do add a few kilometers in your quest of quiet roads, you'll find they're well worth it for the solitude, safety, and scenery they'll provide.

Try to make your helmet a habit. It's easy to remember to reach for the plastic "brain bucket" when you're forced to cycle heavily traveled routes, busy city streets, or dangerous terrain (steep downhills, for example), but unexpected tumbles on ordinary roads can be every bit as dangerous—more so when your helmet is tucked inside a bike bag instead of cinched beneath your chin. We've tumbled on slick railroad tracks and mischievous curbs, and the falls came without warning and without time to prepare. Knees and hands and pride may take a beating when you topple, but if you can discipline yourself to lash on your helmet every morning, your skull should survive unscathed.

Another key element of safety is bicycle maintenance. If you get into a daily checkup routine, you'll avoid unnecessary breakdowns and accidents. Check tire pressure, brake pads, cables, spokes, and wheels on a daily basis. Make sure your bags are mounted securely when you load your bicycle, too.

One tedious task that will save you time in the long run is a daily "sliver search." Examine your tires regularly for tiny shards of glass imbedded in the tread and dig them out gently with the tip of a pocketknife blade to prevent them from working into the tube and producing those hated flats. Don't forget to lubricate your derailleur and chain at least once a week, more often if you're cycling through rain.

*You're never too young (or too old) to start using a helmet.*

Of course, you'll want to keep your body in good working condition, too. Eat enough food to replace the calories you're burning each day. This won't be a difficult task, especially with the endless selection of European delicacies tempting you from every store window you'll cycle past. But choose your fuel with care. We shared part of our ride in Spain with an English tourer whose daily breakfast and lunch consisted of three giant chocolate bars—tasty and calorie packed, but not exactly a nutritionist's ideal.

It's also important to leave your American "7-Eleven" mentality behind when you enter Europe. Once you're away from the 24-hour shopping options in the United States, you'll find that having a dollar, a franc, or a Deutschmark in your pocket doesn't mean you'll always be able to find a place to spend it. Familiarize yourself with the shopping hours (and the unfamiliar holidays) of the countries you'll be visiting, and take those opening and closing times seriously. Ignore them, and you may go hungry. We've listed general shopping hours in the introductory section of each tour.

**INFORMATION, PLEASE.** You'll find additional information on shopping, holidays, culture, and courtesy in the companion travel guides you buy for your routes. Michelin *Green Guides* have helpful sections that cover these subjects, as do Rand McNally *Blue Guides,* and the *Let's Go* and *The Real Guide* series. A guidebook's cost and weight is well worth the increased understanding and appreciation you'll gain from it, and the small city maps that often accompany the text can come in handy in a pinch.

Of course, the thousands of tourist offices scattered throughout Europe serve a similar function, and they have the added advantage of providing most materials free. Relying entirely on tourist offices does have its drawbacks, though. You'll have to battle lunch-hour closures, crowds, and occasional inconvenient locations, and some tourist-office brochures are full of superficial "fluff" designed to convince all comers that their town is the gem of Europe.

**ROUTE FINDING.** One important rule to remember as a bicycle tourer is this—"Pride goeth before a wrong turn." We learned this lesson the hard way, after too many dead ends and extra miles. When you're confused, ask for help. Europeans will be delighted to come to your rescue. They won't ridicule your ignorance or laugh at your despair. So what if the husband and wife you question argue for 15 minutes before agreeing on which road to point you toward? In most cases, the people you seek out will know a lot more about the area than you do, and their friendly aid will save you from a host of wrong turns. And occasionally, these roadside conversations will result in dinner invitations, impromptu picnics, refreshments at local cafes, and delightful new friendships as well.

Your main information sources as you ride will be the maps fastened atop your handlebar bag, the tours you're tracing from Part II of this book, and the road signs you'll constantly be searching for. Make a point of getting acquainted with the shapes and colors of the signs for the country you're riding in. They follow definite patterns, and knowing them can help you with your route-finding chores. Often, signs indicating motorway routes are one color, signs for primary roads are another, and signs for secondary roads are yet another. Think of yourself as a detective with several sets of clues to piece together. Use them all and you'll arrive at your destination with a minimum of difficulty.

We've included a page of international road signs you'll encounter frequently in Europe, with explanations from a cyclist's point of view.

To help with the daily task of route finding, we suggest you take a few minutes each morning to study your map, your guidebook, and the tour you're following from Part II of this book. Use a yellow highlighter to draw the day's intended route on your map. This will help you make quick decisions at junctions, and you can refer to our detailed route descriptions whenever you get stumped.

We've used kilometers as the distance unit in all tours except Tours No. 1 and 2, as these trace roads in Britain, where miles are the standard road unit. This way, you'll be operating in the units employed by the country you're in. A simple formula for kilometer-to-mile conversion is 8 km = 5 mi. So an 80-km day amounts to a 50-miler, the basic distance we aimed for as we planned our cycling days. When there's a lot to see or tough terrain to ride through, you'll shorten your rides accordingly. No single distance is "right" or "respectable." Find the pace that works for you, and go from there.

**MEMORIES.** Each day of your tour will bring you a host of new sights and sounds, and you may start to find the castles and cathedrals, forests and fields, honks and hellos blending together in a happy blur. Try to slow down long enough each day to open up a notebook and scribble a few lines about your experiences—a face, a place, a taste, or a feeling. The time you spend recording those moments will be a small investment for the future, and you'll go home at the end of your tour with a treasure of experiences that fading memories and jumbled recollections can never erase.

### Circular Signs—Give Orders

White bar on red background. No entry for vehicles. (One-way traffic coming at you!)

Red ring around motorcycle and automobile. No motor vehicles. (OK for nonmotorized you!)

Red ring around bicycle. No cycling. (Tunnel, freeway, busy road, or bike-eating dog ahead!)

White bicycle on blue background. Pedal cyclists only. (Sometimes obligatory. Follow local custom.)

### Rectangular Signs—Give Information

Black letter "i" on blue field. Tourist information. (Where am i?)

White bar with red tip on blue. No through road. (This sign can lie—check it out if you feel adven-turesome.)

### Triangular Signs—Give Warnings

Black bump in red border. Uneven road. (Look out for potholes!)

Black gate in red border. Railroad crossing with barrier. (Slow down for tracks or trains!)

Black train in red border. Unguarded crossing. (Slow down for tracks and look for trains!)

Parallel lines bending closer. Road narrows. (So long, shoulder!)

Black hill in red border. Steep downhill. (Yahoo!)

Black hill in red border. Steep uphill. (Could be a "pusher"!)

# PART II

# 18 TOURS GEARED FOR DISCOVERY

*A budget hotel in France provides an interesting window on the world.*

# TOUR NO. 1

# CATHEDRAL COUNTRY
## Oxford to Newhaven, England

*Distance:* 253 miles (407 kilometers)
*Estimated time:* 8 riding days
*Best time to go:* June, July, or September
*Terrain:* Lots of gutsy English hills
*Connecting tours:* Tour No. 2

Keep left! Keep left! Now, with that critical detail out of the way, what should you know about cycling in England? Well, it's rewarding, stimulating, challenging, and often wet. You'll be surprised by the toughness of the English hills and delighted by the lovely countryside and tidy villages you'll pedal through.

Seriously, though, remembering to keep to the left may be a problem, especially if you're cycling alone. Try taping a warning note to your handlebars or map case, at least for your first few days of cycling. Even after we had 1,000 miles of English roads behind us, it still took a great deal of concentration for us to head to the left side of the road after a lunch stop or sightseeing break. Turning into correct lanes, negotiating roundabouts, and dealing with merging traffic presented new challenges. And the shock of seeing cars pass each other on the right or approach us from the "wrong" side of blind curves had us grabbing for our brakes more than once.

English roads have lots of traffic and English drivers are the worst we encountered in Europe, so always use your helmet and stay on secondary routes whenever possible. More cautious than their Continental counterparts, many English drivers seem unwilling to swing wide to pass a bicycle, and they'll crowd you on the narrow roads.

Route finding in England can be a challenge, too. Many of the rural signposts are either ancient, defaced, or missing entirely. And junctions seem to multiply in direct proportion to the obscurity of the route. You'll have to watch your map carefully to keep track of your location, and you'll probably want to invest in the most detailed road maps you can afford. As another route-finding aid, you'll surely want to take advantage of one benefit that cycling in England offers—you can ask for directions from the locals and be confident that you'll receive a reply in your own language (more or less)!

**CONNECTIONS.** If you fly into London or arrive by ferry from the Continent, you can make use of the remarkably biker-friendly British

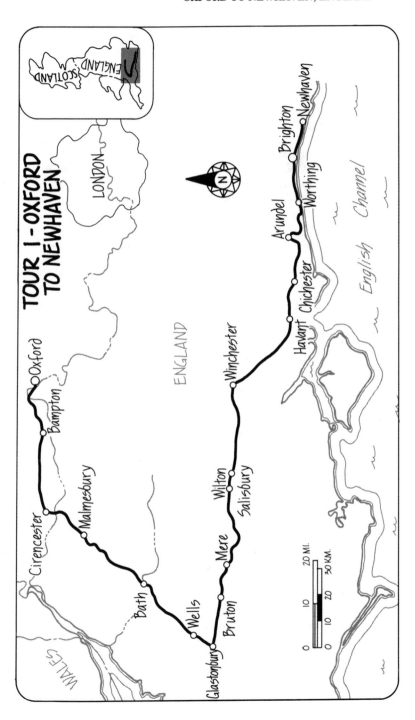

TOUR 1 – OXFORD
TO NEWHAVEN

rail system to get your bicycle to Oxford and the start of this tour. You'll probably have to go through London's rail hub to get to Oxford, but that'll provide an opportunity for sightseeing in the British capital, if you're interested. You can take your bike right into the passenger car with you when riding many short and/or off-hour commuter trains. On long-distance and high-use trains, you'll need to choose a train with a baggage car and purchase advance reservations for your bike. The reservation fee is a small price to pay for the privilege of loading your bicycle into the baggage car with your own hands.

**INFORMATION.** There's always an abundance of printed literature available at tourist offices in England. You'll be able to get campground listings and information on B&Bs (bed and breakfasts) or hotels. Even though you'll be traveling in an English-speaking country, it's a good idea to do some research in advance. To request information before you go, write to the British Tourist Authority, 40 West 57th Street, 3rd Floor, New York, New York 10019. Ask for free city maps, information on cycling and camping, and general tourist hype.

If you plan to do some solo cycle exploring, try contacting the Cyclists' Touring Club, Cotterell House, 69 Meadrow, Godalming, Surrey GU7 3HS, England, to request information on club membership and bicycle touring in England.

Rand McNally's *Blue Guide England; Let's Go: Britain and Ireland;* and Michelin's *Green Guide Great Britain* and/or *Green Guide England: The West Country* are just a few of the many commercial guidebook choices you'll have for your trip.

Although England certainly has a wealth of worthwhile sites to visit, only the wealthy can afford to see even a fraction of them. If you're serious about sightseeing, consider joining either the National Trust or English Heritage. The National Trust is a historic-preservation group that owns and maintains more than 200 properties in England, Wales, and Northern Ireland, from deer parks to manor houses to elaborate flower gardens. Trust properties are free to members of the organization, and, although the one-year membership fee is hefty, you'll save a "ton" of pounds and see a fortune of British treasures if you spend much time in England. A membership in English Heritage is equally beneficial and provides free access to the properties owned by this organization. Memberships can be purchased at tourist sites belonging to the respective organizations.

**MAPS.** The English are great map lovers, so your selection will be enormous. Take advantage of the excellent detailed maps that are widely available—you'll need them to negotiate the sometimes confusing British road junctions and the often unmarked secondary roads. The *Ordnance Survey Routemaster Series* at 1:250,000 is an excellent choice, since these maps provide helpful (if daunting) contour lines.

**ACCOMMODATIONS.** The nosedive of the American dollar in the past few years has made travel in Britain a challenge for the budget cyclist. When compared to other European countries, British prices are in the high to middle range. Lodgings in hotels can be quite expensive, so try out bed-and-breakfast options if you're looking for a better bargain. These rooms in private homes, though seldom cheap, provide a pleasing introduction to British habits and hospitality.

Campgrounds in England are generally clean, well maintained, and pleasant. Prices are reasonable, although often higher than you'll find in France or southern European countries. Unfortunately, the British are avid "caravanners," and you'll have to share your sites with fleets of camping trailers, complete with "tellies," lawn chairs, and teapots. Some campgrounds are licensed only for trailers and will not accept tents. If you'll be spending several weeks here and camping exclusively, the Michelin camping guide, *Camping and Caravanning in Britain,* is a great investment.

**SUPPLIES.** A "supermarket revolution" in 1991 challenged the age-old British practice of a nationwide Sunday shutdown of stores. Still, you'll be safest shopping ahead on Saturday afternoon, as only big towns and large stores offer a chance for Sunday shopping. Be prepared for the possibility of Wednesday- or Thursday-afternoon closures in small towns, too. General shopping and banking hours are Monday through Saturday, 9:00 A.M. to 5:30 P.M.

For picnicking, be sure to sample the delightful variety of English cheeses. They vary widely from county to county, and each region is proud of its specialty. Add slices of flavorful corned beef to hunks of grainy brown bread, throw in a handful of sinfully greasy English "crisps," and you'll have the makings of a delicious lunch. The sweet, bubbly English cider makes a cheery picnic beverage. Shop selectively, as cider can vary from a mildly alcoholic thirst quencher to a high-octane steamroller known as "scrumpy."

Pay your respects, too, to British institutions like fish and chips, Cornish pasties, and Chelsea buns. And be sure to join in the nation's almost religious adherence to afternoon tea, with a handful of the ever-present "biscuits" thrown in to soothe your cyclist's appetite.

If you find time to cycle between all these excuses to eat and drink, remember that bicycle touring is very popular in England, so you should find replacement parts without difficulty.

## Oxford to Cirencester: 35 miles

If you like university towns, you'll love Oxford. A serious campus cruiser could spend days here, moving from one famous college to another. Each of Oxford's colleges has its own unique architecture and setting, as well as a list of notable alumni that often reads like a who's who of British writers, scientists, rogues, and politicians.

You'll land on the west side of town if you arrive by train. Look for Oxford's **tourist office** across from the city hall on St. Aldates Street.

You can pick up a city map, information on visiting the colleges, and a list of lodging options here. Oxford boasts a youth hostel, a score of B&Bs, and a pleasant campground on the south side of the old town. To find the campground on Abingdon Road, take the bike route signed for South Oxford and Kennington and watch for campground signs about 1½ mi from the center.

Christ Church College is a definite "don't miss." The college chapel (also Oxford's cathedral) is a treat, as is the candlelit interior of the great dining hall. Be sure to admire the regal lines of the grassy Tom Quad, too. In between college hopping, take a stroll along the length of High Street, a busy thoroughfare lined with attractive buildings.

From the train station on the west side of town, continue west on **Botley Road** to the suburban community of **Botley.** At Botley, watch for a turn to the **right** onto **Road B4044** for **Eynsham.** Much of Oxford's traffic will appear to accompany you for the early portion of this ride as you cycle flat terrain to cross the Thames/Isis River on a tiny **toll bridge** (free to bicycles) and continue to a roundabout where you'll go **left** for **Stanton.** Keep with signs for **Stanton** as you go **left** at a **second roundabout,** and continue with **Road B4449.**

Yet another roundabout will direct you **straight** for **Hardwick,** and you'll savor quieter riding as you pass through a relatively unattractive landscape of flat farmland and gravel pits. Push on to **Road A415** and continue **straight** toward **Yelford.** You'll love this tiny road that runs like a thread through the fabric of encroaching fields. Yelford is a "don't blink or you'll miss it" town. It's rural Britain at its best.

Continue past Yelford, pedaling **straight** ahead for **Lew,** then veer **left** for **Aston.** More quiet cycling leads to Aston and a **junction** with **Road B4449.** Go **right** here to cycle into the attractive stone-built town of **Bampton.** Hit a **T** as you enter Bampton, and go **right** to find the **town center.** Even the pubs in this handsome little city are worth a few photographs.

Leave Bampton on **Road A4095** for **Faringdon,** and endure a short stretch of busier cycling. Then veer **right** onto a tiny road signed for **Black Bourton.** Pastoral scenery and charming villages await. Cycle to **Alvescot,** then angle **left** for **Kencot** and continue past **Filkins** to a junction with **Road A361.** Go **left** on A361 for **Lechlade,** but dive off shortly after as you turn **right** for **Southrop.**

A tiny road will take you into the region of Gloucester and through the enchanting settlement of Southrop. Sliced by a tiny creek overlooked by stone-walled houses, Southrop epitomizes a Cotswold village. Once one of the richest areas of Britain due to a thriving medieval wool trade, the Cotswold hills have been home to limestone cottages and flocks of grazing sheep for centuries. It's a lovely (if punishing) area to explore by bike, and you might want to consider a 2- or 3-day detour to explore the heart of the region to the northwest.

From Southrop, continue with the route signed for **Fairford.** You'll begin to encounter gently rolling hills as you go **right** at the junction signed for **Hatherop** and **Bibury.** Stay with signs for **Bibury** to pedal on (and up) to the charming National Trust property known as **Arlington Row.** This well-kept Cotswold village is a picture-perfect example of the architecture that characterizes the region.

From Arlington Row, you'll have a couple of options to get to **Cirencester.** You can "main road" it in on **Road A433.** It's a straight shot through rolling terrain, and traffic was tolerable when we cycled it in late August. Or you can dive **left** off **Road A433** just past Arlington Row to cycle a much quieter paralleling road for part of the way to Cirencester.

If you're planning to camp in Cirencester, angle **right** off Road A433 at **Barnsley** to cycle west to **Road A435** and the Mayfield Touring Park. If you're considering a day ride into the Cotswold hills, this campground 2 mi north of Cirencester might be a good base of operations. There's also a youth hostel 5 mi northwest of Cirencester at Duntisbourne Abbots.

Enter Cirencester and follow signs to the **center** and the city's pride—one of England's largest parish churches. Pause at the handsome structure and admire its gorgeous stone porch, then cross the street to visit the **tourist office** down the block. Office personnel can help you with lodgings, provide you with information on the Cotswolds, and direct you to the city's highly rated Roman museum. Cirencester is a comfortable city with lots of shopping opportunities. Don't forget to buy some Gloucester cheese to tuck into a pannier.

## Cirencester to Bath: 35 miles

From Cirencester's parish church, take **Cricklade Street** past the city's upscale shopping complex, then go **right** on **Ashcroft Road.** Pedal onward to the unsigned **roundabout** and go **left** to gain **Somerford Road** out of the city. Cross over a howling **motorway** and continue with this signed route for **Somerford Keynes.** You'll enter a rather confusing resort area to the south of Cirencester. Follow signs for **Oaksey.**

Resort developments give way to farmland as you pedal through level terrain to **Oaksey,** another attractive stone village. At the far end of Oaksey, veer **left** for **Crudwell,** but abandon the Crudwell route as you follow signs for **Hankerton** and **Charlton.** Pass through Hankerton and reach a **junction** with **Road B4040,** where you'll go **right** to cycle into **Malmesbury.** Watch for the majestic form of Malmesbury's abbey church as you endure a traffic-heavy finish into town.

Descend into Malmesbury's old center and swing **right** to arrive at the city's famous **market cross.** The nearby abbey church, erected in

1180, is a wonderful blend of ruin and standing stone. You'll be amazed by the rainbow of Romanesque stone carvings above the entrance and amused by the window dedicated to Elmer the flying monk.

From the abbey church, descend to the **intersection** signed for **Foxley,** and take **Foxley Road** away from town. More quiet cycling awaits as you pedal through farmland to a **left** turn signed for **Norton.** Ride to Norton and sneak a look at its lovely village pub, then stay with signs for **Hullavington** from there. Continue with the main road through Hullavington, sneaking a peek at the Norman tower on its parish church, and arrive at **Grittleton,** yet another enticing village. In Grittleton, go **left** for **Yatton Keynell** to cross over the **M-4 motorway.**

Look for a **right** turn for **Castle Combe** just after crossing the motorway, and take this quiet route to a **T** where you'll turn **left** toward Castle Combe. Descend past a large car park that's a good indicator of the popularity of this "preserved" village, and wind downhill into the heart of town. If you're fortunate enough to visit Castle Combe when hordes of tourists aren't tiptoeing past the tea rooms and gift shops that line the main street, you'll probably decide that it's a delightful spot. Ancient stone houses, a tidy village church with a creaky cemetery, and a covered market cross all beg a photographer's attentions. Linger and enjoy—for now your work begins.

Cruise downhill to the outskirts of the village and enter a shady creek-fed forest. When the road branches, keep to the **right** for **North Wraxall.** A steep and agonizing ascent leads out of the ravine. Follow signs for **Colerne** and **Bath** to gain a straight-arrow road along a breezy ridge. Vistas of the rolling hills and green agricultural valleys will soothe you as you ride.

**Cross Road A420** and continue straight with signs for **Colerne.** You'll never actually cycle through this town, but it's the only one in the area that seems to advertise. Continue straight, shunning turnoffs to the right and left. A **diving descent** to cross a tiny creek will lead you into an **exhausting climb** to another ridgetop. Pedal onward, cursing British roads with every stroke, then leap into a **wild, curving downhill plunge** that leads to an **intersection** with the suicidally busy **main road (A4)** into **Bath.**

Hug the shoulder and hope for the best as you cycle through Bath's suburbs and begin following signs for the **center.** Be sure to take the **nontruck route** toward the city core. Watch for the towering form of Bath Abbey looming above the city snarl as you near the center. You'll hit a maze of pedestrian streets around the abbey. Get off your bike and let your trembling knees follow the well-signed route to Bath's **tourist office.**

Bath's campgrounds are inconvenient at best, especially if you're hoping to do much sightseeing. There's a youth hostel about 1 mi (uphill!) from the center, or ask about other budget accommodations at the tourist office. You can wander Bath's streets for hours, looking at mansions and townhouses, museums and churches. Visits to Bath Abbey and the nearby Roman Baths are practically obligatory, and you can join the English tourists for a "cuppa" in the Pump Room above the Roman Baths. (You'll definitely need something to calm your nerves after cycling into this traffic nightmare.)

## Bath to Glastonbury: 25 miles

The next two days of your tour will be physically and mentally challenging. You'll encounter dozens of killer hills and confusing junctions. If you haven't purchased a map with good detail up to now, do it before you leave Bath. Even a 1:50,000 map won't be an overkill for this stretch of cycling. Your pence will be well spent.

Bid a reluctant farewell to Bath's pedestrian-friendly center and prepare to do battle with Bath's biker-hostile suburbs as you work your way south from the tourist office. Gain **St. James's Parade** and follow it to the banks of the **Avon River** and a terrifying roundabout. Then follow signs for **Exeter** onto **A367** and endure a **gruesome climb** out of the sinkhole that holds the city. Too much traffic and too much hill will combine to make your departure less than enjoyable.

Reach the crest of your climb and watch for an escape route to the **right** signed for **Tunley** and **Timsbury.** Cycle a much quieter **Road B3115** onward. The hills will challenge you nearly all the way to Wells. Descend a long slope after **Tunley,** and angle **left** at a sign for **Radford** when the main route angles right.

Continue downhill to cross a creek, then tackle a long, steady incline to gain the edge of **Paulton** and another **intersection.** Go **left** here for **Midsomer Norton** (don't dive back down the hill with the straight-ahead route), and climb to a busier road through Paulton's center. Turn **right** onto this main drag, but dive **left** soon after when you reach the little city's **market cross.**

If you think things have been complicated up to now, hang onto your helmet—it gets worse! We listened to 20 minutes of detailed directions from a local citizen at the Paulton supermarket, then we set off in quest of a small church, a big hill, and a red phone booth. From the left turn at the market cross, climb steeply to the **little church** that marks the intersection with **Tennis Court Road.**

Go **left** on Tennis Court Road and continue battling the British hills, ascending to a ridgetop on a quiet byway, then descending to **Road A362.** Go **left** here, then take the **first right** (it's unsigned—look for a **red phone booth**) to continue on with a quiet road into the hill country of Somerset. Keep straight ahead on this rolling route (hang in there—a long descent is just ahead) to reach **Road B3139.**

Join Road B3139 as you go **right** to pedal on toward Wells. You'll pass the grassy Old Down Campground ½ mi later, then cruise on to an **intersection** with **Road A37.** Go right very briefly, then left again to regain **Road B3139.** Look for the Mendip Hills huddled to the north as you ease into a glorious **downhill glide** that will carry you to Wells. If you're interested in a detour to the famous **Cheddar Gorge** (campgrounds and a hostel), watch for a junction with Road B3135. It's signed for Cheddar.

Breeze into Wells on B3139 and head for the dominating form of the cathedral. Set on a vast green lawn that begs for picnics, Wells Cathedral rules the tiny city. The church's carved facade deserves long study, and the interior is a pleasing blend of cavernous emptiness and Gothic intricacy. Walk to the nearby Bishop's Palace and take a peek at Vicars' Close. Wells's **tourist office** is on Market Place, near the cathedral.

From the tourist office, follow **High Street** to **Road A39** signed for **Glastonbury.** You'll endure a busy main road ride for the flat 5 mi to the city. Road A39 will deposit you at a junction with Glastonbury's **High Street.** Angle **right** on High Street to cruise past many of the city's medieval attractions—The Tribunal, St. John's Church, and the George and Pilgrims Inn.

High Street leads to an intersection with **Magdalene Street.** Go **left** here to find Glastonbury Abbey, the city's main attraction. Glastonbury's **tourist office** is just to the right of the intersection, on Northload Street. Continue out of town about ½ mi on Northload Street to find a deluxe and delightfully convenient campground. The nearest youth hostel is in Street, 4 mi southwest.

Glastonbury is a glorious blend of legend, architecture, tourism, and the sixties. You'll find shops selling incense and pottery side by side with proper British tea rooms. Don't neglect a visit to Glastonbury Abbey. Founded in 678, the abbey is the legendary burial place of King Arthur, and it's considered by many to be the birthplace of English Christianity. Even if you're not a fan of "romantic" history, the evocative ruins are worth a stroll.

## Glastonbury to Salisbury: 54 miles

You'll want to get an early start for this one. It's a typical English toughie—lots of hills, scores of confusing junctions, and plenty of pleasing pastoral scenery. From Glastonbury's **High Street,** retrace your route to the **junction** with **Road A361** for **Frome.** Cling to the shoulder of this narrow, busy road as you cycle past the turnoff for the Chalice Well and Glastonbury Tor, then watch for a turn to the **right** signed for **West Bradley.**

Abandon the terrifying main road for quieter riding through hilly orchard land. You'll see where much of the Somerset "scrumpy" originates as you pass tree after tree loaded with juicy cider apples. Please don't indulge quite yet—you'll need your wits about you to negotiate the maze of roads ahead.

Angle **left** with signs for **East Pennard,** then continue with this through road, ignoring turnoffs to the left and right. Signs for **Ditcheat** lead **straight across Road A37** as you cycle past quiet farms and grazing sheep. Pause in Ditcheat to admire an enchanting parish church floating on a lush sea of green, then ride onward to

*A quiet road leads past the parish church of East Dean.*

eventually reach a junction with **Road A371.**

Go **right** on **A371,** then **left** soon after for **Bruton.** More hilly, scenic cycling awaits. Struggle through a **long climb** before Bruton, then enjoy a quick descent through the handsome town. Ride your brakes enough to notice the many fine buildings lining High Street. Keep to the **right** at the bottom of High Street, and gain **Road B3081** toward **Wincanton.** A 1-mi climb leads away from town.

Now comes the part of the day you'll surely curse us for. Follow our route if you want to stay on tiny roads, but be forewarned—this hill is brutal! Watch for a road sign for **Stourhead House,** and turn **left** off B3081 as the climb from Bruton fades. Descend toward the village of **Hardway** (a more fitting name was never given), with views of the monolithic Alfred's Tower ruling the forested ridge ahead. Guess what ...

Angle **right** for **Stourhead** at the bottom of the hill, and begin a gradual climb toward your goal. We began to wonder what we were in for when several grinning locals watched us pass, then informed us that the hill got much steeper in voices trembling with sadistic glee. The incline picks up intensity like a runaway truck. Battle through it as long as possible. Then get off and push.

You'll be thankful for the trees dripping shade on your sweat-stained back as you gain the crest of the hill and the National Trust property known as **Alfred's Tower.** Built in 1772 to commemorate a ninth-century battle in which Alfred the Great repelled the Danes (this hill would repel anyone!), it makes a pleasant spot to catch your breath. Continue into a gradual descent and hit a junction with a larger road. Go **right** here for **Stourhead,** then **right** again onto **Road B3092** to continue toward one of Britain's most famous landscaped gardens.

The National Trust site of Stourhead is well signed off B3092. It's a wonderful place, but the entry fee is almost as steep as the hill you've just come over. If you're neither a garden lover nor a National Trust member, don't bother.

Continue with B3092 to arrive at **Mere,** an attractive village with several neat old inns. If you decided to bypass the "horrible hill" with some main-road riding, you might rejoin our route here. Swing to the **left** through the center of town, then watch for an unsigned turn to the **right** onto **Boar Street.** It's marked by a small **Wiltshire Cycle Route** sign.

Depart Mere on Boar Street and stay with this through road past the charming Walnut Tree Inn before swinging **left** for **West Knoyle** and **East Knoyle.** Another **left** for **East Knoyle** leads on to **two unsigned junctions.** Go **right** at the first and **left** at the second to continue toward **East Knoyle.**

If you can manage to get your nose out of your map through this confusing section, you'll love the sturdy thatched-roof houses that characterize the region. Negotiate **two right turns** (signed when we were there) for **East Knoyle,** then keep with this winding road as you ascend a cottage-dotted hillside with views of the farmland below.

Wind downhill past **East Knoyle's church** and emerge onto **Road A350.** If you're a fan of English architecture, you might be interested to know that East Knoyle is the birthplace of one of Britain's most famous architects, Sir Christopher Wren. Swing **right** onto **A350,** then dive **left** immediately after with signs for **West Tisbury.** More quiet cycling follows.

Continue with signs for Tisbury to a **junction** where you'll go **right** for **Wardour.** Descend to cross the **train tracks,** then veer **left** to cycle along a gentle river valley. Pass the turnoff for Wardour Castle. You'll go **left** again to recross the tracks and climb into **Tisbury.** As you enter Tisbury, take the route to the **right** signed for **Salisbury.**

Signs for **Teffont** lead on as you enjoy easy pedaling and pastoral surroundings. Join **Road B3089** to the right to cycle through **Dinton** and on to **Barford St. Martin** and a junction with **Road A30.** Although Road A30 leads directly to Salisbury, it's perilous with flying cars. Avoid the hubbub by going **right** on **A30** (away from Salisbury), then take the **first left** for **Burcombe.**

Trace this quiet route to **Wilton,** and angle **left** into Wilton's center. There's a fine parish church here, boasting 800-year-old stained glass. Take a **right** at the traffic light to cycle past the highly rated **Wilton House.** A subsequent **roundabout** will dump you back onto the main road into Salisbury, but you can abandon it once again by taking **Road A3094** to the **right,** then grabbing the **first left** to enter Salisbury via quiet suburbs and the train station.

You'll spot the tallest spire in England, crowning one of the loveliest cathedrals you'll ever visit, as you approach Salisbury's center. Salisbury Cathedral was built in the incredibly short span of 38 years, in an era when many cathedrals took centuries to complete. The church is well worth an afternoon of sightseeing, especially if you can tag along on a tour of the heights (tours start at 11:00 A.M. and 2:30 P.M.). You'll never forget the stairs, the stones, or the stories you'll hear on the climb.

Salisbury's **tourist office** on Fish Row can provide you with information on the city's myriad attractions and give you help with lodgings. There's a pleasant campground about 2 mi north of town, just off Road A345 for Amesbury. (With a good town map, you can find it without cycling the main road.) Salisbury's youth hostel is on our route to Winchester. Read on to find it.

## Salisbury to Winchester: 25 miles

The ride from Salisbury to Winchester is moderately hilly but mercifully brief. No doubt your legs will be ready for a rest after the tough terrain you've just cycled through. From Salisbury's **High Street,** head east along **New Canal/Milford Street.** Pass under the ring road and ascend on Milford Hill. You'll see signs for the youth hostel on the left. Keep with this route as it becomes **Shady Bower** and then **Milford Mill Road.**

You'll emerge onto the busy **Road A36.** Go **left** here for **Southampton,** then swing right for **Alderbury** not long after. Relish much quieter cycling as you ascend toward Alderbury, then angle **left** for **West Dean** just before the village proper. Cross **over A36** and stay with this road through subsequent junctions. You'll hit a **T** near East Grimstead, and keep **right** for **West Dean.**

Go **right** for **Lockerley** at the next junction and continue on delightfully peaceful pavement past thatched-roof cottages, shadowy hedgerows, and lots of rolling hills. Lockerley is just one of many pretty villages you'll see today, each with its own dignified parish church. Hit another **T** just past Lockerley, and take a **right** for **Romsey.** Swing **left** for **Mottisfont** soon after.

You'll hit a town sign long before you see the town. Cycle on to **Road B3084** and go **left.** Climb briefly to go **right** on a **tiny unsigned road** guarded by thick hedges. This thoroughly English lane leads on to Mottisfont, a charming village that boasts a National Trust house and garden.

From Mottisfont, continue to **Road A3057** and go **left,** then take the **first right** to climb steadily toward **Michelmersh.** Keep **right** at the **unsigned Y,** then angle **left** for **Braishfield.** We encountered several vandalized signs and unsigned junctions through this section of the ride, so keep a close eye on your map to pedal on to Braishfield.

Hit a **T** at Braishfield, and go **left** for **King's Somborne,** then **right** for **Winchester.** Winchester road signs lead onward to **Road A3090.** Suffer on with speeding vehicles as you gut it out on A3090 for the final 4 up-and-down miles into Winchester. You can add distance and distraction to your day by angling left onto smaller roads into the city. Decide for yourself if it's worth the work.

Signs for the **center** lead into the heart of Winchester. There's a zooish but extremely convenient tents-only campground at North Walls Park, behind Winchester's "Leisure Center" (roller disco and swimming for those who still have the energy). Winchester also offers a centrally located hostel in an eighteenth-century watermill (a National Trust property).

You'll find the **tourist office** in the guildhall on Broadway, not far from Winchester's somewhat squatty but oh-so-regal cathedral. The cathedral's west front is particularly pleasing when the stones blush pink with the last rays of the setting sun.

## Winchester to Chichester: 35 miles

We should preface the final few days of this tour with a warning. From Winchester onward, the roads in southern England become increasingly busy. The coast is nothing short of bedlam and small-road options are almost nonexistent. Still, Chichester is charming, Arundel Castle is magnificent, and Brighton is infinitely English. If you detest traffic and have better things to do, do them. If not, ride on!

From Winchester's **High Street,** cycle past the guildhall and King Alfred's Statue, cross the **River Itchen,** and angle **right** at the **roundabout** to gain **Road A272.** A second **roundabout** will put you on the small road signed for **Morestead.** Endure a **1-mi climb** with entirely too much motorized company, then continue with this roller-coaster route past a series of junctions. The riding is challenging.

Reach a **T** 9½ mi from Winchester, and go **left** onto **Road B3035.** Dive **right** just afterward for **Droxford.** Go **left** for **Hambledon** at the next junction and stay with this through road to **cross** the frightening **Road A32** and cycle on to Hambledon. The punishing terrain finally eases as you continue from Hambledon with the route signed for **Waterlooville.**

Pass through **Denmead** and pick up more cars, then keep with **Road B2150** to **Waterlooville.** Stay with signs for **Havant** from here. You'll negotiate several roundabouts and endure harrowing roads to the edge of Havant. Reach a **roundabout** signed for the **HyperMart** and **Leigh Park.** Go **left** for **Leigh Park** to push on to the next roundabout, and continue straight for Leigh Park Center. Yet another roundabout leads straight for the "shopping center" (it's the truth!).

Dazed by exhaust fumes and dizzy from roundabouts, you'll emerge onto a very busy auto road. Go **left** very briefly, then take the **next right** signed for **North Havant** and **Stansted House.** This small thoroughfare leads out of the snarl of Havant. Toss back a "good riddance" as you cross a larger road and continue **straight** with signs for **Chichester** on **Road B2178.** Chichester signs lead on from here.

Gentle terrain and glorious solitude will heal the wounds left by Havant. Cross a larger road roaring toward the coast, and continue with **B2178** for **Chichester.** Forest, farms, and small villages make the cycling pleasant. Reach a turnoff signed for **Stansted House,** regal residence of the Earl and Countess of Bessborough. If you still haven't taken the opportunity to wander through one of these British mansions plump with paintings and antiques, here's one more chance.

As you near Chichester, a turnoff for **Fishbourne Roman Palace** offers yet another detour. Fishbourne is the largest Roman palace yet to be excavated in Britain, and the "digs" here are accompanied by an excellent Roman museum that's certainly worth a look.

Arrive on the outskirts of Chichester, and angle **left** on the busy **ring road.** Then dive into the city center with **North Street.** North Street soon becomes a pedestrian route, but you'll want to go **right** on **West Street** to find the city's impressive market cross (erected in 1501). Continue on to Chichester Cathedral, a lovely building ringed by lawns that invite sun-seeking picnickers.

The city **tourist office** is just beyond the cathedral. They'll be able to direct you to a local B&B or to the campground southeast of town.

## Chichester to Brighton: 34 miles

Depart Chichester on the small road signed for **Oving.** It's difficult to find. Cycle to the **east end of town,** and look for your route taking off from the **north side** of the **Four Chestnuts Inn.** You'll have the usual crush of coastal traffic accompanying you as you pedal away from Chichester. Stay with **signs for Oving** through a series of junctions. Reach Oving and continue **straight** for **Barnham.** (We encountered several vandalized signs through here, so trust your map more than your eyes.)

Arrive at the larger and busier **Road B2233** and go **right,** then veer **left** onto **Road A29** for a short stretch. Hit a roundabout and stay with signs for **Barnham** to regain **Road B2233.** Cycle through Eastergate and Barnham, then push on to **Yapton.** In Yapton, dive **left** for **Walberton** to gain less hectic cycling.

Watch for a turn to the **right** signed for **Ford** and **Arundel.** Take it, then pedal on to another junction where you'll go **left** for **Arundel.** There's a no-frills campground near the junction, if you're hunting for a site. Continue toward the touristy little city of Arundel, crouched beneath the majestic **Arundel Castle.**

You'll hit a **roundabout** on the edge of town. Stay with **city center signs** (not the auto route signed for the castle) to climb into the attractive city. Cycle onward to reach the signed castle entrance. Arundel's cathedral is worth a look, but save the bulk of your time for the castle. This is a castle of fairy tales and legends—in short, the castle of your dreams. Outside, its stout walls are flanked by lush green lawns and blossoming pink orchards that are spectacular in May. Inside, the richly furnished rooms are flush with books, tapestries, and sculpture.

Arundel Castle is open to visitors only in the afternoon, so you'll need to keep this in mind when planning your arrival. If time gets away from you as you stroll the vaulted halls, Arundel offers many accommodation options (however, few of them are cheap). The city's youth hostel is signed on our route toward Brighton.

Fortify yourself like a medieval knight preparing for battle as you get ready to face the coast from here to Brighton. It's nothing short of awful. Leave Arundel with the frantic **Road A27** toward **Worthing.** Watch for an escape route to the **right** onto **Road A284** for **Lyminster** and **Littlehampton** (there's a campground at the junction), and coast downhill on this busy road to the edge of Littlehampton. Veer off A284 with signs for **Angmering** and **Worthing.** You'll be back on another branch of the dreaded **Road A27** from here.

This is a truly horrible stretch of cycling. Some sections of the road are four lane, there's a constant roar of traffic, and enough trucks will thunder past to send a continual trickle of chills down your spine.

Mercifully, the riding is flat and fast. Reach a **roundabout** beyond Angmering and swing **right** onto **Road A259** for **Goring** and **Worthing.** At a second **roundabout** in **Ferring,** abandon A259 and cycle toward the sea.

You'll finally have some pleasant riding as you swing east along the coast. Enjoy the seaside houses, glimpses of the English Channel, and the delightful absence of terrifying traffic. Unfortunately, you'll be forced to rejoin **Road A259** at Worthing. As traffic intensifies, your enjoyment will probably fade. Push onward through **South Lancing**

*A royal figure bows to the power of time in southern England.*

and continue to **Shoreham.** The coastal settlements are a fascinating mix of seaside resorts and hard-working harbor towns.

Continue paralleling the coast through Shoreham and on to Hove. Then enter the carnival-like beachfront city of Brighton. Brighton is entertaining (if a bit bizarre), with a waterfront area that looks more like a state fair than a city. Get off your bike and stroll the sidewalks if you want to see the sights from a safer vantage point.

After you've ogled the waterfront for a while, turn into the city streets and pedal to the Royal Pavilion, a wacky building that looks right at home in the carnival atmosphere of Brighton. The city **tourist office** is nearby, in Marlborough House at 54 Old Steine. The staff there can direct you to a B&B, to the youth hostel (4 mi north in Patcham), or to Brighton's campground on the east side of town.

## Brighton to Newhaven: 10 miles

If you're not planning to hop a ferry to France from Newhaven at the end of this tour, you may want to skip this final day of cycling and put bike and baggage aboard a London-bound train in Brighton. Although the coastal scenery between Brighton and Newhaven is spectacular, the hills are even more impressive, and the traffic is thick.

From Brighton, continue east on the suddenly hilly **Road A259,** and cycle through Rottingdean and Peacehaven. You'll cross the Greenwich Meridian as you pass through Peacehaven, then climb steadily away from town. Savor glimpses of the white cliffs that make this section of the British coast so scenic as you labor on toward Newhaven.

A final breezy descent leads into the maritime city of Newhaven, guarded by its clifftop fortress. Follow signs for the **ferry** to find the harbor and a ferry office where you can purchase your ticket to Dieppe, France. The Channel crossing takes about four hours and bicycles travel free.

# TOUR NO. 2

# HEAVEN ON EARTH
### York, England, to Edinburgh, Scotland

*Distance:* 264 miles (425 kilometers)
*Estimated time:* 8 riding days
*Best time to go:* June, July, August, or September
*Terrain:* Fabulous scenery and fierce hills
*Connecting tours:* Tour No. 1

You'll see some of Britain's most incredible scenery on this challenging ride from York to Edinburgh. Much of the route passes through the borderlands of England and Scotland, an area with a long history of conflict. Lighten up, toughen up, and prepare yourself to do battle with some horrendous hills. But rest assured that your "war wounds" will be soothed by the quiet countryside and spectacular scenery you'll pedal past.

Please refer to Tour No. 1 for information on cycling in England. Much of that data will carry over as you cross the border into Scotland and head north toward Edinburgh. Scotland claims the same language (more or less) as England, and government agencies (post office and transport) cross the boundary, too. Keep to the left when you enter Scotland—this country's driving regulations mirror England's. And, although Scotland does have its own pound note, English notes and coins are widely circulated here.

So, what differences will you notice when you enter Scotland? It's a lonelier land, that's for sure. Although the main thoroughfares are quite busy, especially in the summer months when tourists raise the auto count, Scotland's secondary roads are delightfully deserted. Towns are smaller and more scattered, and the entire border area has an unspoiled and undeveloped air to it. Despite the close association of England and Scotland, the Scottish people will be the first to tell you that they are indeed unique. Acquaint yourself with Scottish history, observe the local customs, and benefit from the widespread friendliness and good humor, and you'll certainly agree.

**CONNECTIONS.** York is served by frequent trains from London, and you should be able to get your bicycle and gear onto a train with a baggage car to make the leap. If you fly into London or arrive by ferry from the Continent, you'll probably have to go through London's center to catch your train to York. However, there is a ferry that travels from Rotterdam, Holland, to Kingston upon Hull, England. This will leave you one long-day's ride to get to York. It's an excellent option if you're coming from that direction.

You can finish the tour in Edinburgh with a train for London or a plane for home. If you have good weather and more time for cycling, consider exploring farther north. According to the reports of most travelers we met, Scotland just gets better and better. We cycled east along the Firth of Forth when we left Edinburgh, passing scores of ruined castles and deluxe golf courses before calling it quits at Dunbar and hopping a train toward the south. The major problem with riding out of Edinburgh is traffic—no matter which direction you head. It's difficult to avoid busy roads in this intensely populated slice of Scotland.

**INFORMATION.** The British Tourist Authority (address in Tour No. 1) will send you materials on Scotland when you write. Be sure to mention that you'll be cycling to Edinburgh. With any luck, you'll get some special touring information and a map of the enormous city. Michelin's *Green Guide Scotland* is a wonderful companion for your ride in Scotland, and all of the countrywide guidebooks listed for England in Tour No. 1 will take you into Scotland, too. Do your homework, and read about what makes the two countries different. Your time in Scotland will be richer for your efforts.

If you decide to join one of the historical organizations listed in Tour No. 1, you'll be able to visit properties in Scotland as well. Historic Scotland is the counterpart of English Heritage, and the National Trust reaches across the border to administer several noteworthy properties in Scotland.

**MAPS.** Maps are no problem in Scotland. Choose the amount of detail you desire, and you'll find a map to match your wishes. Our favorites were from the *Ordnance Survey Routemaster Series* at 1:250,000. These maps provide wonderful route-finding detail. Supplement them with freebies from tourist offices and/or a camping guide (e.g., *Scotland: Camping and Caravanning Parks*).

**ACCOMMODATIONS.** As in England, you'll find the price of Scottish lodgings on the top half of the European scale. Campgrounds are excellent but sometimes difficult to reach. Freelance camping is allowed on public land, but it's always a good idea to ask permission. Hostels and B&Bs are your best bet for indoor budget accommodations.

**SUPPLIES.** Although the Scottish shopping practices and hours are quite similar to the English ones, you'll find a delightful new splash of Scottish specialties to make your grocery bag more interesting. Scottish shortbread is a delectable national institution, and don't neglect the mouth-watering (and filling-spoiling) chewy Scottish caramels. For more nourishing fare, sample a repast of Highlands game meat or fresh fish while dining out, or carve yourself a picnic from a hunk of excellent Scottish cheese.

You may have some difficulty locating large bicycle shops in Scotland, at least until you arrive in Edinburgh, as most of the towns you'll pedal through aren't as large as their English cousins to the south.

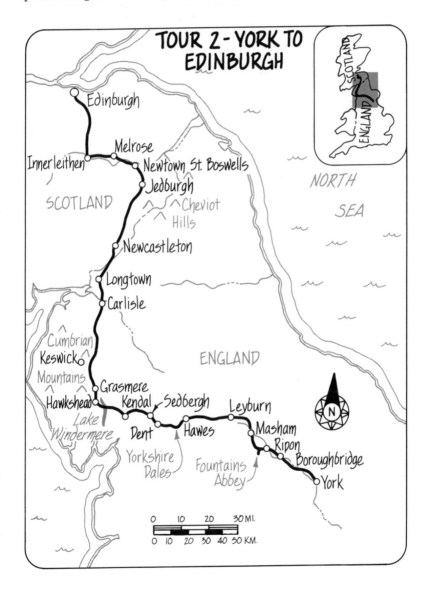

TOUR 2 - YORK TO EDINBURGH

# York to Fountains Abbey: 28 miles

If you arrive in York by train from London, make your first stop at the small **tourist information** office in the station. Pick up a city map and a list of accommodation options while you're there. In the busy months of July and August, York is literally glutted with tourists and competition for rooms can be fierce. However, the city has scores of B&Bs and an excellent hostel, so you should come up with something. If you're hoping to camp, keep your fingers crossed and try the deluxe Rowntree Park caravanning site on Terry Avenue. It's worth reserving in advance to claim one of the handful of tent spots this place offers. You simply cannot beat the location. If you strike out here, there are several campground options a few miles out of the city.

York Minster is one of England's most majestic cathedrals, and you'll want to reserve a good part of your day to pay it your respects. Begin with a free tour of the interior. There's so much to see here, you'll need a guide to help you sort it out. With your eyes still squinting from their introduction to the Minster's world-renowned stained glass, emerge from the building to pace the surrounding lawns, and savor Britain's largest Gothic cathedral from a host of angles. Some of the finest views of the cathedral and the city can be gained from York's perimeter walls. Access is free and the stroll is lovely.

You'll want to get an early start on your first day of cycling away from York, as one of the most magnificent abbey ruins in Europe awaits you at day's end. From the train station, follow the road beside the Ouse River, cycle past York Minster, and leave York on **Road A19** signed for **Thirsk.** There's a bike route signed into town all the way from Skelton, but we couldn't spot any counterparts heading our direction.

Stay with the busy **A19** as you pedal out through York's suburbs, and pick up a bike lane near the hamlet of **Rawcliffe** (campground here). Continue on to **Shipton** and swing **left** with signs for **Newton-on-Ouse** and the National Trust's **Beningbrough Hall.** Savor much quieter cycling as you push on through pleasant flat farmland. We encountered a tenacious wind from the west when we rode this section. We'll hope you don't.

Pass through Newton-on-Ouse and on to **Linton-on-Ouse.** Hit a **T** beyond Linton and go **left** for **Ouseburn** to cross the Ouse River on the Aldwark Toll Bridge (no charge for bikes). Keep **right** at the next junction to pedal through **Great Ouseburn.** You'll enjoy a string of typical English villages as you ride today, each with its own parish church and parish pub.

Gentle hills commence after Great Ouseburn—a hint of bigger things to come. Join the busy **Road B6265** toward **Ripon** as you continue. Recross the **Ouse River** in **Boroughbridge,** then look for a

**left** turn off the main road. It's signed for **Skelton** and **Langthorpe.** More serene cycling follows. Pedal past **Newby Hall** and rejoin **B6265** just before **Ripon.** The city's hilltop cathedral will lure you onward.

Ripon is worth a pause. It's a pleasant town with an attractive old core. Peek inside the cathedral for a look at the intricate wood ceiling and inhale a breath of the damp air emanating from the church's ancient crypt (671). If you're not camping, you'll probably want to hunt for a bed in Ripon, then make the 6-mi roundtrip ride to Fountains Abbey without your baggage.

Leave Ripon on the route signed for **Pateley Bridge** (Road B6265). The hills begin in earnest now. Climb out of town and watch for a small road to the **right** signed for **Galphay** and **Kirkby Malzeard.** If you're skipping Fountains Abbey (please don't!) or if you've already completed your visit, this is the road you'll want to take as you continue with the tour. To ride for Fountains Abbey, struggle onward with the route toward Pateley Bridge, and look for a turn to the **left** for **Studley Royal Park.**

Ride most of the way to the ruined abbey through the surrounding deer park, then walk the final 1/4 mi through the landscaped grounds. Fountains Abbey is one of the largest monastic ruins in England, and it's surrounded by the lush lawns and gardens of Studley Royal Park. Bring a picnic and hope for a sunny day. This is sightseeing at its best.

If you're looking for a campground to end your ride, please read the first paragraph of the next section for directions.

## Fountains Abbey to Hawes: 42 miles

From Fountains Abbey, backtrack to the **junction** signed for **Kirkby Malzeard** and go **left.** Climb steadily on this tiny road. Ride through **Galphay** and continue toward **Kirkby Malzeard.** (If you want to camp, go left after Galphay, then angle right toward Grantley. Don't be lured in by the campground sign leading left—they don't take tents. Watch for signs for Woodhouse Farm Campground about 1 mi later. Set on enormous grassy fields and blessed by hot showers, a small store, and laundry facilities, this will look like heaven after the horrendous hills you've just encountered.)

Cycle on through **Kirkby Malzeard,** then battle through rolling hills to **Masham.** Gaze to the west for views of the mounded Pennines, spread beneath the sky like purple piles of woven cloth. Descend a long hill before Masham, then feast your eyes on this lovely town of somber stone. Reach a **junction** with the main road and go **right** for **Ripon** to cross the River Ure. Veer **left** immediately after for **Richmond.**

You'll have fairly steady traffic to contend with as you climb away from the Ure and continue ascending for approximately 5 mi. Watch for a turn to the **left** signed for **Spennithorne,** and take this tiny road past farms and fields. Revel in much quieter cycling as you pass half a dozen junctions, staying with the main route for **Spennithorne.** A quick descent leads into Spennithorne.

Go **right** for **Harmby** and **Leyburn** just after you enter town, and climb **very steeply** to the main road. Go **left** on the main road to pedal into **Leyburn,** a hopping little tourist town with a well-signed **tourist office.** From Leyburn, descend with the **main road** (Road A684) toward **Hawes** and **Aysgarth Falls.** In **Wensley** (namesake of Wensleydale cheese), veer **right** onto the small road signed for **Bolton Castle.**

Exquisite scenery will ease your pain as you climb once more, with tantalizing views up the valley toward the Yorkshire hilltops. Look for the square towers of Bolton Castle tucked into a hillside as you pedal on. Keep **left** at the first junction and continue cycling for **Redmire.** You'll enter the Yorkshire Dales National Park as you ride past Redmire and stay with signs for **Carperby** and **Aysgarth Falls.**

Pass a **turnoff** for **Bolton Castle** (it's a ½-mi climb) and continue on a delightful small road through undulating terrain. You'll gain elevation steadily but pleasantly as you pass piled stone fences portioning brilliant green fields. Grazing cows and sheep dot the pastures like black-and-white chessmen on an emerald playing board. Cycle through the small settlement of **Carperby** and shun the turn for Aysgarth Falls (this is a worthwhile detour if you have the time).

Continue with your tiny byway to **Askrigg,** an attractive stone village with a twelfth-century church and scores of tourists. Portions of the BBC series *All Creatures Great and Small* were filmed here in the heart of James Herriott's beloved Yorkshire Dales. Cycle past the turn for Bainbridge as you follow your quiet route to **Hawes,** another busy tourist town.

Unless you're feeling incredibly energetic, make Hawes your stopping spot for the night. The hill out of town would give any cyclist nightmares—better to face it on fresh legs. Hawes offers a campground, beds at the aptly named Herriott Hotel, and brews for hikers and cyclists alike at the many pubs and tea rooms in town. Stop in at Hawes's **tourist information** office for help with lodgings. There's a Yorkshire Dales National Park office in town, too.

## Hawes to Dent: 14 miles

The party's over as you leave Hawes on **Road B6255** signed for **Ingleton.** A ridiculously steep pitch just out of town will make you feel as though you've ridden 80 mi instead of 80 meters. Do the best you can—and push it if you can't. The next 7 mi are unforgettable, painted against an incredible backdrop of Yorkshire vistas and punctuated by a series of incredibly punishing inclines. Short level stretches allow quick breathers, but you'll be sweating all the way to the crest of the pass.

Reach the top and descend briefly to take a **right** turn signed for **Dent** and **Sedbergh.** You'll feel your muscles as you climb once more, but the pain is soon over. Check your brakes and tighten up your chin strap as you dive into a sometimes hair-raising descent. You'll pass the picturesque **Dent Head Viaduct** (an old train bridge) in the midst of a **1:7 downhill grade** through a steep-sided gorge. It's difficult to stop for photos at this pace, but you won't regret it if you do. The scene is unforgettable.

Pass a secluded youth hostel, then an isolated campground, as you accompany the **River Dee** on its hasty journey down Dentdale toward the little town of Dent. As the incline mellows, the route becomes a narrow byway lined with moss-flecked walls of rock. Be very cautious here—it's one-way traffic, even on a bicycle.

Enter the tiny town of **Dent,** a personable village surrounded by working sheep farms and set in a deep valley contained by a sky of rushing clouds. There are campgrounds on either end of town, and limited indoor lodgings are available. Join the hordes of hobbling hikers wearing rain gear and heavy boots as they stroll along Dent's cobbled streets, and peek inside the town's souvenir shops, tea rooms, restaurants, and small groceries. Linger here to watch the locals work their sheep, to hear the sharp yelps of collies as they move the flocks, to listen to the bleating of the distant animals, scattered like cottonballs on the vivid hills.

## Dent to Hawkshead: 27 miles

You'll have more hauntingly beautiful scenery ahead as you depart Dent and cruise toward **Sedbergh** along the **River Dee.** It's a roller-coaster ride along the valley's sloping hillsides, with lots of short, steep uphill pitches and some precipitous downhills. Look for distant sheep grazing in lofty fields, and feast your eyes on the region's characteristic stone walls, rock houses, and rock roofs. Look for scores of English hikers, too. This area is a walker's paradise, and, as one English outdoorsman told us, "You can't throw a brick without hitting a tourist if you visit the Yorkshire Dales in August."

Follow road signs into **Sedbergh's center.** It's an attractive mid-size town, with plenty of shops and a **tourist information** office for the national park. Pause for a sticky bun from a local bakery while you consider your options here. The first (and probably sanest) choice is to take **Road A684** for **Kendal** from here. The route is busy but

*An ancient bridge tempts a cyclist in the Yorkshire Dales.*

direct. We opted for the nearly carless road for Howgill as we headed out of Sedbergh, then went on to Grayrigg before joining Road A685. The scenery was incredible, but so were the hills. If you're not feeling masochistic, take Road A684.

Either way, you'll be ready for a break when you cycle into Kendal, a bustling market city with lots to see. Visit the city's parish church and museum, or simply stroll the shopping streets to gather a hungry cyclist's picnic lunch. Leave Kendal on the busy road northwest signed for **Windermere,** and **climb steeply** away from the city. Savor a farewell vista of the Yorkshire Dales to the east, then arrive at a **roundabout** and follow signs for **Hawkshead (via ferry).**

Abandon the busy route toward Windermere as you cut across the ridgeline. It's a tough haul, with many steep pushes interspersed with brief level stretches. Mercifully, the traffic is mellow and the surroundings are delightful. Gaze northwest toward the enchanting silhouettes of the Cumbrian Mountains, and pedal between thick hedges in the shadows of twisted oak and piled stone walls.

A **gruesome incline** beyond the small settlement at **Crook** will steal some of your delight, but the grade eases as you struggle on toward Hawkshead. **Descend steeply** to a turn for **Bowness,** but stay with the signed route for the **ferry** to gain the shore of **Lake Windermere.** If you're cycling in spring, you'll be cheered by the bluebell-carpeted forest that covers the hillsides here. Pedal on to the ferry landing and hop aboard for the inexpensive 10-minute ride across the lake. Ferry waiting lines are hours long for auto passengers in August—the line will make you glad you're on a bike. Alas, the hill on the opposite shore will not.

Leave the ferry landing and climb **very steeply** away from Lake Windermere. Cycle through **Far Sawrey,** and push on to **Near Sawrey,** site of Beatrix Potter's Hilltop. The house where Potter wrote many of her best-loved children's stories is still furnished with her desk and stove, and the wood-scented rooms offer visitors a touching glimpse into the writer's life and work.

Pedal onward, with a fine vista of **Esthwaite Water** against its backdrop of peaks, and reach a signed turn for **Wray Castle.** You'll find a delightful lakeside campground (remember, "lakeside" means back down the hill!) if you take this route. The campground is administered by the National Trust and is open only to tents. Continuing from Wray Castle, it's possible to visit the touristy village of Ambleside on Lake Windermere's northern tip (youth hostel and scads of B&Bs).

We opted for a quieter route through **Hawkshead** instead, shunning the turn for Wray Castle and pedaling into the small town to look for a campground. With loads of tidy tea rooms and busy pubs, Hawkshead is a pleasant, if tourist-heavy town. Indoor lodgings are somewhat scarce, but there is a youth hostel in the vicinity. Hawkshead is the boyhood home of the famous Lake District bard, William Wordsworth, and it boasts a wonderful Beatrix Potter Museum, too.

To find the campground, continue with the route signed for **Ambleside.** The vast and often crowded site is on the right, a short walk from Hawkshead's center.

## Hawkshead to Carlisle (Campground): 41 miles

Leave Hawkshead on the road for **Ambleside,** and veer **left** after about 1/2 mi on a tiny route signed for **Barngates.** Silent and exquisite cycling follows as you pedal past stone farm buildings and stone walls and stone-faced sheep. With no cars to crowd you, you'll be able to hear the sheep chewing as you pass. Climb steadily to cross a larger road, and stay with signs for **Skelwith Bridge.** Enjoy peaceful pedaling to **Road A593,** where you'll go **right** for **Ambleside.** Dive **left** immediately after for **Langdale.**

Stay on this main road for about ½ **mi of steady climbing,** and watch for an **unsigned turn** to the **right.** The tiny byway is marked by a width-clearance warning proclaiming it passable for vehicles skinnier than 6 feet, 6 inches. If you qualify, climb unrelentingly on this ribbon of asphalt, keeping to the **right** at an **unsigned junction,** then to the **left** with signs for **Grasmere.** You'll encounter a wild **25 percent grade** on the descent into Grasmere. If you don't have a lot of confidence in your brakes, walk it!

Grasmere is yet another Lake District town built on the pence and pounds of literary pilgrims. Join the faithful in a tour of Dove Cottage, home of William Wordsworth and his sister Dorothy (and hangout of Samuel Taylor Coleridge) from 1799 to 1808, and stop in at the adjacent museum, too. If you decide to linger in this poetic setting, Grasmere has two nearby youth hostels and a score of B&Bs.

Depart Grasmere with **Road A591** for **Keswick,** and endure a steady ascent on a much-too-busy thoroughfare. Fortunately, there's a wide shoulder, so you'll still be able to appreciate the striking scenery as you climb between glowing green hills. Approach the south end of **Thirlmer Lake** and veer **left** for **Armboth** to gain a much quieter road along the lake's **west shore.** Enjoy forested, level cycling with views of the water as you continue.

Another route decision awaits at the north end of the lake. You can stay with signs for Keswick when the road angles left and rejoin the hectic Road A591 to ascend to the ridge above Derwent Water and the city. Keswick makes a great stopping spot if you would like to abandon your cycling for a few days to do some wandering in the countryside. We climbed Mount Skiddaw on our first tour through the Lake District, and we loved every minute of it. Keswick offers lots of lodging options, and you can easily regain our route by taking Road A66 toward Penrith when you leave.

If you opt for the less-traveled route from Thirlmer, go **right** at the **north end** of the lake when the road for Keswick angles left. **Cross** the main road (**Road A591**) and cycle onward to an **intersection** with another route heading north toward Threlkeld. Go **left** for **Threlkeld** and pedal on with views of the heather-blanketed peaks (purple in August). Reach a **junction** with the main **Keswick/Penrith road** and go **right** for a brief stretch of unpleasantly busy cycling.

Climb toward the small settlement at **Scales,** and watch for the **White Horse Inn** on the left side of the road. Dive **left** here to gain a **small road** that takes off behind the inn and savor a wonderful

close-up look at the hillside farms that have characterized this countryside for centuries. You'll ride within inches of unblinking curly-
horned sheep as you pedal this narrow, roughly paved route across the
hillsides. This is not a road for someone in a hurry—half a dozen live-
stock gates span your asphalt trail, and you'll be forced to dismount to
open and close each one.

Trace your rolling route to the stone village of **Mungrisdale,** where
handsome old farmhouses will charm you anew, then continue
through the equally picturesque settlement of **Mosedale.** The terrain
opens up into more gentle hill country as you keep to the **right** with
the **main (low) route,** then follow signs for **Caldbeck** to **Hesket
Newmarket.**

Revel in a speedy descent to the edge of Hesket Newmarket, then go
**right** for **Carlisle** to dive down even more. Angle **left** at the bottom of
the hill and climb to an **intersection** with a busier road (**Road
B5305**). Go **left** here to ascend toward **Sebergham.** Another swift
downhill plunge will carry you across the **creek** that runs through
Sebergham. Just across the **bridge,** veer **right** on a tiny road beside
the water.

Stay with signs for **Welton** as you follow this small byway along the
creek, then endure more uphill chugging as you abandon the water's
course to climb to **Welton** and **Road B5299.** Swing **right** onto Road
B5299 and ride toward **Dalston.** If you need groceries for supper,
Dalston should fit the bill. Leave the midsize town, cross some **train
tracks,** and watch for the **Dalston Hall Caravan Park/Golf Club**
on your right. Pull in here to find a charming little campground. It's
quiet, well tended, and inexpensive. (If you're looking for a room, read
on and ride on to Carlisle.)

## Carlisle (Campground) to Newcastleton: 29 miles

Continue toward **Carlisle** on **Road B5299.** Traffic is tolerable on
this route into the city, although things pick up as you near the center.
Arrive at a traffic **roundabout** (just before a tall **smokestack**) as you
enter Carlisle, and turn **right** to get on **Junction Street.** Pedal this
thoroughfare a short distance, then angle **left** across the **River Cal-
dew.** Cross above the railroad tracks on the **Victoria Viaduct,** and
angle **left** from there to find Carlisle Cathedral and most of the city's
historic attractions.

Carlisle's **tourist office** is in the Old Town Hall on English Street.
They can help you locate a B&B or direct you to the youth hostel in
the city. Take a tour of Carlisle Castle (administered by English Heritage), and be sure to visit Carlisle Cathedral. It's a somewhat squatty
building of reddish stone, but it boasts a wonderful interior with an
intricate painted ceiling and lovely stained glass.

While you're in Carlisle, you might consider using the city as a base for a one-day exploration of the nearby excavations of Hadrian's Wall. Check on tours at the tourist office, or stow your baggage and cycle northeast on Road B6264, then Road A69, then Road B6318 to find the National Trust site known as Housesteads Fort. The site contains 3½ mi of the Wall, and it provides wonderful insight into the hilly line of defense built by the Romans between 122 and 128.

When you're ready to introduce yourself to Scotland, leave Carlisle to the north by crossing the **River Eden** on the **Eden Bridge**. Stay with **Road A7** as you head northward with far too much traffic for comfort. The route is particularly unpleasant as you work your way through Carlisle's suburbs. Hit a **roundabout** 3 mi from the center and continue with signs for **Longtown** and **Galashiels** on A7.

You'll have level cycling to **Longtown.** As you enter the city, watch for a turn to the **right** for **Netherby** and **Penton.** Take this route and gain a wonderfully quiet road through forest and grazing land as you follow the valley cut by Liddel Water. You'll be pedaling in England, but simply gaze to your left across the ribbonlike stream to see the mounded hills of Scotland smiling their welcome.

The gently rolling route leads through scattered villages, but it's quite a solitary ride. Reach a **junction** with **Road B6318** and go **left** for **Penton/Station Road.** Veer **right** just after to continue on your quiet route toward **Kershopefoot** (the turn is signed for Station Road). Pass scattered farm complexes and marvel at their wonderful stone buildings. When the road branches near Nook, keep to the **left** with the main route.

Push on to another **junction** just before **Kershopefoot** (it's 5½ mi from the Penton junction), and go **left** to descend to **Liddel Water** and cross into Scotland. Climb briefly to **Road B6357,** where you'll veer **right** to pedal toward **Newcastleton.** Newcastleton is an excellent example of a Scottish "planned village," with its wide main street and standardized houses clustered around a large square. The small city offers two hotels, ample shopping, and plenty of friendly locals.

If you want to camp, there's a caravan park in town that *might* take in a desperate tenter. However, it's spendy and they don't really want anyone without a caravan in tow. If you don't mind free camping, the city offers an undeveloped and unsupervised camping area (no water, toilets, or fees) along the banks of the small river that runs along the east edge of town.

## Newcastleton to Melrose: 41 miles

Leave Newcastleton with **Road B6367** and continue along the verdant valley floor. The road branches about 2 mi beyond town. Angle **right** for **Jedburgh** and stay with signs for this midsize city past **Old Castleton** and **Larriston.** Pedal through gently rolling pastureland, with the cries of scattered sheep for company. After the small settlement at **Saughtree,** the day's work begins.

**Ascend steeply** (definitely a low-gear hill!) for about 30 minutes, and try to forget the pain in your muscles by concentrating on the lovely forms of the dark Cheviot Hills to the east. More mounded hills rule the scene ahead, their flanks dotted with wandering sheep, and bright bluebells and blossoming purple heather line the road in August. Climb and climb, with solitude and scenery to cheer you, then revel in a **long, swift descent** to **Road A6088.**

Go **left** on **A6088** and dive downhill to **Bonchester Bridge,** a tiny community astride a small creek. There's an attractive waterside campground here. Abandon Road A6088 in town, and go **right** on **Road B6357** for **Jedburgh.** You'll face another (less-punishing) climb, then enter rolling terrain as you cycle on. Arrive at a junction with the perilous **Road A68** about 2 mi short of Jedburgh, and go **left** here to endure a busy finish into the city.

You'll pass Ferniehirst Castle (sixteenth-century border castle, open on Wednesdays) on your way into Jedburgh. Look for the ruin of Jedburgh Abbey ahead as you near the city center. The abbey is a beautiful sight, its roofless walls rising heavenward from an emerald lawn, its shattered arches piercing a timeless blue sky. If you're looking for a picnic spot, there's a car park and picnic area on the left, with a fantastic view of the abbey on its hillock above Jed Water.

*Scotland's Jedburgh Abbey is a haunting skeleton of stone.*

Stop in at the abbey and consider purchasing a short-term membership in Historic Scotland while you're there. You'll gain free admission to Jedburgh Abbey, Melrose Abbey, and Edinburgh Castle (all along our route), as well as scores of other Scottish sites. Jedburgh Abbey, founded in 1138, was host to many historic events across the centuries. A devastating raid in 1545 left the abbey church in ruin and put an end to abbey life.

Continue into the city with the main road (Road A68). You'll find a **tourist office** on the right, not far from the abbey entrance. Jedburgh boasts a busy core, with hotels and shopping, and you might pause to visit the Jedburgh Castle Jail and/or Mary Queen of Scots House. Leave town on the horrid **Road A68** toward **Edinburgh,** and grit your teeth through 3½ to 4 mi of unpleasant cycling (spurning an escape onto Road A698 toward Kelso). Keep with Road A68 to **cross** the **River Teviot,** then look for a turn to the **right** onto **Road B6400** for **Nisbet.**

Make your escape joyfully and pedal the serene Road B6400 through a pleasant forest. You'll cross the route of an ancient Roman road (Dere Street), pass a garden, then look for a large **manor/farm complex** marked by a low stone wall on both sides of the road. Just beyond the farm, take the **unsigned turn** to the **left** to climb steeply through the trees. Skirt along the base of Peniel Heugh, a 744-foot hill that was once the site of Roman camps (now crowned by the impressive Waterloo Monument).

After the auto inferno of Road A68, you'll love the pastoral peacefulness of this route. Pedal on to **Maxton,** then go **left** on **Road A698** for **St. Boswells.** An unwelcome return to **Road A68** awaits you at St. Boswells, as you continue with signs for **Edinburgh** and **Melrose.** (There's a signed turn for Dryburgh Abbey at St. Boswells. It's a 4-mi detour to the majestic ruins. Or, you can try the footpath route signed to the right off Road A68, just beyond St. Boswells.)

Escape the busy road beyond St. Boswells by swinging **left** onto the quieter route through **Newtown St. Boswells.** Stay with signs for **Melrose** and **Galashiels** from here. You'll climb steeply out of Newtown, and endure a narrow and hill-studded route to Melrose. Hug the shoulder and pedal hard. Leave the main road to swing **right** into Melrose's **center** and coast down into this pleasant town, made popular by the presence of yet another striking abbey ruin.

There's an excellent campground at the far end of town, and it's an easy walk back to the abbey from the site. Melrose has a youth hostel, a hotel, and B&Bs galore, if you need a bed. Check at the **tourist office** near the abbey for help with lodgings. Another property of Historic Scotland, Melrose Abbey was the great love of Scotland's great man of letters, Sir Walter Scott. Backed by the three heather-blanketed peaks of the Eildons, the haunting ruins are an artist's or photographer's dream. Let your imagination prowl across the centuries, then wander into town for a "cuppa" and a square of shortbread.

If you're inclined to linger an extra day in Melrose, a visit to Abbotsford (2 mi west) should be on your itinerary. This mansion was the home of Sir Walter Scott for 20 years, and he wrote many of his poems and novels here. Hikers would do well to spend the day exploring the Eildon Hills or the banks of the River Tweed. Ask at the tourist office for walking routes.

## Melrose to Edinburgh (Campground): 42 miles

Continue on the main road through the city as you depart Melrose, then go **right** for **Gattonside** to shun the busy Road A6091. Veer **left** for **Galashiels** immediately after, and pedal **Road B6374** to the large city. Just after entering **Galashiels** (look for the town sign), take an **unsigned road** to the **left** to descend to the quiet banks of the **River Tweed.** Keep to the **left** to cycle **under Road A6091** (a lofty bridge across the Tweed) and stay with your scenic route beside the river.

Enjoy pleasant, peaceful cycling as you trace the water's course. The River Tweed is one of Scotland's longest waterways, and it's famed as the "queen of the salmon rivers." You'll see plenty of sheep as you cycle the Tweed Valley, as the woolen industry is one of the traditional mainstays of the area. Join the hectic **Road A7** toward **Selkirk** and **Hawick** for a short stint, then dive **right** onto **Road B7060** for **Yair.**

Quiet riding becomes a bit less so as you go **right** onto **Road A707** and continue along the Tweed Valley with signs for **Peebles.** Enjoy scenic, easy cycling through **Walkerburn** (Scottish Museum of Woolen Textiles) and on to **Innerleithen.** Traffic is moderate and the surrounding hills are lovely. Arrive at Innerleithen, a midsize town with a yen for tourists. The city's Traquair House is worth a visit, especially if you passed on Abbotsford. The house's history goes back as far as 1107 (visit of Alexander I) and its historical guest book reads like a who's who of Scottish royalty.

If you're running late (or running out of energy) by the time you cycle into Innerleithen, you might consider ending your day here. It's another 24 hilly miles to Edinburgh's campground (29 mi to the city center) from Innerleithen, and there aren't many lodging options along the way. You'll probably be able to rustle up an affordable B&B in Innerleithen without too much difficulty. One added note—if you haven't purchased a street map of Edinburgh by now, do it before you leave Innerleithen. You're going to need it!

To continue for Edinburgh, leave Innerleithen on **Road B709** headed north (it's signed for **Heriot** and the **golf club**). Delightful cycling follows as you begin with a gentle climb up the long, broad valley carved by Leithen Water. Sheep are everywhere—in the fields, on the hillsides, even on the road! And the heather-draped hills are regal and silent in their purple robes. The climb gains intensity as you continue. You'll crest one scenic pass and cruise downhill to a road **junction.** Continue **straight** with signs for **Gorebridge.**

Ascend once more as you pedal through a lovely basin ringed by hills. You'll feel like whooping as you reach the summit and begin a **long descent** with fantastic views all the way to Edinburgh and the Firth of Forth. Watch for a **left** turn for **Middleton** at the end of your descent, and cycle through this small village, then dive downhill to cross a **small creek.** You'll see the extremely unappealing Road A7 off to the right. Veer over to join its crash course toward Edinburgh.

Endure awful cycling with lots of traffic for a time, then grab a **left** turn onto **Road B704** for **Bonnyrigg.** Climb again to pedal through the bustling development of Bonnyrigg/Lasswade, and continue **straight** across a main road signed for Rosewell. Reach a **junction** with **Road A768** and go **left** here for **Loanhead.** Continue with this busy thoroughfare as it angles **right** for **Edinburgh.** If you haven't already figured it out by now, you might as well admit it—this city won't be fun to cycle into.

We opted for a stop a few miles short of Edinburgh's center, putting up our tent at Mortonhall Campground. To find the campground, watch for a **left** turn off the main road in. It's signed for **Gracemount Leisure Center.** Pedal along **Captains Road** toward **Mortonhall,** and continue straight with **Captains Road** through the next main junction (stay with signs for **Mortonhall** and **Fairmilehead**).

You'll find the vast and popular Mortonhall Campground on the right, a bit farther on. Prices are high, but that doesn't deter the huge crowds that make this modern facility their base for sightseeing in Edinburgh. You'll find hot showers, a laundry, and a small store here, and there's convenient bus service into the city center from just across the street.

If you're planning to cycle into town or to continue in to the youth hostel at 7-8 Bruntsfield Crescent (on the route toward the center), stay with Captains Road past the campground, arrive at a **main intersection,** and go **right.** The youth hostel is signed to the right of the road. You'll have 4 or 5 miles of busy pedaling to make the city center.

Edinburgh has more B&Bs than you can shake a bike pump at, but you'll find lodgings tight in August when the world-renowned Edinburgh International Festival is taking place. Unless you're a fiend for culture, movies, music, and crowds, you might want to schedule your visit to avoid the festival weeks. There are a handful of hostels and scores of hotels in Edinburgh, and the city runs a much "campier" municipal campground on the Firth of Forth, if you can't stand the caravan fleets at Mortonhall.

Begin your sightseeing at the main **tourist information** center near the central train station, then climb the hill to Edinburgh Castle, walk The Royal Mile, and explore the carefully designed "New Town." Gray, dingy, and somewhat bleak under overcast skies, Scotland's capital comes to life when the sun sparkles on its buildings. If the clouds part for an afternoon, hustle to the castle ramparts for a fantastic vista of the sprawling city and the vibrant Firth of Forth.

*Nearsighted horses study a road sign in the Lake District.*

# TOUR NO. 3

# A CHEESY PROPOSITION

*Brussels, Belgium, to Amsterdam, Holland*

*Distance:* 438 kilometers (272 miles)
*Estimated time:* 9 riding days
*Best time to go:* May for tulips, June for sun, September for solitude
*Terrain:* Flatly undemanding
*Connecting tours:* Tours No. 2 and 4

If you're unsure of your conditioning or courage for bicycle touring in Europe, there are few countries more ideal to "get your feet wet" than Holland, a land so flat it's practically underwater and so overrun with bicycles that cyclists rule the road. Belgium, although a bit less biker friendly, offers yet another hefty dose of easy terrain, mixed in with the almost constant hum of urbanization. If you're seeking adventure, wide-open spaces, or great physical challenge, however, perhaps you can combine this tour with a more demanding ride in northern England or France.

Flemish Belgium sometimes seems like one eternal city, and you'll have to deal with busy roads and plenty of urban cycling as you begin this tour. Main roads in Belgium usually have bike lanes—unfortunately, they also possess unpleasantly heavy traffic. Be sure to invest in a good map, as we found smaller Belgian roads to be poorly signed and difficult to negotiate. Fortunately, the cities you'll pedal through are well worth visiting, and you'll find unimagined delights in Mechelen, Gent, and Brugge.

Because you'll be cycling through "Flemish Belgium" on your way to Holland, keep in mind that this country is still openly divided on one issue—language. Don't risk offending local sensibilities by seeming unaware of Belgian diversity. It's best to leave your French in Brussels. Attempt your greetings in Flemish (a variant of Dutch), or simply bungle along in English. Belgians are skilled language jugglers.

Holland, though one of the most heavily populated countries in all of Europe, has a more rural feel to it than northern Belgium does, and the land's 30,000 km of cycle routes make it a pleasure to explore. The Dutch people are hospitable, helpful, and amazingly skilled in languages. You'll seldom find a young Hollander who doesn't speak at least some English. One Dutch fellow shrugged off our amazement with his language prowess with a wry smile. "We're a small country, and we like to do business," he explained.

Bicycling is a national pastime in Holland, as evidenced by the more than 14 million bicycles that call the country home. You'll see city women toting tots and groceries and country men hauling hoes and vegetables. Holland's bicycle path system is incredible, and most cities are crisscrossed with scores of bike lanes and illuminated with dozens of bicycle traffic lights. Watch for signs showing a white bicycle on a blue background—they mean that use of the bike paths they mark is compulsory. Dutch cyclists are conscientious about complying with traffic laws—you should be, too.

**CONNECTIONS.** The busy Brussels International Airport (Zaventem) northeast of Brussels is a major European entry point for travelers from the United States and Canada. Airfares to Brussels are competitively priced, so it's an economical spot to begin your cycling trip. Amsterdam boasts a busy airport, too, so if you're flying in and out of the same city, you can easily close the loop with a quick train ride.

Train travel with bicycles is delightfully hassle free in Holland and quite convenient in Belgium, too. Many Dutch trains have baggage cars where you can simply wheel your bike aboard, secure it snugly for the ride, then unload it yourself at your destination. Please note that bicycles are prohibited on certain trains during peak commuter hours (6:30 to 9:00 A.M. and 4:30 to 6:00 P.M.). If you really want to cover the country, you can purchase a week-long "go anywhere" ticket for your bicycle and hop trains to hither and yon.

If you'd like to do some cycling in France as well, you might consider tracing this tour in reverse, then continuing on with Tours No. 4 and 5, our Brussels-to-Angers ride. Another option for those who might like to see a bit of Britain on their European adventure would be to catch a ferry from either Oostende (near Brugge), Rotterdam, or Hoek van Holland and blend some English or Scottish cycling into their trip. (Please check the "Connections" sections in Tours No. 1 and 2.)

**INFORMATION.** Write to the Belgian and Dutch national tourist offices before you leave. They'll send bundles of literature, plus campground and tourist maps. The address for Belgium is Belgian National Tourist Office, 745 Fifth Avenue, #714, New York, New York 10151. Ask for a street map of Brussels to make your arrival go more smoothly, and mention that you'll also be visiting Gent and Brugge. Once in Belgium, you'll find well-stocked tourist offices in almost every midsize city, and it's usually easy to obtain guidance in English.

For information on Holland, write to The Netherlands Board of Tourism, 355 Lexington Avenue, 21st Floor, New York, New York 10017. Request specific information on cycling and camping (if you're interested), and ask them to send you a street map of Amsterdam (you might get lucky!). Holland's tourist offices are known as VVV. They are abundant and helpful. However, you should expect to pay a slight fee for maps and city guides. If you plan to do much sightseeing, check into Holland's *Museumkaart*. It's good for free admission to more Dutch museums than you'll ever have time to visit.

Despite the Hollanders' mastery of language, you'll want to familiarize yourself with a little Dutch in preparation for your ride. It's especially critical to recognize the Dutch phrases used in signing bike routes and roads. Here is a brief list of words and phrases you'll need to know. *Fiets* is a bicycle, and *M.U.V. fietsers* means a route is acceptable for cyclists (this sign is sometimes placed on one-way streets and dead ends). A *fietspad* is a bike path, and *fietsers oversteken* means bikes must cross the road. *Dorgaand verkeer* means "all directions" (as in, no matter where you're headed *this* is the road you want).

Potential reading material for Belgium and Holland includes *The Real Guide: Holland, Belgium, and Luxembourg,* the *Blue Guide Holland,* the *Blue Guide Belgium and Luxembourg,* Michelin's *Green Guide Netherlands,* and Michelin's *Green Guide Belgium and Luxembourg.*

**MAPS.** Michelin produces an excellent map series for route finding in Belgium, and the 1:200,000 detail will probably satisfy all your needs. There are special cycling maps available for Belgium (they provide greater detail and indicate cycle routes), but you'll find them rather expensive if you're covering much ground. Maps are readily available in bookstores in the country, but it's a good ideal to *arrive* with your first map already in your handlebar bag.

Map choices verge on mind boggling in Holland. Depending on how much detail you want and how many guilders you're willing to shell out, you can purchase cycling maps at scales of 1:50,000 and up. The *ANWB Toeristenkaart* series at 1:100,000 is an economical option. Look for your maps at tourist offices or bookstores.

**ACCOMMODATIONS.** Dutch campgrounds are pleasant, abundant, and affordable, and you can get listings of sites from the Dutch tourist offices (VVV). If you're visiting in high season (July and August), coastal campsites will be crammed and most others will be crowded. Belgian campgrounds, although less abundant (and often less convenient) than their Dutch counterparts, are equally well equipped. Because many campgrounds in Belgium operate as "camping clubs," with regular visitors who know just where they're located, campsites are often very poorly signed. Expect to hunt when you're looking for a Belgian campground.

Camping in either country is an accommodation bargain, when compared to the price of hotel rooms. Look for youth hostels, student hostels, university lodgings, or unpretentious hotels if you're on a budget.

**SUPPLIES.** Shopping should be fairly effortless in both of these modernized countries. However, in Holland, grocery stores are often tucked away in a main square and sometimes difficult to find. Look for *Winkel Centrum* (shopping center) signs to clue you in to a store's location. Shopping hours are usually Monday through Saturday from 9:00 A.M. to 6:00 P.M., with an occasional afternoon or morning off. Banks in Holland keep similar hours.

Belgium adheres a bit more closely to the French custom of lunch-time closures, so you'll have to watch out for midday shutdowns if you're shopping in small stores or in rural areas. Don't expect to buy groceries on Sunday in either country.

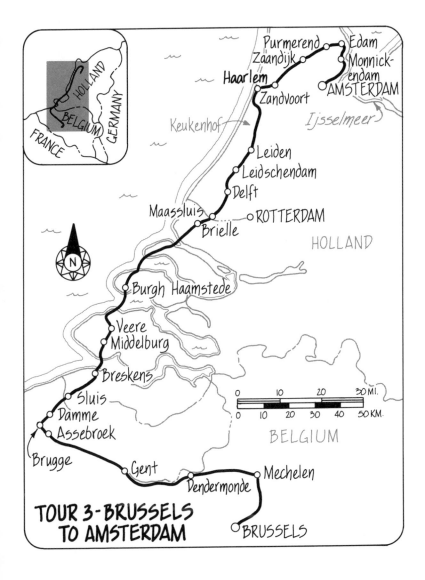

TOUR 3-BRUSSELS TO AMSTERDAM

Dutch food is hearty and simple, from the famous cheeses such as Edam and Gouda to pickled cabbage and salty herring. The Dutch people have been traders and travelers for centuries, and their cuisine is heavily influenced by the countries they've visited. Indonesian restaurants are particularly abundant here. Try one out if you need a break from bread and cheese. One thing the Dutch don't need to import is beer—Dutch brews are famed throughout the world.

Belgium boasts its own beer prowess with more than 300 varieties brewed within the country. Sample a seafood dinner at a Belgian restaurant—the people's passion for fresh mussels borders on fanatical. And be sure to try a sweet Belgian waffle for breakfast some morning. Buy it warm from a street vendor (not cold and sugary from the supermarket shelf). One more thing—you haven't been to Belgium if you haven't eaten *frites*. This greasy pile of fried potatoes, topped with a huge scoop of mayonnaise or a river of curry catsup, puts American french fries to shame. (It may also put your arteries into total panic.)

Since cycling is incredibly popular in both Belgium and Holland, you'll find an abundance of bicycle shops to serve you. Try to seek out a shop that doesn't have a total racing emphasis, however, as touring parts sometimes run a distant second to the passion for racing gear.

## Brussels to Mechelen: 30 kilometers

We're going to preface this 30-km section of your tour with a recommendation that may seem rather strange for a cycling guidebook. Take the train! Brussels is huge, and the traffic around this city is horrendous. Add in the fact that drivers here are less than biker friendly, and you've got a good argument in favor of the train. On our first visit to Brussels almost 10 years ago, an English-speaking friend told us about his first driving lesson in the city. "What do I do if someone gets in my way?" he asked his aggressive driving instructor. "Why, ya kill 'em!" his tutor replied. Enough said ....

If you arrive in Belgium at Brussels International Airport, you can load your bicycle and gear (boxed or unboxed) aboard the quick commuter train into the city center (we took our bikes right into the passenger compartment), then transfer your baggage to a northbound train for Mechelen. The ride to Mechelen takes less than an hour, and this little city offers a much more placid introduction to Belgium than Brussels does. When you purchase your train tickets at the airport office, inquire about making the switch to a Mechelen-bound train.

Of course, you'll want to do some sightseeing in Brussels. It is an attractive city and the Grand-Place is undoubtedly one of Europe's most impressive squares. Hotels in Brussels are steep, but there are several youth hostels. Stop in at the **tourist office** in the town hall on the Grand-Place for help with your accommodation search. If you don't find the train cost to be prohibitive, you may want to find your lodgings in Mechelen and simply "commute" into Brussels. After all, it's the European way.

For those set on cycling this section, we recommend trying to time your ride for a Saturday or Sunday when urban thoroughfares are a bit more friendly. Purchase a cycling map in Brussels, tighten up your helmet's chin strap, and go for it!

Once in Mechelen, head for the central square (*Grote Markt*) to find the city's well-stocked **tourist office** in the *Stadhuis*. Mechelen, once a center of great power and wealth, is today a comfortable city for exploring on foot. You'll find admirable architecture and plenty of activity, wherever you roam. Begin in the impressive *Grote Markt,* then visit Saint Rombout's Cathedral, which boasts a lacy choir and a fifteenth-century bell tower with 98 bells and a world-famous carillon. Free carillon concerts are given on Monday nights during the summer months.

## Mechelen to Gent: 64 kilometers

You'll have few hills and very little solitude on this ride west toward Gent. Fortunately, Belgian cities filled with architectural treasures will repay you for your unsuccessful search for quietness. From Mechelen's *Grote Markt,* follow **Ijzeren-Leen** south across the **Dijle River,** cycle past a massive city gate, and continue with signs for **Hombeek.** Hit a **T** at **Hombeek,** and go **left** toward **Kapelle-op-den-Bos.** The road has entirely too much traffic for comfort, but there's a bike lane to lend a little security.

Cross under a set of **train tracks,** then over a **large canal.** Parallel the train tracks past **Kapelle** (the city will be on your right), and follow signs for **Londerzeel.** As you enter Londerzeel, you'll meet a one-way street coming at you from the center of town. Follow it (carefully) to a main **intersection** and go **right.** Veer **left** shortly after for **Merchtem** and **Steenhuffel.** Cycle onward about **1 km** to where the road makes a **sharp left;** continue **straight** (unsigned) instead. Pedal this small road to an **intersection** with a larger, busier road, and go **right.** Endure this route for **1 or 2 km,** then dive **left** at a turn signed for **Buggenhout.**

Keep the railroad tracks on your right as you approach the small town (the road branches before town, with both ways signed for Buggenhout—don't cross the tracks). Buggenhout offers shopping opportunities and an incredibly hard-to-find campground (it took us nearly an hour). Cruise past the small community, keeping the train tracks on your right.

When your route swings away from the tracks about 1½ km beyond Buggenhout, zig **right** to pedal on the north side of the train line for a

*Brugge is a delight of piled roofs and lively streets.*

short time. **Recross** the tracks soon after, hit a town sign for **Lebbeke,** and veer **left** to leave the tracks at last. Ride about ¹/₂ km and take a **right** onto the route signed for **St. Gillis** and **Dendermonde.**

Cycle toward the center of St. Gillis, and go **left** to ride toward the city's **large church.** You'll arrive at a **main road** cutting through the town just in front of the church. Go **right** here to pedal on toward **Dendermonde.** Cross the railroad tracks (yes, the same ones!) on the edge of town, and continue toward the *centrum* (don't get on the ring road) as you cycle **Brusselsestraat** past the city's 1822 Brussels Gate and across a large canal (the Dender).

Continue to the delightful *Grote Markt,* with an outstanding fourteenth-century town hall (**tourist office** inside) and several noteworthy old buildings. You'll probably want to take a break to admire the city's architecture. Consider taking a stroll through the *beguinage,* an enclosed community of seventeenth-century dwellings that is unique to this region.

Leave Dendermonde's *Grote Markt* with the route signed for **Gent** and **Aalst,** then go **left** onto **Kerkstraat** to cycle past the Gothic Church of Our Lady and continue out of the city. Heavy traffic will accompany you as you skinny into a litter-strewn **bike lane** along **Road N416** toward **Gent.** Cycle through Wichelen and Wetteren with the busy main route. You'll have bike lanes most of the way.

At **Wetteren,** you can attempt a quieter approach to Gent by taking the signed route for Laarne and zigzagging from there. We opted for the main-road route, having found little in the way of solitude on *any* road near a large Belgian city, and pedaled on from Wetteren to join **Road N9** into town. Traffic was as awful as expected, but an almost constant **bike lane** made cycling a bit less harrowing.

Ride in toward Gent's **center** and head for the town hall (*Stadhuis*) to find the **tourist office.** You'll want a city map (if you don't already have one), and the office staff will be able to give you help with lodgings, too. Gent's university provides cheap rooms between mid-July and September, and there are two campgrounds west of the city center. The closest is Camping Blaarmeersen, at Zuiderlaan 12, but you may find it fully booked in high season.

Once the accommodation problem is solved, settle in to enjoy a truly remarkable city. Gent once rivalled Paris in power and prestige. Although it's a small player on the European board these days, the city still possesses a wealth of architecture from the Renaissance period. You'll easily blow half a day strolling along Gent's canals, ducking inside its churches, and wandering the city streets with your nose turned skyward as you admire one lovely building after another.

## Gent to Brugge: 45 kilometers

From Gent's **center,** ride past **St.-Niklasskerk** and cross the canal on the picturesque **St.-Michiels-Brug.** Stay with **Hoogstraat** to cross another canal, then turn **right** onto a small road paralleling the water. Enjoy surprisingly serene cycling as you pedal beside the canal for about 4 km. Ride through **Vinderhoute** and go **right** on a busier road to **cross** the **canal.** Next, veer **right** for **Lovendegem** to swing around and under the main road and gain additional canalside cycling.

Share your route with Belgian day trippers as you pedal beside the water, pass **Lovendegem,** then cross under the bridge to **Durmen** and go **right.** You'll reach a **junction** signed for Lovendegem (straight)—go **left** here. A miserable stretch of roadway, paved with rough stones, leads into **Zomergem.** You'll pick up signs for **Brugge** from Zomergem (let's hope you don't have to pick up a few fillings, too).

The well-signed route for Brugge leads through **Ursel, Knesselare, Oedelem,** and on to **Assebroek.** Pedaling is effortless, traffic is steady, and an endless succession of small towns, farms, and fields dotted with cows will entertain you. There's a **bike lane** most of the way along **Road N337,** and as long as you're not fighting a headwind, you should make excellent time.

You'll come face to face with a very busy **ring road** as you approach

Brugge's lovely **Gentpoort** (one of several city gates). To find camping, go right on the ring road, then right again on Road N9 signed for Gent. Watch for campground signs on the right after about ½ km (just before a massive GB Maxi store), and swing right to find the crowded but adequate Camping Memling. It's a long walk or a quick bus ride to the city center from here.

If you're looking for indoor accommodations, cross the canal and head for the **city center** from Gentpoort. You can get help at Brugge's **tourist office** at Burg 11, just east of the *Markt* (central square). Brugge has a few centrally located hostels and one "official" youth hostel in Steenbrugge, south of town. If you haven't made reservations in advance, expect to scramble for lodgings in July and August. This town gives new definition to the word "popular." You won't believe the hordes of tourists you'll encounter here. Despite all that, Brugge is worth the effort.

Begin your sightseeing at the *Markt,* a central square enclosed by an incredible collection of captivating buildings. If you do only one thing in Brugge, climb the 366 steps of the *belfort,* a soaring tower that provides a breathtaking view of the canal-cut city. Brugge's churches are justifiably famous, and its Church of Our Lady cherishes a *Madonna and Child* painted by Michelangelo. More than anything, Brugge is a city for strolling. Follow one of the walking tours on the tourist-office handout (or follow them all!), and spend a day savoring one of Europe's most captivating cities.

## Brugge to Veere: 48 kilometers

You'll have a delightful day of cycling ahead of you as you leave Brugge's center via the **Kruispoort** (or return to the ring road via Road N9 from the campground), and cycle north in the bike lane along the **ring road.** Swing **right** with signs for **Damme** just before crossing the **Canal Brugge-Sluis,** and ride **Damsevaart Zuid** beside the water. Savor easy, scenic cycling as you follow the paved bike lane next to the canal, surrounded by lots of cows and quiet fields.

Pick up signs for the **Noordzee Route LF1** (long-distance bike trail) as you approach Damme, a quaint little canalside town with an attractive *Stadhuis* (**tourist office** inside). Continue along the southeast bank of the canal until you reach a **crossing** signed for **Oostkerke.** Go **left** here, then veer **right** as soon as you're across the water to cycle a paved canalside bike route (ignore dead-end signs) that will take you all the way to **Sluis** and your entry into Holland.

Entertain yourself by studying the scores of fishermen along the banks of the canal, decked out in rubber boots and huddled beneath huge umbrellas. Cross the Belgian/Dutch border without fanfare and arrive in **Sluis,** a busy tourist town with inviting shops and streets.

You'll bid a reluctant farewell to your canalside cycling here, as you continue with the route for **Breskens.** The road is paralleled by a paved bike path, and it's heavily signed with bike-route directionals.

Watch the signed **Noordzee Route** veer off to the left toward Cadzand—it's more direct if you simply continue **straight** for **Breskens,** cycling through flat (what else?) farmland dotted with your first Dutch windmills. As you near **Breskens,** your route will intersect with **Road N58.** Go **left** here to cycle a roadside bike path signed for **Vlissingen** and the **ferry.** (If you'd like to take a look at the fishing town of Breskens before hopping on your ferry across the Western Scheldt, stay with the route signed for Breskens's center. You can continue to the ferry landing from town.)

The 20-minute ferry ride to Vlissingen is frequent and free to bicycle riders. Simply cycle past the lineup of automobiles and go right into the ferry building. There's a special set of bicycle doors that leads out to the belly of the boat. If you're cycling in August, as we were, you'll have lots of company.

Debark at Vlissingen and cross the road with signs for the **Noordzee Route LF 1b.** Pedal past the **train station** and across the **canal,** then swing **right** to gain a lovely canalside route all the way to **Middelburg.** Stay on the west bank of the Kanaal door Walcheren, admiring pleasure boats and windmills as you ride. Follow the **bike signs** for the *centrum* to cycle into Middelburg's enchanting town square. The *Stadhuis,* although partially destroyed during fighting in World War II, has been restored to all its Gothic exuberance, and the city's main square forms a lovely setting for the building. Look for Middelburg's **VVV** just off the square.

The Noordzee bicycle route takes a more westerly course from Middelburg, while we opted to leave town on the road signed for **Veere.** Traffic is fairly steady, but you'll pick up a bike lane not far from Middleburg. The riding is effortless as you approach Veere. When the road branches 1 km short of town, keep to the **right** for **Veere.** You'll spot a magical-looking windmill in a field off to the left. If you're planning to camp, watch for a campground sign on the right as you near the outskirts of the city. Swing off the road to find a small, pleasant campground that's an easy walk from town.

Continue into Veere, passing a **tourist office** on the way, then pause at the village's muscle-bound fourteenth-century church. The unfinished tower gives the building the appearance of a stumpy giant, ruling the town with a good-natured scowl. Veere's streets are charming (and often filled with charmed tourists), and its little pleasure boat harbor is a lovely sight on a sunny afternoon. Contrast the elegance of the belfry in Veere's old town hall with the humorous homeliness of the church tower. There's a respectable grocery store in town if you need to shop, but you'll find indoor lodgings to be scarce and dear.

# Veere to Brielle: 69 kilometers

Pack your sunscreen, your bathing suit, and your camera where they're easy to reach today—if the skies are friendly, you may need all three. In fair weather, the coast winds blow from the southwest in this part of Holland. You'll fly if you're fortunate enough to hit a sunny day. In fact, if the skies are foul and you're not in a big hurry, you might consider waiting out the weather for a day or two. Battling up this section of the coast could be murder with a stormy wind from the northwest.

Leave Veere with the road signed for **Vrouwenpolder,** and pedal a nice **bike lane** past a wonderful windmill as you depart the city. As long as you're not fighting a headwind, you'll have an easy ride to the edge of Vrouwenpolder, where you'll join a busier road toward the **Veersegatdam.** Cross under the road to pedal the **bike lane** on the **seaward side** of this dam that connects the islands of Walcheren and North Beveland. It's very exposed to storms, so if you're riding on a blustery day, expect to suffer.

You'll have bike-route signs for **LF1b** and **small red bike signs** to decorate your course as you continue onto the **Oosterscheldedam.** Keep pedaling along the seaward side to get the best vistas. Again, this 3-km dam is extremely exposed to coastal storms and wind (it's often closed in stormy weather, and you'll want to use the Zee-landbrug in these conditions). We were lucky enough to have cloudless skies and a stiff tailwind when we cycled this—it was incredible!

If you're fascinated by the Dutch technology invested in these dams, or simply impressed by the Dutch courage and ingenuity displayed in their constant battle against the sea, consider a stop at the **Delta Expo.** This exhibition, situated on one of the artificial islands of the Oosterscheldedam, does a wonderful job of highlighting the construction of the delta dams, their function, and engineering technology. (You'll see signs for the Delta Expo from the bike route.)

Continue on to **Burgh Haamstede** with the **red bike signs.** (If you don't mind adding some kilometers and time to your route, you might consider a detour to the town of Zierikzee. It's really a charmer.) Basically, we ignored the ramblings of LF1b through here, as we knew where *we* wanted to go, and weren't too sure where *it* wanted to take us. If you're cycling in July or August, **Burgh Haamstede** and everything around it will be a total zoo, overrun with sunbathers, windsurfers, and campers. Continue **straight** through town with the **bike route** signed for **Renesse** and **Brouwershaven.**

There is a small road to the east of the main route toward Renesse, but it's lined with campgrounds and seemed equally busy in August. Either way, you'll have plenty of company. Enter **Renesse,** another hopping little tourist town, and continue with the **bike route** for

**Brouwershaven** and **Scharendijke.** Leave the Brouwershaven route as you swing up onto the **Brouwersdam,** built between 1963 and 1972. You can ride up on top of the **embankment** that protects the road from the sea (you'll probably want to be down beside the road if the winds are hostile), and enjoy wonderful views of the sparkling water and sandy beaches while you pedal.

Continue with the **red bike signs** for **Ouddorp,** then begin picking up **bike signs** for **Brielle** as you pedal onward. This route will take you across your final dam for the day, the 5-km **Haringvlietdam.** Stay with signs for **Brielle** to shun the main-road route toward Rotterdam and cycle quiet countryside for a time. Brielle is an ancient fortified town, surrounded by water. It boasts a fifteenth-century Gothic church and a host of interesting streets and byways. You can end your day here with a hotel room, or ask at the city **tourist office** to find a nearby campground.

## Brielle to Delft: 33 kilometers

From Brielle, follow **bike-route signs** for **Maassluis** to gain the short **ferry** crossing from **Rozenburg,** across the mouth of **Rotterdam's yawning port,** and on to the busy little town of **Maassluis.** Crossings are frequent and inexpensive. (If you're considering a visit to the sprawling city of Rotterdam, you'll pick up bike-route signs at Maassluis to lead you into the mouth of "the beast.") From Brielle onward, bike-route signs grow a bit more scarce, but look for **bike signs** for **Maasland** and **Delft** to take you north from Maassluis.

**Maasland** is a watery wonderland—pure Holland for any tourist with a drop of romantic blood in his veins. Pedal slowly through this tiny canal-crossed city, and pause for what must be one of the best photo opportunities in Holland as you leave town with signs for **Delft.** A canvas of cows, windmills, and a placid canal begs for photographs. The **bike route** for **Delft** zigs to the left side of the Schipluiden-bound canal, then zags back to the right bank shortly after. Pleasant canalside cycling follows, as you pedal on for **Schipluiden.**

Things get rather confusing in Schipluiden, with bike signs leading everywhere and nowhere at once. Swing off into the city center if you want to see more of town, or simply hug the **canal** to get out as fast as possible. You can *try* to follow the bike signs, but you'll need more patience and luck than we had. Depart Schipluiden with the **bike route** signed for **Delft,** and enjoy more canalside cycling toward the city.

You'll hit a **busy main road** as you enter Delft. **Cross the canal** here, and pedal a small road beside the canal to find the center of town. Delft's enormous and usually crowded campground is on the north side of the city, about 1½ km from the center. Ask for directions at the **VVV** office in the market square, as older maps place the campground incorrectly. If you're looking for a bed, Delft has several hotels (spendy), pensions (not so spendy), and student flats (cheap—but only available in the summer).

Allow yourself at least an afternoon to explore this captivating Dutch city on foot. Canals are everywhere, as are porcelain shops (hawking the famous Delft blue-and-white plates, cups, windmills, and "wooden" shoes). You'll be amazed by the sheer numbers of bicycles you'll see (where did all those balloon tires come from?) and you'll be delighted by a climb to the top of the tower in Delft's Nieuwe Kerk. The church's exterior, covered with somber red brick, seems unnaturally glum in the midst of the glittering china that fills Delft's shop windows.

## Delft to Zandvoort: 61 kilometers

From Delft's market square, follow **Oude Langendijk** toward the **Rijn-Schiekanaal. Cross the canal** and go **left** with the road beside it (it's a one-way street, but bicycles are allowed to ride against traffic). Stay on this route to cycle out of Delft. You'll remain on the **east bank** of the canal all the way to the outskirts of **Leiden.** The road is fairly busy, but you'll have a bike lane to ease the worry. There aren't many bike-route signs, so simply keep the canal on your left and pedal.

Cross under the **A12 freeway** in **Voorburg,** then begin following signs for **Leidschendam.** Stay beside the canal through the picturesque city of Leidschendam (swing down to the **left** when the road curves away from the water), and gain much quieter cycling from here. Continue on this small, virtually car-free route as you pass dozens of attractive canalside homes with lace-trimmed windows and neat, flower-bedecked yards. You'll find yourself waving to the boaters on the canal and exchanging greetings with fellow cyclists as you ride.

Enter the **Vlietland Recreation Area** (a large lake with a campground on your right), and swing away from the canal briefly as you stay with **bike signs** for **Leiden.** You'll circumvent a large marina, then regain your canalside path as you approach Leiden. The canal splits as you near the city. Keep to the **right** branch. Bike signs for **Leiden** will direct you up and around to gain a **main auto road** across the canal, then stay with the bike route toward the **center** to pedal into the heart of town.

Cycle **Breestraat** past Leiden's town hall, then look for **bike signs** for the **station** to lead you to Leiden's **VVV** (across from the train station). You can get a city map here, as well as a listing of the city's many fine museums. Leiden boasts Holland's oldest university

*A quiet bike path near the coast of Holland.*

(founded in 1574), and it possesses a rich intellectual heritage. North Americans will find a special connection here, as the city is also the home of the Mayflower pilgrims.

Follow **bike signs** for the **station** as you're leaving town, and cycle past the handsome **De Valk Wall Mill.** Abandon the station route with **bike signs** for **Warmond,** pedaling out of town beside the railroad tracks. **Bike signs** for **Voorhout** take priority next. Cycle into **Voorhout** on the main road, then go **right** on **Herenstraat** when the main road crosses the canal. Follow **bike signs** for **Lisse** as you leave Voorhout, **cross** a **main road** signed for Sassenheim, and continue **straight** onto **Loosterweg.**

Savor a flat and scenic ride past scores of bulb farms as you cycle onward. If you're lucky enough to ride through when the flowers are in bloom (late April and early May), you'll be rewarded with a dazzling display of daffodils, hyacinths, and tulips. Cycle on into a pleasant forest, go **left** on **Lyndenweg,** then swing **left** again on **Stationsweg** to pedal past the gates of the **Keukenhof.** The Keukenhof garden is open from late March to late May—flower lovers will think they've died and gone to heaven in this haven of five million blossoming bulbs.

Continue past the Keukenhof (praying you won't be trampled into the fertilizer by the 900,000 tourists who visit here each spring), and follow **bike signs** for **Noordwijker-hout,** first swinging **left,** then joining a main road, then pedaling across a canal. Angle off onto a **small road** toward the coast with signs for **Langevelder-slag,** and press on into an area of rolling dunes, bending grass, and wind. Stay with the route for **Langevelder-slag** as you parallel the coastline northeast toward **Zandvoort.**

Enjoy wonderful coastal cycling as you join the bevies of cyclists and walkers exploring this dune-dominated recreation area. You'll see everything from hard-core bicycle racers who look as though they're racking up 200-km days, to picnicking families loaded down with bread, cheese, and beach towels. Pass a large snack bar/bathing center at **Langevelder-slag,** and continue northward with the bike route to arrive at **Zandvoort.**

Zandvoort is an absolute zoo on sunny days in August, as hordes of Hollanders vacate the urban strongholds at Haarlem and Amsterdam and head for the beach. If you like carnivals, you'll love Zandvoort. The seaside city has shopping, restaurants, a casino and a race track, and lots and lots of young people. Seek out the well-signed **tourist office** if you need a bed, or continue with the seaside promenade to the north end of town to find two nearby campgrounds. The first site, next to the race track, is crowded, dingy, loud, and convenient. The second, a bit farther on, is more pleasant, more expensive, and caters to families and caravans.

## Zandvoort to Edam: 58 kilometers

From Zandvoort, continue north on the **seaside promenade,** and stay with the main road to **Bloemendaal aan Zee.** A bit more reserved than Zandvoort, this seaside town offers camping, too. Swing inland toward **Haarlem** with the signed **bike route,** and leave the dunes behind as you regain the flat farmland that characterizes this virtually hill-less country. Enter the outskirts of **Haarlem** and stay with signs for the *centrum* to visit this pleasing city of canals and church towers.

Haarlem's Grote Kerk (St. Bavo's Church) and the adjacent *Grote Markt* provide a look at some of the city's finest architecture. Some excellent museums, the Corrie Ten Boomhuis (a refuge for Jews during World War II), and lots of lively streets will make Haarlem worth whatever time you choose to spend there. Stop in at the **VVV** beside the train station if you would like more information on the city. One more detail—if you haven't acquired a street map of Amsterdam yet, do it in Haarlem (the *Falk Plan* is an excellent choice). You're going to need it!

From Haarlem's *Grote Markt,* follow **Jansstraat** north toward the **station.** Hit the main road in front of the train station, and angle **right** to follow **bike-route signs** for **Spaarnwoude/Amsterdam** under the train tracks and away from the center of town. Stay with the **Spaarnwoude signs** to swing **left** onto **Spaarndamsveg** beside the **Spaarne Canal.** Pedal along the canal/lake with signs for **Spaarndam** (keep **left** at one unsigned branch) to arrive at Spaarndam.

Cycle through the attractive little town, then go **left** along a **main road** heading northeast (auto signs for **Buitenhuizen**). There's a bike lane to make your riding comfortable. Stay with this route to reach a free **ferry** across the wide **Noordzee Kanaal** (Amsterdam's outlet to the sea). Roll aboard and sail across, then resume riding with **bike signs** for **Westzaan.** Savor peaceful pedaling past farms and grazing land, and arrive at Westzaan, a charming little community made up of tidy Dutch houses with canal-bordered front yards.

The main road angles right just before a **large windmill,** but you'll continue **straight** with the **bike path,** paralleling the A8 freeway. Reach a **T,** and go **left** on the **main road** (no sign) to enter **Zaandijk.** Keep **right** with the **bike signs** at the next intersection, then watch for more bike signs for **Zaanskanse** ("Zaanse Schans" on your map). This route will lead you across the **Zaan.** Go **left** onto a **paved pathway** immediately after you cross the water, and enter Zaanse Schans, a delightful open-air museum of working windmills and centuries-old houses. Several of the buildings are open to visitors (admission fee), and you'll be able to observe the inner workings of windmills, a wooden shoe workshop, a dairy, and more.

Without paying a guilder, savor the pleasure of a stroll along Kalverringdijk, a grassy embankment adorned with picturesque windmills. An asphalt pathway leads along the **dike,** then you'll emerge onto a **small road** and go **right.** Cycle onward to another intersection, and swing **left** with **bike signs** for **Purmerend** and **Neck.** Quiet, pastoral riding follows as you pedal to the banks of the **Noordhollandsch Kanaal;** cross it to enter **Purmerend.**

If you'd like to stop in at the **VVV** or view this midsize city's church or town hall, simply continue **straight** from the bridge, and walk your bicycle along the **pedestrian street** that leads into the center of town. From the **center,** angle **left** (north) to gain a **main auto road.** Go **right** along this route, cross under the **train tracks,** and veer **left** onto another busy road with signs for **Edam.** Dive **right** at the next opportunity, and cycle on about ½ km to gain the banks of a small **canal** that runs all the way to Edam.

**Cross** the canal and begin pedaling along its **east bank,** then settle in to enjoy some of the finest cycling Holland has to offer. This is why Holland is famous with bike tourers all over the world—kilometer after kilometer of paved, carless cycling through lovely pastoral surroundings. Truly, "it doesn't get any better than this."

Cross the busy **Road N247** on the outskirts of **Edam,** then stay with signs for the **center** to pedal into this attractive little city of canals and cheese. Although Edam cheese is now produced in other regions, this mainstay of the Dutch table originated here. Walk the city's quiet streets, peer into its ever-present canals, and absorb the atmosphere of yet another Dutch charmer. If you can tear yourself from the city streets, Edam's Grote Kerk contains a fine collection of stained-glass windows.

Seek out the **tourist information** office for advice on indoor lodgings. If you're camping, there is a campground near the city. Edam also makes an excellent base for exploring northward to Hoorn and the beaches along the Ijsselmeer, if you'd like to see a bit more of Holland before your rendezvous with Amsterdam.

## Edam to Amsterdam: 30 kilometers

Between Edam and Amsterdam, a proliferation of bike-route signs awaits. You'll be tracing sections of the Waterland Bike Route as you turn south from Edam, and you'll have two route choices when you leave the city. You can take the **dike road** toward **Volendam** (this pleasant 5-km ride follows the coastline all the way to town) or you can opt for the shorter, more direct route to Volendam, pedaling along the main road with **bike signs** for **Volendam.** Suburbia or sea—cycle the route of your choice and arrive in Volendam, then follow signs for the *haven* to gain the shop-lined promenade along the harbor.

Once a thriving port on the former Zuiderzee, Volendam has become a major tourist center. Its inhabitants sometimes don the traditional Dutch costume on Sundays and feast days, although the practice is fading as modernity encroaches on the town. Even so, the city boasts a lovely harbor, and the narrow streets below the dike are worth investigating, too.

From Volendam, follow **bike signs** for **Monnickendam** and **Katwoude** as you shun the main-road course and pedal a lovely **seaside route** to Monnickendam. Monnickendam is a wonderful coastal city, with a main street lined with attractive buildings and overlooked by a sixteenth-century brick tower. Continue with signs for **Marken** from here, and cycle a **bike lane** beside the coastal road. Enjoy exhilarating riding **atop the dike,** with views of flat fields on one side and dancing sailboats on the other.

Cross the access road to Marken as you turn **right** for **Uitdam** and cycle onward with the bike route. There's a sprawling, busy campground beside the sea at Uitdam, if you're in the market. Pedal on along the dike and savor scenic cycling past the Uitdammer Die and the Kinselmeer. You'll begin picking up **bike signs** for **Amsterdam** from here. Pass scattered campgrounds and resorts as you press south along the coast.

Cross under the **A10 freeway,** then ride under another **main road. Bike signs** for **Amsterdam** will lead you up and onto a massive **bridge.** Ride across one expanse of water, then stay on the bridge as it "rests" briefly on an island (there's a zooish youth campground here, with bus service into the center). Pedal above more water as you stay in your **bike lane,** then keep to the **right** to come down off the bridge and onto **city streets.**

The bike lane continues for a time, then comes and goes as you follow **Zeeburgedijk Street** toward the city center. Reach an **intersection** ruled by a large **windmill,** and go **right** with the signed route for **Havens** to pedal toward the central **station** and the main **tourist office.** (If you have another goal in the city core, angle left for Utrecht and continue looping around the center on the ring road S100. You can turn right at any time to hit the center.) Wherever you're headed, ride cautiously. Although Amsterdam is undisputedly one of the world's most cycle-friendly big cities, cars here still outnumber, outweigh, and take out bikes—so stay alert.

Hostels (both official and unofficial) abound in Amsterdam, as do inexpensive rooms and luxury hotels. Even though the city is literally crammed with tourists during the summer months, you can almost always find a bed. Amsterdam's youth campgrounds tend to be pretty wild—if you don't like all-night parties, look elsewhere. Whatever you do, *don't ever* leave your bicycle or gear unattended in Amsterdam. Only take a room if the manager will provide a safe place for your bike. Holland has 900,000 bicycles reported stolen every year. Don't let yours be one of them.

Amsterdam has far too many top-notch attractions to list here. Our highest recommendations go to the Van Gogh Museum, the Rijksmuseum, and the Anne Frank House. Of course, the city itself is a living museum you can explore for days. Plan to do lots of walking, or hop one of the canal boat tours to get an overall look at this enormous city.

If you're headed home via a plane from Schiphol Airport, you can hop a quick train from Amsterdam's central station. Those wishing to cycle to the airport can follow the Den Haag bicycle route past Osdorp, Badhoevedorp, and on to Schiphol. We were headed for England from here, so we did a one-day, 80-km forced march from Amsterdam to Hoek van Holland, following signed bike routes virtually the entire way.

# TOUR NO. 4

# WAFFLES AND CHAMPAGNE
## Brussels, Belgium, to Versailles, France

*Distance:* 662 kilometers (411 miles)
*Estimated time:* 11 riding days
*Best time to go:* May, June, July, or September
*Terrain:* Gentle hills; lots of quiet secondary roads
*Connecting tours:* Tours No. 3 and 5

France and bicycles—the two words just seem to go together, don't they? And anyone who has done much bicycle touring in this beautiful, varied, and uncrowded country will tell you, "France and bicycles are a perfect match!" French roads are among the best in Europe. The secondary road system is excellent, with well-maintained surfaces, light traffic, courteous drivers, and surprisingly direct routes. While planning our tours here, we often found that our "sacrifice" in using the small French roads instead of the major ones actually resulted in fewer kilometers to pedal rather than more. Sure, the French drivers routinely travel at suicidal speeds, and you'll be shocked by the "rockets" that catapult past you during your first days on French roads. But you'll also be delighted by the consistent, careful courtesy extended to cyclists here.

This tour from Brussels, Belgium, to Versailles, France, will provide you with a wonderful mix of riverside riding, farms and fields, cities and sightseeing. You'll see the vine-covered hills of Champagne and the cathedrals of Reims, Troyes, and Sens. Continue with our Tour No. 5 to Angers, and you'll pedal through the château-scattered Loire Valley as well. Best of all, you'll meet the French people, who, despite the reputation cultivated by rude Parisian waiters over the last few decades, are not unfriendly, hostile, or unwilling to speak English. In the nearly twelve months we've spent exploring France, we've been invited into the homes of dairy farmers, computer programmers, teachers, and grape growers. We've been given directions, stuffed with homemade crêpes, provided with beds, had our bicycles repaired ... the list goes on and on. In short, *vive la France!*

**CONNECTIONS.** The busy Brussels International Airport is the starting place for this tour. However, you can pick up the tour's beginning by air or train or pedal power. If you choose to ride either Tour No. 3 or Tour No. 4 in reverse, you could hook the two together for a ride between Versailles and Amsterdam. As mentioned earlier, a natural continuation of this route is the tour from Versailles to Angers, so keep that in mind when you're planning, too. This tour also has several potential connecting points with routes in our book, *France by Bike,* so please refer to that volume if you would like to do additional cycling in France.

Transporting bicycles on trains isn't too difficult in France, although troubles multiply in direct proportion to the distance you wish to travel. Short local trains often allow cyclists to load their own bicycles and ride with them (restrictions usually occur during high-use periods). On long-distance or international trains, you'll probably have to send your bike a few days in advance. We recommend removing all luggage, lights, and computer paraphernalia, taping down cables, and perhaps even unfastening your derailleur and taping it to the frame (to prevent it from getting caught on something and ripped off your bicycle). If you're really serious about protecting your bicycle, you might even box it (in the same way it was boxed for air travel). If you'd only heard the horror stories we've heard....

**INFORMATION.** Please refer to Tour No. 3 for suggestions about obtaining information on Belgium. Write in advance to the French National Tourist Office, 610 Fifth Avenue, New York, New York 10020-2452. Don't forget to mention that you'll be cycling, camping (if you are), and visiting Paris (if you are). Once in France, be sure to make use of the local tourist offices to collect English-language literature. If you're camping, the regional campground listings they provide are extremely helpful. Most city tourist offices offer detailed accommodation guides, too. Offices in France are called *Office de Tourisme* or *Syndicat d'Initiative.*

It's also a good idea to bring along at least one tourist guide for your trip through France. The *Blue Guide France* is an extensive (if somewhat dry) sourcebook on the entire country, while *Let's Go: France* and *The Real Guide: France* are a budget traveler's fountain of practicalities. Michelin's *Green Guide France* takes on the Herculean task of covering all of France in a single volume. Fortunately, Michelin also divides the country into more than twenty regions, each covered by a separate *Green Guide.* Guides for Champagne, Paris, and the Île-de-France are applicable to this tour (the Champagne guide is not yet offered in English, however).

**MAPS.** Michelin produces an excellent map series for route finding in France, and the 1:200,000 detail will satisfy all your needs. Maps are readily available in bookstores, and they're considerably cheaper than the Michelins in the United States. If you're conserving francs, wait until you arrive to buy (maps are usually a few francs cheaper at monster supermarkets, such as *Hypermarché* or *Mammoth*). Please refer to Tour No. 3 for Belgian route finding.

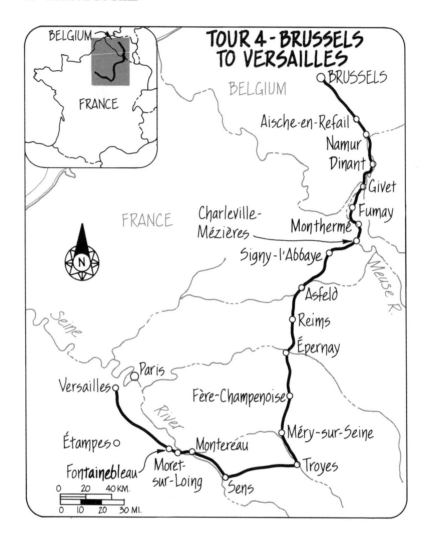

**ACCOMMODATIONS.** Campgrounds abound in France, although they're more scarce in the rural and less-touristed areas of the country. Municipal campgrounds are excellent bargains here, and they're usually easy to find and well maintained. There are no campgrounds in Europe more consistently wonderful for cyclists than the French ones, in our opinion. Many French cities seem to take their most delightful patch of ground, with the most superlative view of the city's cathedral, château, or citadel, and turn it into the municipal campground. Although hot showers are pretty much standard equipment at French campgrounds today (they weren't 10 years ago), you'll still encounter lots of pit toilets. It's a good idea to carry a spare roll of toilet paper in your panniers when camping in France. For some reason, BYOTP (bring your own toilet paper) seems to be the accepted policy in many French campgrounds.

The hotel system in France is delightful, too. A one-, two-, three-, and four-star rating scheme allows you to select your luxuries (and your approximate price range) in advance, then shop around in the right "neighborhood." One- and two-star hotels vary greatly in their quality, but, with a little hunting, you can usually find something entirely adequate at a very comfortable price. Room prices are usually posted at the front of the hotel, either on a window or in the lobby, and you can always check out your room in advance. Best of all, French hotel managers are usually friendly to cyclists. We'll never forget the hotel manager in Carcassonne who took in two drenched, mud-splattered cyclists and one very energetic toddler in a very dirty bike trailer, leading us to our room with a smile that made a wintry day turn warm.

**SUPPLIES.** Shopping hours in France can be troublesome, especially outside of the big cities. The monster supermarkets that inhabit nearly every midsize and larger city in France are usually open from 9:00 A.M. to 8:00 P.M., from Monday through Saturday (with some exceptions). But in rural areas, French shopkeepers adhere to a strict set of opening and closing times that will have your stomach growling in dismay. Watch out for Sunday afternoons and Mondays, in particular. These are sacred times to shopkeepers, and you can often search high and low for sustenance—without luck. Also, the hours between 12:30 and 2:00 or 3:00 P.M. are dedicated to crazily hung *fermé* signs and lots of locked doors. But if you shop for lunch early, shop for dinner by 6:00 P.M., and buy for the weekend on Saturday, you'll be able to enjoy some of the most delicious food you'll find anywhere in Europe.

If you're a cheese and bread lover, France is just short of heaven. If pastries are your weakness, it may be even closer! Hunt down breakfast feasts of buttery croissants or *pain au chocolat;* enjoy wonderful picnic lunches of crusty brown baguettes and creamy cheese; and make your dinners special with a glass of one of France's score of outstanding regional wines.

Cycling is a way of life in France, although racing still outstrips touring in popularity. If you can make it to a midsize city, you should have no difficulty finding a bicycle shop and, with any luck, the replacement part you need (or a workable substitute).

# Brussels (Airport) to Aische-en-Refail: 51 kilometers

Belgian tourist literature laments the fact that many tourists consider Belgium to be simply a place to set off from on their way to other European destinations. Indeed, it's a shame to skip the things that Brussels has to offer in your haste to hit the cycling trail. So, if you won't be returning to Brussels for your flight home, plan to delay your cycling a few days and take a look around while you recover from jet lag. (Please refer to the first riding day of Tour No. 3 for more information on Brussels.)

On our past visits to Brussels, we've conducted our sightseeing from two locations—from a pleasant hotel in the little community of Zaventem (near the airport) and from the quiet enclave of Camping Paul Rosmant at Wezembeek-Oppem (about 6 km from the airport). This saved us from the hassle (and danger) of cycling into the enormous capital of Belgium and allowed us to do our "touristing" from a convenient base. You can pick up a map and information on Brussels at the airport information office when you land.

From Brussels International Airport, follow road signs for **Zaventem Centrum** to find the small town a few kilometers from the airport (indoor lodgings here). Stay on the main road through town, passing a grassy **park** on the left, then turn **left** on **Road N2** at the next **light.** Ascend a small hill and go **right** on **Leuvense Steenweg,** then descend to pass under the **freeway.** Angle **left** at the following **Y,** and stay with the main route past the MP-guarded **American School,** descending a slight hill along the way. Go **left** onto **Tramlaan** at the **stop sign** at the bottom of the hill.

If you're looking for Camping Paul Rosmant (also known as Camping Wezembeek), take the first **right** onto **Warandeberg** (this may or may not be signed for the campground, depending on whether the sign has been knocked over lately). Climb a gentle hill and look for the campground **entrance** on the **right.** This pleasant spot offers nice facilities, hot showers, and a cozy clubhouse. It's open April to September, and it provides a good base for trips into Brussels via public transport. (There's an enormous shopping center about 1½ km away. Ask at the clubhouse for directions.)

If neither camping outside the city nor a room in the suburbs appeals to you, there are plenty of accommodation options in Brussels, including some youth hostels. You'll find lots of cars and congestion in this very international city, so please enter with caution. After you've gotten dizzy spinning and staring in the Grand-Place, overwhelmed your senses in a few of Brussels's superior museums, and had your first taste of warm Belgian waffles, Belgian *frites* topped with mayonnaise, or a bar of the country's famous Godiva chocolate, you'll be ready to pedal.

From **Tramlaan** (the street before the campground), follow signs to the small town of **Moorsel.** Pedal through Moorsel, and veer **left** onto **Groenlaan** (a small, easy-to-miss street—look for the water tower). Keep to the **right** as you leave Moorsel, and **descend briefly** before taking the **first left** onto **Kruisstraat.** Stay on this road to a **junction** with **Road N3.** Cross this busy thoroughfare and enter

**Leefdaal.** You'll have fairly quiet riding through gently rolling terrain as signs for **Neerijse** lead you on from here.

Cycle through Neerijse's **center,** first making a **left** to ride past the **church,** then veering **right** for **St.-Agatha-Rode.** A short, **steep hill** will take you out of Neerijse, then watch for a small town sign marking a road to the left for **St.-Agatha-Rode.** Go **left** here to pedal on to this quaint village settled around its small Gothic church. From the town **center,** swing **left** for **Archennes,** then cycle to an unsigned **T** and go **left** again.

Ride through Archennes and push on to the busy **Road N25. Cross** carefully to enter **Grez-Doiceau,** and hit the main route through the town soon after. Go **left** here, following signs for **Jodoigne,** then dive **right** about ½ km later, turning off for **Longueville** and **Bonlez.** Keep with the main route to **Bonlez,** then go **left** for **Gistoux** on the far end of town. In **Gistoux,** swing **right** at the **stop sign,** then take the **next left** to gain the unappealing **Road N243.** Endure 11 km of unpleasant cycling as you follow the hectic, roller-coaster ride of N243 all the way to **Perwez.**

There's a rough **bike path** on the left side of the road. It makes for slow, bumpy, but safe riding—use it! At least the scenery is pleasant as you pass through rolling green farmland and small settlements. Cruise into **Perwez,** a busy Belgian market town. You'll find shopping and indoor accommodations here, if you're looking. To push on for Aische-en-Refail and the campground, leave Perwez with signs for **Aische-en-Refail,** and cycle **Road N972** toward this small town. Ride through Aische, then follow signs for the **château** and **camping** to reach your goal.

Here you'll find a pleasant, well-equipped campground crouched beside a moated château. The price is friendly, as is the management, and cyclists erect their tents right on the lawn of the castle, shunning the caravan "slums" across the way. Nice!

## Aische-en-Refail to Dinant: 50 kilometers

You'll want to get an early start today, as a midday pause at Namur will surely be on your itinerary. From the campground at Aische, **retrace** your route through town and go **left** for **Liernu.** Hit a larger road (**Road N912**) about 4 km later, and swing **right** for **Namur.** Grab the next **left** (signed for **Dhuy**) and pedal on to this small community. Just beyond the **church** in **Dhuy,** watch for a small sign for **Warisoulx.** Veer **right** here.

Cross under the freeway, ride to **Warisoulx,** then swing **right** for **Villers-lez-Heest.** Signs for **Namur** lead on from Villers with **Road N934.** You'll begin the breezy descent to the Meuse River at **St. Marc.**

Enter the sprawling city of Namur several quick kilometers later. Signs for the **centre** will lead you to the neighborhood of Namur's major attractions—the citadel and the cathedral.

Visit Namur's provincial **tourist office** at 3, rue Notre Dame, to gather information on the city and surrounding region. The city's massive hilltop citadel is well worth a few hours of exploration, and the streets below offer a cathedral and a dozen museums to tempt you to linger even more. If things get out of hand and it's just too late to cycle on, Namur has a youth hostel and plenty of hotels for overnight visitors.

From Namur, you'll have two route options on your journey to **Dinant.** You can cycle the less-traveled but hillier road that traces the east bank of the Meuse River, enjoying lofty views and cooling forest shade, or you can take the flatter and busier west-bank route. If you do opt for the west side of the river, you'll have lots of opportunities to escape the main road. Simply dive off onto the intermittent riverside pathways that hug the shore. You'll find quiet waterside cycling with pleasant views of the river and its mansions, but you should expect a

*Cyclists can follow the lovely Meuse River between Namur and Dinant.*

few dead ends and a bit of cobblestone along the way. We've cycled both sides of the Meuse and enjoyed both equally, so it seems you'll have to decide for yourself.

If you plan to camp around Dinant, there's a campground just opposite the town of Bouvignes. It's on the east bank of the river, about 2 km north of Dinant. Set right on the water, the campground is a somewhat spartan, but very typical European "trailer town." It comes complete with a healthy scoop of local flavor in the form of a busy *frites* stand and an even busier *boule* (French "bowling") area, and it offers a convenient base for sightseeing in Dinant.

Dinant itself is an unqualified delight, a charming small city nestled beneath a stout fortress that towers above its onion-domed church. Take the tour of Dinant's citadel and listen to your guide tell jokes in three languages. Then descend to admire the striking stained glass in Dinant's church or join the crowds of ice-cream-eating tourists strolling the city's narrow streets. A handful of hotels provide indoor lodging options. Check at the city **tourist office** at 37, rue Grande, for more information.

## Dinant to Monthermé: 73 kilometers

Leave Dinant with the main road toward **Givet** along the **west shore** of the **Meuse River.** You'll have flat and effortless cycling. We found the route pleasantly quiet on a Sunday morning in April; however, the road certainly gets its share of traffic in the summer months. If you have the time and patience, scattered snatches of **riverside pathway** allow brief escapes from the main road. Either way, you'll enjoy lovely views of Belgian towns and country mansions, water-loving kayakers and floating swans, speeding cycle racers and cruising tourers.

Cross the **Belgian–French border** just before **Givet** and continue into the handsome French city, overlooked by its hilltop fortifications. From Givet, stay with the Meuse and **Road N51** toward **Fumay.** The first portion of the ride is the pits, with lots of traffic and challenging terrain. Look for a neat fortified church in **Hierges,** and enjoy mellower cycling after **Vireux-Molhain,** a personable little town with good shopping opportunities. Your legs will enjoy the break as you follow the river toward **Fumay.**

Abandon N51 as you **cross** the Meuse at **Haybes,** then follow the shoreline to **Fumay** on a much quieter road. You'll **recross** the Meuse, then endure a **stiff climb** to Fumay's attractive **central square.** This is a town worth lingering over, if you have the time. From Fumay, follow signs for **Revin** as you stay beside the Meuse and bid adieu to N51. The route is narrower from here, but cars are scarcer, too.

Signs for **Monthermé** lead on from Revin, as you hug the suddenly snaking **Meuse** and fight your way through a succession of short ups and downs. The cycling is scenic and pleasant, made more so by the loneliness of the route, and you'll arrive in **Monthermé** via the stout fortified church of St. Leger. Situated at the confluence of the Semoy and Meuse Rivers, Monthermé is an attractive little town, popular with Belgian and French tourists.

The city's campground is a treat, plunked down in the grassy triangle where the Meuse and Semoy flow together. To find this pleasant and inexpensive spot, ride through town on **Road D1,** with signs for **Bogny-sur-Meuse** and **Charleville-Mézières.** Watch for campground signs just beyond a small *supermarché* on the edge of town. If you need indoor accommodations, you should be able to rustle up a bed in Monthermé. Otherwise, Charleville-Mézières is a relatively easy 21 km away.

## Monthermé to Charleville-Mézières: 21 kilometers

Depart Monthermé on **Road D1** for **Bogny-sur-Meuse** and **Charleville-Mézières.** You'll get a glimpse of the four rock spires of the Rochers des 4 Fils Aymon to the left as you pedal the narrow riverside road through a handful of small towns. **Climb** away from the Meuse after **Bogny,** then make a **left** turn onto **Road D1A** (signed for **Joigny-sur-Meuse**). Escape the main road for a forested break from traffic, then **descend steeply** to cross the Meuse River and pedal on. You'll **rejoin D1** at **Nouzonville.**

More tree-lined climbing awaits after Nouzonville. Watch carefully for a **left** turn signed for **Montcy** about 3 km short of Charleville-Mézières. Take it to gain the tiny **Road D69** toward the city. You'll descend to the river once more, then pedal into Charleville on a delightfully quiet road.

Reach the **Vieux Moulin,** a riverside museum dedicated to the city's favorite native son, the poet Arthur Rimbaud. Here, a **camping sign** leads left to the city's wonderfully situated municipal campground on the banks of the Meuse River. It's a short walk from here to Charleville's impressive Place Ducale and the **tourist information** office.

Charleville has several hotels, extensive shopping opportunities, and loads of interesting pedestrian streets. You'll love the remarkably homogenous Place Ducale and the typically flashy Hotel de Ville (town hall). Duck inside a few of the city's myriad churches to round out your visit.

## Charleville-Mézières to Asfeld: 69 kilometers

You can look forward to a day of small roads, pastoral surroundings, and an abundance of half-timbered buildings as you set out from

Charleville-Mézières. Unfortunately, you must fight your way out of one very large city before you reap the benefits of France's delightful countryside. From the campground beside the Meuse, cycle to Charleville's **Place Ducale,** then go **right** to pedal on to **Road N43.** Follow **N43** out of town, enduring heavy traffic for a time, then dive **left** on a small road signed for **Warcq.**

Ride this quiet route to **Warcq,** an interesting village with a squatty fortified church (look for the lofty arrow slits) and a communal washing area. From Warcq, follow the serene and gently undulating **Road D9** through **Belval** and **Haudrecy,** marveling happily at how quickly city turns to country in France.

Leave Haudrecy with signs for **Signy-l'Abbaye** and **St. Marcel.** If you like stained-glass windows, pop inside the town church at St. Marcel. The pleasant **Road D2** leads from here through quiet, rolling farmland. Cycle past cows, tractors, and unassuming villages to arrive in **Signy-l'Abbaye.** With an excellent municipal campground beside the city soccer field, Signy-l'Abbaye may tempt you to call it a day. It's a charming French village, untouched by the terrors of mass tourism.

Pedal **Road D2** toward **Lalobbe,** and settle in for more quiet roads through rolling countryside. If you're riding in the spring and you're an allergy sufferer, you may be sneezing with each stroke—the fields are brilliant with the blossoms of pollen-heavy yellow rape. In **Lalobbe,** veer **left** onto **Road D102** signed for **Wasigny.** The tiny route climbs steeply through fields, then winds through small villages as you continue from **Wasigny** through **Herbigny, Hauteville,** and **Ecly** (now on **Road D11**).

Watch for the bell towers of the village churches—the design is characteristic of the area. Also characteristic are the abundant half-timbered buildings you'll see. Signs for the ***Route du Porcien*** will indicate you're on a "tourist itinerary" of local architecture. **Road D11** runs smack into the much less friendly Road D946 in **Ecly. Cross** it, then continue on **Road D3** toward **Château-Porcien.** You'll join **Road D926** as you pedal into the midsize town (this may be your best chance for indoor accommodations this afternoon).

Continue with **D926,** pedaling through the green fields above the Aisne River as you cycle to **Gomont.** Then go **right** onto **Road D18B** toward **Juzancourt.** Enjoy quiet riding through Juzancourt, then look for a turn to the **left** for **Asfeld.** Take it, and glide downhill to cross the **Aisne River** and enter the outskirts of the little town.

We were exhausted by the time we got here, so we put up our tent beside the canal and watched the barges pass all evening. (Please remember that you free camp at your own risk. There is an official campground at Guignicourt, about 15 km southwest.) There's a grocery store on the right as you enter Asfeld, and the little town boasts a unique brick baroque church that's worth a look. If you're hunting for indoor accommodations, you may have to search a bit.

## Asfeld to Reims: 28 kilometers

You'll have a quiet, pastoral ride ahead as you set out for the bubbly capital of France's Champagne region—Reims. Leave Asfeld with signs for **Vieux-les-Asfeld** on **Road D926,** then veer **left** beyond Vieux onto **Road D37** for **Poilcourt.** Cross the regional border after Poilcourt-Sydney. Now you'll be pedaling in Champagne! You'll also notice an oddity of the French road system here—often, when French roads cross regional boundaries, their numbers change as well. Continue with the renumbered **Road D274** through St. Etienne and **Bourgogne.**

Signs for **Reims** lead onward through vast fields of grain, and you'll spot the dark towers of Reims Cathedral from about 10 km out. Begin to encounter Reims's urban sprawl not long after. Enter the suburb of **Bétheny,** and follow the **rue Bétheny** into the city. Signs for the *centre* and *cathedrale* will lead you to the **rue Jean Jaurès.** Cycle this busy thoroughfare to a roaring roundabout, and continue **straight** toward the **cathedral.**

Reims Cathedral occupies a royal position among French cathedrals. A soaring Gothic structure with a lofty nave and exquisite stained glass, the cathedral has seen the coronation of French rulers since 498. We carried the memory of the building with us for an entire year of cycling. Its golden stone exterior and breathtaking interior will delight you, too.

Reims's efficient **tourist office** is a stone's throw from the cathedral at 2, rue de Machault. Pick up a free map and ask for help with lodgings here. There's a youth hostel and university housing in Reims, and the campground is 3–4 km from the center. If you're interested in a tour of one of Reims's champagne cellars, the tourist-office staff can point you in the right direction. But don't spend too much time underground in Reims. The city has too many architectural treasures to miss.

## Reims to Épernay: 34 kilometers

With a population pushing 200,000, Reims is a *big* city, and you'll have to fight your way out of the suburbs to find the vine-covered hills you're looking for. Either buy a detailed city map or do what we did— stop frequently to check out the transit maps at the bus stops. Follow signs for **Cormontreuil** (a suburb on the city's southern flank) as you begin. You'll gain **Road D9** south, then cycle past a vast development of **megastores** about 6 km out of the city center.

Watch for a turn to the **right** signed for **Trois-Puits** just beyond the super mall, and swing off onto this tiny road to begin your tour of sparkling champagne villages surrounded by acre after acre of vineyards. The day's ride is rolling, challenging, but delightfully pic-

*A succession of famous names makes pedaling through the vineyards of Champagne a bubbly pursuit.*

turesque as you cycle through **Trois-Puits, Montoré** (ride past the village church, then continue out of town), and on to **Rilly-la-Montagne.** Rilly is a charmer, with a main street lined by family mansions, their doorways labeled like a shopping list of fine champagnes.

Pedal on to **Chigny-les-Roses** and **Ludes** from here. **Climb steeply** from Ludes, and **rejoin Road D9** toward **Louvois.** You'll have more climbing (about 2 km) ahead as you ascend through trees to **Craon-de-Ludes,** then revel in a wonderful downhill glide through the Forêt de la Montagne de Reims. Watch for a regal château at the road junction near **Louvois,** and stay with **D9** for **Épernay** from here.

Avenay-Val-d'Or boasts a handsome church. As you depart **Avenay,** take the turn to the **right** signed for **Mutigny** to gain the silent **Road D201** as it tiptoes through more of the region's famously named hillside vineyards. You'll join the much less inviting **Road D1** in **Ay,** and follow signs into **Épernay** from here. Épernay offers a wonderful municipal campground beside its soccer stadium (well signed from the bridge across the Marne River as you enter town) or continue into the center to find the **tourist office** in the Hotel de Ville.

You can ask about Épernay's indoor lodgings at the tourist office (they're few and dear from June to September) and stock up on champagne-related literature, too. Although Épernay has little in the way of historical monuments or great architecture, it does boast miles of subterranean champagne "rivers." Tour the cellars at Moët and Chandon or ride the underground train at Mercier. You can't admire flying buttresses forever....

# Épernay to Troyes: 103 kilometers

You'll have a challenging day of hill-studded riding ahead as you leave Épernay. Vineyards, grain fields, and small villages are the rule between here and Troyes, so if you need a room, you may want to get an early start and go for a 100-km forced march (we did it once, but it wasn't fun). There are some camping possibilities along the way, so you'll have more flexibility if you're carrying a tent.

Getting out of Épernay isn't fun either. Traffic is thick and the roads are confusing. Look for **Road RD51** to the south toward **Sézanne,** and follow it to a harrowing **roundabout,** where you'll dive off onto the much quieter **Road D40** for **Avize.** Hilly cycling through endless vineyards awaits. Climb and descend, climb and descend (now on **Road D10**), passing through **Cuis** and struggling on to **Cramant.** Despite the rather tacky champagne bottle that marks the town, Cramant does boast a wonderful view of the surrounding hills.

From Cramant, pedal to **Avize** and **Oger,** then join **Road D9** soon after with signs for **Vertus.** Vineyards give way to rolling wheatland now, and you can watch dozens of tractors crisscrossing the fields as you continue. **Cross** the busy **Road RD33** at **Bergères,** and stay on D9 to **Fère-Champenoise.** We shared this section of our ride with far too much truck traffic, but the pedaling is much more pleasant after Fère-Champenoise. Pause to explore the cool stillness of the church in Fère-Champenoise, then ride on with signs for **Corroy.**

A smaller, quieter **D9** leads to Corroy, a tiny town with a wonderful twelfth-century pilgrimage church. Enjoy flat cycling to **Fresnay, Faux-Fresnay,** and **Courcemain** before abandoning D9 to ride for **Boulages.** (If your legs are beginning to fail you by this point in the day, there is a campground at Anglure, about 12 km from

Courcemain.) In Boulages, follow signs for **Longueville,** then **Méry-sur-Seine** to gain **Road D78** along the Seine River.

You'll have fairly easy cycling through **Droupt-Ste.-Marie, Droupt-St.-Basle,** and **Rilly-Ste.-Syre,** each with its own church, graveyard, and war memorial. But the hills increase after **Chauchigny,** and the Troyes-bound traffic picks up from **St. Benoît.** Stay with signs for Troyes to reach **Pont-Ste.-Marie,** with a remarkable church and plenty of shopping opportunities. Troyes's municipal campground is just beyond the bridge that spans the Seine. It's crowded and mediocre, but it provides excellent access to the city.

Continue into Troyes, following signs for the **center,** and arrive at the Cathedral St. Pierre et St. Paul. Enter the church's cool interior and watch the lines of stone pillars unfold before you, dappled with colored sunlight and stained by windows of brilliant glass. Check in at the **tourist office** near the train station for accommodation listings and information on the city. The youth hostel is 5 km south of the city core in Rosières, but there are plenty of inexpensive hotels to choose from closer in.

Troyes is a wonderful city for strolling. Visit the old town to walk along the rue des Chats, lined by half-timbered houses, explore the city's wealth of churches, or simply pull up a chair in a cozy *crêperie* and fill your hungry cyclist's stomach with a taste of France.

## Troyes to Sens: 70 kilometers

This ride leads through the breadbasket of France, with endless acres of rolling wheatland, lots of quiet roads, and an often troublesome west wind. Leave Troyes's center on **Road N60** toward **Estissac.** Cross over the **train tracks** and take the **first right** to get on the friendlier **Road D60** out of town. Continue past the busy ring road on the edge of Troyes, following signs for **Grange l'Evêque.**

Stay on D60 through Dierrey St. Pierre and continue on to **Faux-Villecerf,** then angle **right** onto **Road D23** before going **left** onto **Road D29** for **Villadin.** Turn **left** in Villadin, then go **right** to climb for **Pouy-sur-Vannes** on D29 once more. Swing down through town at Pouy-sur-Vannes to pedal past a lovely château, then regain the main road (now **Road D84**) for **Courgenay.** Continue past Courgenay and take a **right** soon after onto **Road D328** for **la Charmée.** Cycle through la Charmée and stay on D328, then go **right** onto **Road D28** for **la Postolle** and **Thorigny-sur-Oreuse.**

In **Thorigny,** angle **left** to ride the final 15 km to **Sens** on the up-and-down **Road D939.** Descend a moderate hill before Soucy, then continue on for Sens through **St. Clément,** arriving in the city with the mass of the cathedral rising up before you. You'll find Sens's **tourist office** near the cathedral. Sens has youth hostels and a municipal campground (south of town along the Yonne River), as well as several hotels to fit your accommodation needs.

Begun in 1140, Sens's Cathedral St. Etienne is a Gothic beauty. The building served as a model for England's Canterbury Cathedral, and it boasts fine stained-glass windows and a delightfully vast interior. Pace the pedestrian avenues around the church to discover the hidden treasures of the city.

## Sens to Moret-sur-Loing: 54 kilometers

Leave Sens by **retracing** your route north to **St. Clément,** then angle **left** onto **Road D23** toward **Cuy** and **Gisy** just after crossing the **N6** auto route. Go **left** again after about 2 km to follow the small road through **Cuy, Evry, Gisy,** and **Michery,** paralleling the winding **Yonne River** along the way. Continue on **D23** through **Serbonnes** and **Courlon,** riding northwest toward Montereau.

Road D23 becomes **Road D29** just before **Misy-sur-Yonne,** where a pretty riverside park awaits. In **Marolles,** 6 km farther on, turn **left** onto the busy **Road D411** and ride toward **Montereau.** Cross the confluence of the Yonne and Seine Rivers in Montereau, a city with a large church. Turn **west** onto **Road D39** immediately after crossing the river, following signs for **Champagne.** This section of the ride is dull, with lots of industrial development, but the scenery improves from here.

Just before Champagne, go **left** to cross the **Seine** and enter **St. Mammes.** This busy little port town, snuggled into the confluence of the Seine and Loing rivers, must have one of the highest barge counts per capita in France. Pedal through St. Mammes, then veer **right** across the Loing to enter the charming city of **Moret-sur-Loing.**

Your infatuation with Moret will begin on the bridge across the Loing, where you'll gain a lovely view of the town church, its flying buttresses perched precariously above the water. Although often packed with strolling tourists, the streets of Moret are fascinating, too, and well worth an afternoon excursion. The little city's **tourist office** is at the Porte de Semois on the rue Grande, straight ahead from the bridge across the Loing. The town makes a great base for exploring Fontainebleau by bike, but you may find indoor accommodations expensive here. (If the day is young, you might consider pedaling on to Fontainebleau itself—the city beside the château has some lodgings.)

If you want to camp, go right immediately after crossing the Loing River and look for camping signs for "du Lido." Stay with the campground signs to cross under a railroad bridge and arrive at a deluxe international site at Veneux-les-Sablons, complete with a bar, tennis, mini-golf, and a swimming pool. Prices are steep for French camping, but the location and facilities warrant the extra francs.

Cyclists who have a day to spare and a yen for a bit of pleasant riding *sans baggage* should consider making Fontainebleau a day trip from Moret or Veneux. The delightful 41,000-acre Forêt de Fontainebleau boasts miles of quiet (try to avoid weekends), shaded roads, and the château itself deserves several hours of exploration. Of course, no visit to France is complete without a sun-warmed picnic, set against the backdrop of a gorgeous French castle, so be sure to pack a lunch.

# Moret-sur-Loing to Versailles (via Fontainebleau): 109 kilometers

Leave Moret via the **rue Grande,** cycling past the Porte de Semois and continuing with the main road to **Veneux-les-Sablons.** Watch for an intersection signed for the **Hotel de Ville, Thomery,** and **Champagne;** go **right** here and begin following signs for **Avon.** Enter the Forêt de Fontainebleau, and pedal through two **roundabouts** with signs for Avon. Continue through **Avon** on **Road D137** (ride straight through town—don't take the truck route).

You'll veer **right** to enter the grounds of Fontainebleau Palace a short time later (no bicycles are allowed on the inner grounds of the palace, so you'll need to lock up outside the gates). A royal mansion was first constructed here in the twelfth century because of the wealth of game in the area, which the French rulers loved to hunt. Today, Fontainebleau Palace is a vast edifice, richly endowed both inside and out. A tour of the interior, although far from cheap, is well worth the time and croissant money you'll invest.

The ride from Fontainebleau will take you along the southern edge of the Paris sprawl, zigzagging on secondary roads and getting close enough to France's overwhelming capital for a mass-transit visit from a safe base at Versailles. If you want to visit Paris (and who wouldn't?), we recommend you find a friendly hotel keeper in Versailles, or set up camp at the city's campground, stow your bike and gear, and utilize the excellent French transit system to get into the city. One word of warning about your ride today—drivers are different in the Île-de-France. We had more close calls and encountered more rude drivers in one day of cycling in this area than we did in a month of pedaling through parts of France more distant from Paris. Please be cautious as you ride.

Leave Fontainebleau on **Road D409** for **Étampes,** passing through fragrant forests on the way. Turn **right** on **Road D11** for **St. Martin** and forsake the busy road for quieter riding. In St. Martin, go **left** for **Courances,** crossing under the **A6** auto route. Follow the quiet country road to Courances. The city boasts a beautiful château with extensive gardens. From Courances, go **left** onto **Road D372,** then swing

**right** onto **Road C3** to continue on to Moigny-sur-École.

Cross Road D948 in **Moigny** and continue with the hilly secondary route toward **Courdimanche.** Merge with **Road D105,** going **right,** then turn **right** again onto **Road D449** for **d'Huison.** There are many lovely châteaux to entertain you as you follow the Essone River northward. Ride to d'Huison, then turn **left** for **Longueville.** Continue on to **Boissy-le-Cutte,** and take **Road D148** to **Villeneuve, Etréchy,** and **Chauffour.** Angle **right** in Chauffour onto **Road D132** for Souzy. Cycle through **Souzy** and pedal on for St. Chéron and **Marais.**

Turn **right** onto **Road D27** just before Marais, catch a glimpse of yet another château, then swing **left** to regain **D132** to **Angervilliers.** Go **right** on **Road D838** for Limours in Angervilliers. From Limours, climb steeply on **Road D988,** then turn left onto **D838** again, following signs for **Versailles** toward **St. Rémy.** Follow the signs for **Milon-la-Chapelle** through St. Rémy, turning **left** onto **Road N306** in town, then swinging **right** for Milon-la-Chapelle.

Reach the picturesque city of Milon and climb a **tough hill** toward **St. Lambert** on **Road D46.** There are several luxurious homes scattered along the way, and you'll have plenty of time to look at them as you struggle up the hill. Go **right** onto the busy **Road D91** after St. Lambert and climb some more. Signs for **Versailles** will lead you on from here.

Head for the **tourist office** at 7, rue des Réservoirs (near the château), and seek help with lodgings there. Once you're settled in, you can pay homage to yet another fantastic French castle and end your tour from Brussels with a "royal" bang. Ask your hotel manager or the Versailles campground staff to explain the complexities of train fees and schedules before you set off for Paris. Then lock up your bike, grab your camera, and make your pilgrimage to the city.

If you're heading home from here, you can make train connections to Brussels (and its international airport) from Paris. You'll need to send your bicycle a few days in advance, then clear it through customs when you get to Brussels. If Orly Airport is your final destination, you can battle the public transit system with your bicycle and gear (a risky proposition) or cycle to the airport from either Fontainebleau (closest) or Versailles (not so close). Better yet—why not hook up with our Tour No. 5 and pedal on to Angers from here?

# TOUR NO. 5

# ME AND MY CHÂTEAUX
## Versailles to Angers, France

*Distance:* 452 kilometers (281 miles)
*Estimated time:* 7 riding days
*Best time to go:* April, May, June, or September; avoid the July/August tourist crunch
*Terrain:* Wonderful river riding with few hills
*Connecting tours:* Tour No. 4

This delightful tour will take you from Versailles to the cathedral city of Chartres, then on to the château-studded Loire Valley. Once in the region of the Loire, you'll wind past a wealth of French castles as you savor riverside cycling, lovely scenery, and superlative French cuisine. To maximize your enjoyment of the area, please avoid high season at all costs. It's no secret—the Loire Valley is one of the pearls of France. Shun the hordes of tourists that "pig out" on its attractions in July and August, and sample the Loire's delicacies in April, May, June, or September. This will be a feast you'll never forget.

**CONNECTIONS.** Combine this ride from Versailles to Angers with our Tour No. 4 from Brussels, Belgium, to Versailles, and you'll be treated to a scenery-rich, attraction-packed route. Although you'll have to contend with a few stretches of intense traffic, quiet cycling on small roads is the norm for both tours. If you end your trip at the château-crowned city of Angers, you'll find good rail connections to other parts of France. Angers's train-station workers are accustomed to handling lots of bicycles in this heavily cycled region, so your hassles should be limited.

This Loire route also has several potential connection points with routes in our book *France by Bike,* so please refer to that volume if you would like to do additional cycling in France.

**INFORMATION.** Read the introductory material in Tour No. 4 for ideas on obtaining information on France. There are a host of books available in English dealing with the Loire Valley. One excellent regional tourist guide is Michelin's *Green Guide* for the area.

**ACCOMMODATIONS.** Please refer to Tour No. 4 for information on French lodgings.

**SUPPLIES.** Check out the supplies section in Tour No. 4 to find out about French food and shopping.

**TOUR 5 - VERSAILLES TO ANGERS**

## Versailles to Chartres: 73 kilometers

Look at the final paragraphs of Tour No. 4 for additional details on Versailles. Of course, you'll need to delay your journey toward the Loire at least a day or two, as you'll undoubtedly want to wander the lush grounds and amazing interior of the château at Versailles for many hours. This building makes even a simple outdoor picnic a regal affair. You won't be able to take your baguette inside the palace, but you will be able to feast your eyes on architecture, furniture, and paintings that bring French history to life.

Versailles makes a great base for seeing Paris, too, either from the safe haven of a hotel or the economical tent spots at the city's campground. The commute into Paris takes less than an hour. After a few exhausting days of sightseeing in the "heart of France," you'll be ready to head for back roads and farmland, so load up your bicycle, strap on your helmet, and head out.

Leave Versailles with the somewhat frantic **Road D91** toward **Dampierre** and **Rambouillet.** You'll face scattered hills along the way, with a real steepie just before Dampierre. Handsome châteaux in pretty settings await you in Dampierre and Senlisse. Road D91 leads into the busy **Road N306.** If you want to see **Rambouillet,** turn **right** to pedal the 10 unpleasant kilometers to your goal. (If you've had enough of châteaux and big-city traffic for a while, consider hopping on Road D72 at Cernay instead. Many quiet and hilly kilometers lead southwest to Sonchamp, across Road N10, and on with Road D101 to Esclimont. Regain our route in Gallardon.)

Cycle into Rambouillet's **center** to arrive at the luxurious grounds of the château. This part of France has an abundance of scenic picnic spots, and Rambouillet is one of them. All you need is a loaf of bread, a hunk of cheese, and a château. When you're finished "sharing" the summer residence of the French president, depart Rambouillet along the **main road south (Road N10),** but turn **right** onto **Road D150** for **Orphin** soon after.

Ride through Orphin and go **right,** then veer **left** to regain **D150** (becomes **Road D32**) for **Ecrosnes** and **Gallardon.** Pause to explore the large church in Gallardon before pushing on along D32 for **Chartres.** You'll see the lovely silhouette of the twin-towered cathedral of Chartres as you approach the city. Road D32 dumps you onto the growling **Road N10** just before town. Follow this to the **center** and the cathedral.

The famed stained-glass windows of Chartres Cathedral glow like a thousand jewels in the velvet-vaulted heights, and the carvings around the front altar are masterpieces of detail, reciting the life of Christ in stone. With its parks and churches, its hilly old quarter, its narrow streets, and its tantalizing alleys, Chartres is a gem of a city to linger in.

Stop in at the **tourist office** across from the cathedral for information on lodgings, city attractions, and cathedral tours. Chartres offers a convenient youth hostel and several hotels to choose from.

## Chartres to Châteaudun: 58 kilometers

Leave Chartres to the **south** with **Road D935** toward **Dammarie.** You'll have 10 fairly busy kilometers to Dammarie, then angle **right** on the far end of town to gain **Road D127** toward **Fresnay-le-Comte.** Swing **right** into Fresnay soon after, and follow signs to **Meslay-le-Vidame,** a small town with a big château. From Meslay, continue on for **Bronville,** and go **right** on **Road D154** for **Bois-de-Feugères.**

Cross the suicidal **Road N10** and angle **left** on **Road D359** for **Alluyes,** riding through flat farmland with few cars for company. Leave Alluyes on **Road D153** and pedal to **Dangeau,** then go **left** on **Road D941** toward **Logron.** Logron straddles the busy Road D955 and offers you a straight-shot 10$\frac{1}{2}$-km route into Châteaudun. This road is not fun. Postpone your entry into Châteaudun (and avoid arriving in the city on the front bumper of one of D955's fleet of automobiles), and **cross D955** to continue with **Road D23** toward **Lanneray.**

In Lanneray, go **left** on **Road D31** for **St. Denis** and **Châteaudun.** Hit the busy **Road D927** in St. Denis and join it for the final kilometers to Châteaudun. (If you need to shop for groceries, you may want to do it in St. Denis, as Châteaudun's central shopping options aren't as good.) Look for Châteaudun's fortresslike château peering down from its rocky perch as you approach the city.

Signs for the **château** and **center** will lead you upward to the hilltop city and its ancient core. If you're planning to camp, don't climb the hill! Instead, head north on Road D955 to cross the Loir River, then go right with campground signs to find Châteaudun's no-frills municipal camping area 1 km later. The inexpensive site features a priceless view of the city's floodlit château by night.

Châteaudun's **tourist office** at 3, rue Toufaire, can help you with indoor lodgings. There is a youth hostel in the city, as well as a handful of hotels.

## Châteaudun to Beaugency: 48 kilometers

To pedal on toward your meeting with the lovely Loire River, leave Châteaudun with **Road D955** as it swings around the base of the hilltop *Vieille Ville*. Jog **left** then veer **right** to gain the wonderfully quiet **Road D31** toward **Meung-sur-Loire,** passing the city swimming pool on the way. You'll have flat farmland from here to the Loire Valley. It's not terribly scenic cycling—but it is quick and easy.

Keep with signs for **Meung-sur-Loire** through acre after acre of corn. Road D31 becomes **D14** and then **D2,** but **Meung** is signed throughout the ride. You can take a shortcut to the river and Beaugency by swinging right onto D25 for Ouzouer-le-Marché in Prénouvellon, then continuing with D25 to its junction with Road D925, 12 km short of Beaugency. We'll give you the slightly longer version, via Meung-sur-Loire. From Prénouvellon, continue with **Road D2** through **Charsonville** and **Baccon.** Pick up a bit of traffic at **le Bardon,** and pedal the final few kilometers to the riverside town of Meung-sur-Loire.

With a medieval château and narrow old streets, the fortified village of Meung is worth a stop. Those wishing to see the immense but stimulating city of Orléans (about 20 km northeast along the river) might choose to make Meung a base for a day trip to the city, and a pleasant riverside campground in Meung invites overnight visitors. Orléans's cathedral is certainly worth a look, and there are many other attractions in the city that sent forth France's greatest heroine, Jeanne d'Arc. Cycling into this vast urban area is less than relaxing, however. Hop one of the frequent trains between Meung and Orléans instead.

To cycle on toward Beaugency, leave Meung from the north end of the **bridge** across the Loire River. Follow the riverside **Promenade des Mauves** away from town and pedal on to **Baule.** You'll be forced to join the busy **Road N152** for the final few kilometers into **Beaugency.** Swing **left** off the main road to enter the city, and look for the **tourist office** on the Place du Martroi. The staff there can direct you to Beaugency's youth hostel or to the campground just across the river.

Visit the city's fifteenth-century château and its twelfth-century Church of Notre Dame, or wander Beaugency's medieval streets and squares in search of buttery croissants. Carry your bounty to the waterfront promenade, absorbing the atmosphere of the Loire while you indulge in the joys of France.

# Beaugency to Blois (via Chambord): 42 kilometers

Depart Beaugency via the **Tour St.-Firmin** and continue on the **rue Porte Tavers.** Stay with this route to **Tavers,** then go **left** just beyond Tavers's **church.** Signs for **Lestiou** lead on to the small village, followed by signs for **Avaray.** From Avaray, look for signs for **Courbouzon,** then veer **left** just past Courbouzon's **church** to descend to the flatlands along the banks of the Loire. You'll work your way through a series of junctions as you pedal effortlessly along the river valley.

Arrive at a **junction** with **Road D112** and swing **left** to cross the Loire into **Muides** (there's a nice riverside campground here). Stay with **D112** as you climb away from the river, following road signs for **Chambord** into the luxurious **Parc de Chambord.** Sunny April weather, a fragrant forest, and the waves from picnicking French families made our first visit to the forest a delight. Be sure to stock up on lunch supplies before you enter the park, as you'll surely want to spread a picnic of your own on the lovely grounds of the château.

Stay with the well-signed route to Chambord Château, set on vast green lawns and framed by carefully trimmed plane trees. This fanciful building, with a roof said to be the work of Leonardo da Vinci, attracts hordes of tourists in the summer months. Even so, the beauty of the castle and its grounds will enthrall you for hours. Take the tour of the interior, too, if you can bear to leave the view outside.

As you leave Chambord, shun the signed route for Blois (it goes to the unappealing Road D951), and follow the route signed for **Huisseau** and **Vineuil** on **Road D33** instead. You'll enjoy scenic, easy cycling to Vineuil, and you may have plenty of company if you're riding on a summer day. Just beyond **Vineuil,** another sign for Blois

will try to lure you toward a main road north. Continue **straight** for
**St. Gervais-la-Forêt** instead, and cross **under the main road** before gaining a smaller road signed for **Blois.**

Go **right** here, and continue straight across the Loire River to
reach the center of the city. You'll find Blois's **tourist office** in the
Pavillon Anne de Bretagne at 3, avenue Jean Laigret (to the left after
you cross the Loire). They'll be able to direct you to the somewhat inconvenient youth hostel or a more centrally located hotel. If you want
to camp, follow Road D951 along the left bank of the Loire River (as
you approach the city, turn right before the Loire bridge), and pedal
about 2 km to a somewhat ratty but convenient campground or 4 km
to a more deluxe site.

Blois is a lively Loire city, and its streets are a delight for strolling.
Visit the Château de Blois, with one of the best-preserved interiors of
all the Loire châteaux, or explore the 800-year-old Church of St.
Nicolas.

*A lone tourer savors the beauty of Chambord Château.*

# Blois to Chenonceau: 46 kilometers

Leave Blois along the **left bank** of the Loire River, pedaling the busy **Road D751** for about 4 km. When the main road swings to the left away from the river, continue **straight** onto **Road D173** for **Candé-sur-Beuvron.** Wonderful quiet cycling follows as you ride to Candé, with a handsome old bridge across the Beuvron River. Rejoin **D751** to push on to **Chaumont.** You'll pass Chaumont's municipal campground and **tourist information** office as you enter town.

Chaumont's hilltop château is worth a look, but you'll need to lock your bike at the bottom and ascend the asphalt pathway to the summit. A spectacular view of the Loire Valley is just one of the perks of this climb—the drawbridge-equipped Chaumont Château is a delight, and tours include a visit to the sumptuous stables.

Retrieve your bicycle and climb away from Chaumont and the Loire on **Road D114** toward **Pontlevoy** and **Montrichard.** Puff up a steady 1-km hill, then swing **right** onto **Road D27** for **Vallières** and **Chissay-en-Touraine.** A gently undulating route leads through fields and forests to Vallières. (If you want to see Amboise, another lively but touristy Loire city ruled by an impressive château, swing right onto Road D30 for Amboise from Vallières.)

To continue for Chenonceau, climb again after Vallières, staying on D27 for the 10 km to **Chissay** and the Cher River. In Chissay, turn **right** onto **Road D176** for **Chenonceaux.** You'll pass a campground in **Chisseaux** on your way to Chenonceau, and there are campsites in Civray and Bléré (farther west) as well. The village of Chenonceaux has a small campground and a handful of hotels.

Spanning the Cher River with its line of elegant arches, Chenonceau Château is a delight for the senses. Thanks to the kindness and popularity of one of the château's former mistresses, it escaped the widespread destruction of the French Revolution. This is one of the most popular châteaux in France, so try to avoid a weekend visit. Hand over the entry fee for grounds, gardens, and interior, and savor the palace's matchless setting in the company of the floods of tourists doing the same.

# Chenonceau to Chinon: 100 kilometers

You may want to consider continuing along the Cher River toward Tours and its St. Gatien Cathedral from Chenonceau, but Tours is an enormous city with a traffic volume to match. We were ready for a break from cities and sights at this point in our ride, so our route from Chenonceau was an end run south of Tours and its sprawl. Leave Chenonceau by continuing west on **Road D176.** At **Civray,** turn **left** for **Bléré** and cross the Cher. Go **left** at the **Y** for **Thoré,** cross under the **main road,** and climb past Thoré and **les Fougères** before turning **right** for **Sublaines.**

Leave Sublaines on **Road D25** toward **Chédigny,** then turn **right** in Chédigny to gain **Road D10** toward **Reignac.** Follow the pretty riverside route through **Reignac** and on to **Cormery** (D10 becomes D17 along the way). Cormery is a lovely village with some noteworthy churches, a windmill, and an old washing house. Intersect with **Road N143** in town and go **left** here. Take the **first right** off N143 (it's signed for the **campground** and **Veneuil**).

Pedal onward past the city campground and keep **left** at the **Y.** Climb briefly but steeply to the green fields above the Indre River. Another challenging dip and climb follows, then enjoy easy terrain to **Veigne,** continuing **straight** with the signed route for the city. Come in beside **Veigne's church,** and go **left** on **Road D50.** Grab a **right** onto the **rue Jules Ferry** just afterward (there's a difficult-to-spot sign for **Montbazon,** too).

Pedal a delightfully quiet route beside the Indre River to arrive in **Montbazon** in the shadow of the city's hilltop ruin and lofty statue of the Virgin. Go **right** on the **main road** through the lively town, then take a **left** onto **Road D17** for **Monts.** Heavier traffic will accompany you as you push on through Monts and **Artannes,** but the cycling is pleasant.

From Artannes, you can stay beside the Indre and pedal west toward the château of Azay-le-Rideau, but this route means a bit less solitude. Unless you're set on visiting Azay, swing **right** in Artannes onto **Road D121** for **Druye** and **Villandry.** Enjoy silent, flat cycling through fields of corn and sunflowers as you head for your reunion with the Loire River. Stay with **D121** through Druye and on toward **Villandry.**

A short, **steep descent** leads past Villandry's Romanesque village church, then go **right** on **Road D7** to gain the entrance to the **château.** Famous throughout Europe for its fabulous gardens, Villandry's château is at its most magnificent in spring and summer. Join the crowds of flower-loving tourists to wander the impressive grounds of the château, then **backtrack** to your **intersection** with D7 and wheel your bike across to find a shaded **picnic area** awaiting your baguette crumbs.

Continue **straight** toward the **Loire River** on this tiny, tree-lined road, then parallel the **Cher River** as it flows into the larger waterway. Keep to the **right** at an **unsigned Y** and endure a short stretch of **cobblestone,** then gain a **paved levee route** along the Loire's left bank. As you pedal on toward **Langeais,** you'll have wonderful views of the river and its many native birds—keep watch for the ungainly herons that are so abundant here.

Enjoy delightful cycling for the next several kilometers, passing under a new bridge that spans the river, then look for Langeais and its

*A sign at the entrance to Villandry Château gives evidence of the plethora of cyclists in the Loire Valley.*

majestic château across the water as you approach the bridge into the city. (If you'd like to visit Langeais Château, famous for its richly endowed interior, pedal across to the city on the opposite bank, then backtrack to the Loire's left bank when you're finished.) To continue on toward Chinon, **cross** the bridge road with signs for **Bréhémont, Ussé,** and **Chinon.**

This second leg along the Loire is a bit busier than the first, but it's still quite wonderful, and you'll revel in French cycling as you glide past Bréhémont, then shun turnoffs for Rivarennes and Rigny-Ussé. Yet another opportunity to view a Loire château will present itself at the **second turnoff for Rigny-Ussé.** Go **left** here and look for the huddled white towers of **Ussé Château** on the tree-clad hillside straight ahead. Cross the **Indre River** (there's a great view of the château from the bridge) and continue to the castle, if you plan to visit. Some say the best thing about Ussé Château is the exterior view of the fairy-tale structure, so decide for yourself if you want to have a look inside.

From Ussé, you can either put up with 3½ busy kilometers on Road D7 or **retrace** your route to the **Loire shoreline** and continue with your quiet riverside road. The river route feeds back into **D7** after a handful of serene kilometers. Continue **straight** across the main road and **climb steeply** to **Huismes.** Then pedal onward with **Road D16** toward **Chinon.**

As you near Chinon, you'll hit a **roundabout** on **Road D751.** Continue **straight** for **Chinon's center** from here, and climb a final ridge before joining another main road into town. Revel in a **wild descent** past the walls of Chinon's fortified château, and fly downhill to the banks of the Vienne River. If you're hoping to camp, there's a great municipal campground on the opposite shore of the Vienne. Position your tent doorway correctly, and you'll have a superb view of the floodlit château by night.

Chinon's **tourist office** is up the hillside in the old core of the city at 12, rue Voltaire. Ask for help with hotels or get directions to the city's youth hostel (back at river level on the rue Descartes). Although the modern suburbs of Chinon are far from enchanting, the old town is a delight, clinging to the hill beneath its ruined fortress. Climb the slope to explore the scarred château, and savor the view of the medieval city, the river, and the surrounding vineyards. Then prowl the steep hillside to stare at the homes burrowed into the rock or stop at a local cave for a taste of Chinon's famous wine.

## Chinon to Angers: 85 kilometers

Leave Chinon on **Road D749 south,** crossing the Vienne and turning **right** onto **Road D751** when the road branches. Go **left** after 3 km onto **Road D759,** then turn **right** for **le Coudray-Montpensier.** Angle **right** again for **la Devinière.** As you pedal along **Road D117,** you'll spot the châteaux of la Devinière and Chavigny on the right and the bulk of le Coudray-Montpensier commanding a hill to the left.

Just after **Chavigny,** turn **right** for **Couziers** and **Fontevraud-l'Abbaye,** cycling through a military area of forest, rolling hills, and rough pavement. Fontevraud boasts the remains of an abbey founded in 1099. Though much altered by time and plunder, those remains compose the largest collection of monastic buildings in France. Pause for a look at the abbey church, then cruise on through the city and gain **Road D145** through the Forêt de Fontevraud.

Continue **straight** through **Champigny,** then pedal into **Saumur** along a ridge above the Loire River. Arrive at the lofty **château** of Saumur, a beautiful towered fortress with a spectacular site above the river. Plan to enjoy a picnic on the grassy grounds while you savor the château and the view. Then proceed through Saumur, following signs for **Gennes** onto **Road D751** along the left bank of the Loire.

Riding is pleasant for the 15 km to Gennes, once you escape the industrial suburbs of Saumur. You can stop at the famed mushroom caves of the Musée du Champignon along the way. In **Gennes,** angle **right** to stay along the Loire's flat **southern shore.** Ride on **Road D132** and pass through the quiet towns of **le Thoureil, St. Rémy,** and St. Jean. Go **right** onto **Road D751** in **St. Jean,** then ride to

**Juigné** and continue **straight** to regain **D132.** Pedal the last few kilometers to a junction with **Road N160** and turn **right** on N160 to gain the **bridge** across the Loire toward **Angers.**

If you want to camp before Angers, you can stop at les Ponts-de-Cé, about 6 km before the city center. Or continue into Angers by pedaling along the busy **Road N160** and following signs for the **center.** The somber black towers of the château will draw you on. But don't let the forbidding exterior keep you from a visit—the château's flower-filled moat is a visual delight and its collection of the Tapestries of the Apocalypse is one of France's great medieval treasures.

The **tourist office** near the château can provide you with information on the city's hotels, hostel, and other campgrounds. If you're ending your cycling here with a train toward Paris or beyond, Angers boasts extensive rail connections and a train station staff accustomed to handling bicycles. Please remember to prepare your bike carefully for long-distance train rides (see "Connections" in Tour No. 4).

# TOUR NO. 6

# BIKING WITH THE VIKINGS
### Stockholm, Sweden, to Copenhagen, Denmark

*Distance:* 632 kilometers (392 miles)
*Estimated time:* 8 riding days
*Best time to go:* Late May through early September
*Terrain:* Gentle hills; lots of easy pedaling
*Connecting tours:* Tour No. 7

For a leisurely look at two very different Scandinavian countries, a pleasant mix of solitude and big-city sightseeing, and lots of beautiful scenery, this tour from Stockholm to Copenhagen is hard to beat. To prepare for your ride, read the introductory material for Sweden provided here, then turn to the information for Denmark at the start of Tour No. 7. If you have time, combine the two tours for a more extensive Scandinavian experience.

Beginning a ride in a new country is always a bit unnerving, and one of the first tasks you'll have in Sweden is discovering a greeting to use for your friendly exchanges on the road. *"Hej-hej,"* Swedish hellos are fun! Practice your *"hej-hej"* (hay-hay) while you cycle, and enjoy the easy warmth and responsiveness of the Swedes you meet along the way. You'll have few difficulties with language here, since most young Swedes speak excellent English, and you'll find people to be hospitable, fun loving, and friendly to cyclists.

Like most Europeans, Swedish drivers fly down the road at terrifying speeds. You may want to dive for a ditch the first time you see the famed "car-passing-a-car-passing-a-car" maneuver, but you'll get lots of "hello" honks and waves to brighten your cycling days as well.

**CONNECTIONS.** Stockholm's Arlanda Airport draws in international flights by the dozens on a daily basis, so reaching the start of this tour should be effortless if you're coming by air. If you have a limited amount of time or are more interested in seeing Sweden than Denmark, you can easily turn this tour into a Stockholm-to-Stockholm loop by swinging north from Kalmar (see Day 4).

If you arrive in Stockholm via air, you'll have about a 40-km journey into the city from the airport. Your best bet may be to find an airport–city center bus that will carry your bicycle and gear into Stockholm for you, or to stow your things at the airport and make the bus trip in to pick up maps and information before you ride. If you plan to cycle into Stockholm, be sure to pick up a good map of the complex urban bike-route system—you'll need it!

Another option for your Stockholm arrival, especially if you intend to stop cycling in Copenhagen (where this tour ends) rather than hooking up with Tour No. 7 and pedaling on through Denmark, is to purchase roundtrip airfare to Copenhagen. You can travel to Stockholm by ferry and train to begin your ride.

**INFORMATION.** Write to the Swedish National Tourist Office, 655 Third Avenue, 18th Floor, New York, New York 10017, for information on Sweden, and request pamphlets on Stockholm, Gotland, camping, and bicycling. Tourist offices within Sweden are well stocked with English-language literature, and be sure to visit the superb library at the Swedish Institute when you call on Stockholm's main tourist office. Additional reading material can be found in *Baedeker's Scandinavia* or *The Real Guide: Scandinavia* to prepare you for your trip.

If you're interested in expanding our route through Sweden and cycling more of this vast country, write to the Swedish Cycling Association, Box 6006, S-164 06 Kista, Sweden. The association sells maps and literature, and they offer a detailed guide to Sweden's extensive network of long-distance bikeways (signposted as *Sverigeleden*). This guide, called *Sverigeboken,* contains 73 pages of maps, as well as 40 city maps. The text is in Swedish, however.

**MAPS.** For route finding in Sweden, use either the 1:300,000 maps published by Esselte Kartor AB or the eight-map 1:300,000 series by Kümmerly & Frey. Check out additional options when you're in the

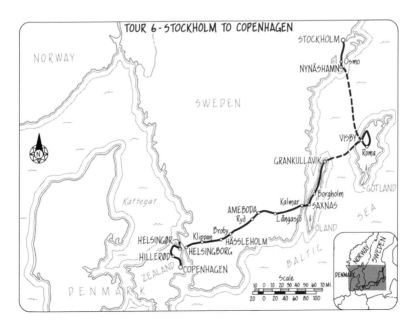

bookstores. Although it's nice to have very detailed maps, you may discover, as we did, that many of Sweden's country roads are not paved and, consequently, not much use to a heavily loaded touring bike.

**ACCOMMODATIONS.** Although Swedish campgrounds cost more than those in most other European countries, they're still good accommodation bargains in a country where indoor lodgings may devastate tight budgets. You'll need an International Camping Carnet (see the introduction) or a Swedish camping card (available in the country) to pitch your tent. You can also take advantage of Sweden's delightful "Everyman's right" (*Allmänsträtten*), a law that allows one-night camping on unfenced land, and plop yourself down in a secluded spot for a free night's sleep. However, it's still wise and courteous to ask permission when you can.

The price of Swedish hotels may be prohibitive to all but the healthiest of pocketbooks. Consider the extensive and well-maintained Swedish youth hostel system instead. Either an international youth hostel card or a membership from Svenska Turistföreningen (STF) is required.

**SUPPLIES.** Sweden's reputation as one of the most expensive countries in Europe is well deserved, so you'll have to scramble if you're on a tight budget. Grocery prices are slightly higher than in the United States, and prepared foods and restaurant meals are sky high. Stick to picnics, supermarket supplies, and camp-cooked dinners (with an occasional splurge for local specialties), and your budget will survive. One of the most delightful things about bicycle touring is meeting local people. Be open to friendly encounters and you may find yourself feasting on priceless home-cooked meals instead of supermarket beans. We did!

Fortify yourself for long riding days with a hearty Swedish breakfast of museli doused with thick sour milk (*filmjölk*) and topped with lingonberries or wild blueberries. For delicious crunchy lunches, try the tasty and mild Swedish cheese (*ost*) on top of ripply brown crackers (*knäckebröd*). Dinner treats include reindeer stew (*renskav*) and a hearty potato, onion, and egg hash (*pytt i panna*).

Swedes are hard workers, and the Swedish economy is one of the healthiest in Europe. Stores keep long hours in this country where the almighty kroner stands tall beside the dollar, but you'll still have to look hard to find a small-town grocery store open on Sunday. Banks are closed on weekends.

There are large bicycle shops in both Stockholm and Copenhagen where you'll be able to find a good selection of replacement parts.

## Stockholm to Nynäshamn: 68 kilometers

Your first priority on arrival in Sweden's capital will probably be accommodations. You can get help from **Stockholm Information**

Service (east of the central train station on Hamngatan). Stockholm has several hostels and some rather inconveniently located campgrounds. Be sure to buy a detailed map of Stockholm's streets if you don't already have one, and ask about the special Stockholm cycling map that is also available. You'll see lots of bicycles on Stockholm's streets, and the extensive network of bike paths makes riding in the city pleasant—*if* you know where you're going.

If you'll be spending much time in Stockholm, check into the Stockholm Card, a pass to city transportation and attractions. After you've done your sightseeing in Sweden's sparkling capital, with walks in the old town (*Gamla Stan*) and visits to the islands of Skeppsholmen and Djurgården, you'll be ready to ride for Nynäshamn and the Gotland-bound ferry. Check on the Gotlandslinjen ferry schedule while you're still in Stockholm. There's an office of the Gotland Tourist Association in the city, and you can get ferry times and prices there.

Hook up with the "purple" bike path (you can get onto it at **Slussen,** on the southern end of **Staden Mellan Broarna**) and follow the small **purple bike markers** through the city and onto a route paralleling **Road 226** south. Pass through **Johanneshov, Älvsjö, Stuvsta,** and **Huddinge,** and ride on to **Tumba,** where you'll cycle along the edge of the busy Road 226 toward **Nynäshamn.**

At **Vårsta,** turn **left** onto **Road 225,** again following signs for **Nynäshamn.** There wasn't a marked bike lane along this 30-km section when we cycled it, and a weekend or holiday ferry rush might make things hectic. Pass through forested countryside and pedal easy hills past clear lakes and countless red farm buildings. At **Ösmo,** swing **right** onto **Road 73** to pedal the final 11 km to the ferry. Traffic increases on this road, so ride carefully. Watch for signs for the **Gotland/Visby ferry** as you enter Nynäshamn.

The Nynäshamn–Visby ferry runs twice a day during high season (June to August), once a day the rest of the year, and it's a five- to seven-hour ride. There is no charge for bicycles, and you'll be amazed by the number of Swedish cyclists who will join you for the trip. As you wait to board, entertain yourself by watching the holiday-bound Swedes around you, and marvel at the suitcases, guitars, and luggage trailers lashed to their bikes.

## Around Gotland: 70 kilometers

The ferry lands at Visby, the largest and loveliest city on Gotland. You'll see hundreds of cyclists in town and throughout the island. They have good reason to be there—Gotland is an enchanting spot for cycling. Its flat fields are carpeted with wildflowers, its Baltic beaches are ideal for lazy days in the sun, its weather is some of Sweden's finest, and its size allows cyclists to do as much or as little riding as they choose.

The Visby **tourist office** is a short distance from the ferry terminal at Strandgatan 9. Request a tourist map of the island. We were able to purchase a *Gotlands Karta* at 1:200,000 scale that showed camp-grounds, churches, hostels, and sights of interest. Ask at the tourist office for information on hostels and campgrounds on the island—there are several youth hostels on Gotland (one in Visby), as well as an abundance of campgrounds. Near Visby, there's a campground on the beach 4 km south.

Plan to spend at least a day exploring Visby. The narrow streets lined with wooden houses and cascading rose trellises, the red slate roofs, and the ruined arches of naked churches, set against an invigorating backdrop of blue sky and sea will make your visit special. Don't linger in the touristy main streets too long. Instead, visit Visby's churches, walk the city wall with its forty-four towers, or explore the botanical gardens for a taste of the town.

You can easily choose your own day trip for cycling on the island. Or take your gear along and hope for a pleasantly situated campground or a secluded beach on which to camp. We've included this sample day ride from Visby back to Visby to give you an idea of what Gotland has to offer.

Ride **south** through Visby on the **main street** and turn **left** just before the **old water tower,** gaining the road marked for **Roma.** Reach an **intersection** with a sign marked **Roma** straight and **Dalhem** to the left. Stop for a look inside the church beside the road. (*K:A* is Swedish road-sign terminology for church—*kyrka*.) Then turn **left** for **Dalhem** and go **right** just past the **church** onto a small paved road.

Follow the road to **Kungsgården,** the ruin of a Cistercian abbey built in 1120. **Retrace** your route out from the grass-encircled ruin, and turn **right** for **Dalhem.** A wonderful series of biblical wall paintings graces the interior of Dalhem's church, and the quiet churchyard makes a great spot for a picnic lunch.

From Dalhem, ride toward **Ekeby,** then continue on for **Fole.** Turn **left** for **Bro** at Fole. Stop to inspect the painted interior of the ancient church at Bro, where a Norman tower rules a Gothic nave. Just past Bro's **church,** turn **right** for **Väskinde,** and pedal on past Väskinde through fields of shimmering wildflowers. Reach a **T** with a larger road and go **right,** then turn **left** for **Krysmyntagården** to pedal south along the coast through **Brissund** and on back to Visby.

## Grankullavik to Saxnas: 100 kilometers

A three-hour ferry ride will take you from Visby to Grankullavik on the northern tip of Öland. Öland is a long, skinny island connected to mainland Sweden by a 12-km bridge. It's as popular with the Swedes as Gotland is, and its accessibility results in heavier tourist traffic.

Nevertheless, the unbroken vistas of sea, fields, wildflowers, and windmills (the island has more than 400) make pedaling on Öland a visual delight.

Leave the ferry dock at Grankullavik and ride to **Byxelkrok.** You may want to stock up on groceries in town, as it has some of the best shopping opportunities you'll encounter for about 60 km. Continue on **Road 136** to **Böda** (there's an Öland **tourist office** here), then escape the main road by turning **right** for **Byerum.**

We encountered rough pavement on this quiet loop, but it was worth it. At **Byerum,** angle back toward **Road 136** and **Löttorp.** Follow Road 136 to **Köpingsvik.** Truck traffic is fairly light on Öland, but a seemingly endless line of cars and campers makes riding less than ideal on Road 136.

Öland's climate encourages the growth of more than thirty species of orchids (don't pick—they're protected), and it's also the favorite stopover for thousands of migratory birds. You'll be cheered by fields of glowing poppies and entranced by the silhouettes of dozens of wooden windmills as you ride.

*A stout windmill searches for a breeze on Öland.*

Köpingsvik and Borgholm are two hectic tourist towns with what must be the highest per capita concentration of putt-putt courses in the world. Roll onto a **bike path** along the right side of the road after **Köpingsvik,** and follow it to **Borgholm.** Swing into town and stop at the busy **tourist office** for literature.

If you're looking for a room, you may want to end your day in Borgholm, as there are hotels and a hostel here. Otherwise, you'll ride past several of the island's score of campgrounds during your final 25 km to Saxnas and the Öland/mainland bridge.

Just outside of **Borgholm,** turn **right** off Road 136 to take a look at **Borgholm Castle** (*slot*). It has twelfth-century origins and 300-year-old walls. The summer castle of Swedish royalty, Solliden, is a little farther down the secondary road past Borgholm Castle. Return to **Road 136** and continue south toward **Glömminge** for about 20 km. Turn **right** at the sign for **Saxnas** and its well-marked campground (a few kilometers north of the bridge) to end a long cycling day. The vast campground is pleasant, quiet, and clean.

## Saxnas to Ameboda: 109 kilometers

Leave the campground and continue on the secondary road to regain the **main route** toward **Kalmar.** Coast down a ramp onto the **12-km bridge** to the mainland (Europe's longest), and claim a piece of the slow-vehicle lane as speeding cars fly by on the left. Bypass the first off ramp, then swing down from the second onto a **bike path** marked for Kalmar's **center** (*centrum*).

You may be tormented by unmarked side paths shooting off the main bike route as you pedal toward Kalmar. Just continue following signs for the **center.** Kalmar's town hall and cathedral and the moat- and garden-encircled Kalmar Castle will greet you in the city.

From Kalmar, an innovative cyclist has several options. You can wander north to close your loop at Stockholm, pedaling through Sweden's world-famous glass manufacturing area and pausing at the glassworks in Orrefors and Kosta. Or you can take a more northerly route toward Helsingborg and Denmark, thus passing through more glass territory than our route offers. Unfortunately, this option means busier roads and more traffic.

We chose to continue our ride toward Helsingborg on secondary roads, cycling through quiet Swedish forests and shunning the traffic-heavy routes to the north and south. The result was three days of peaceful riding through forest and farmland, star-filled nights of camping in the trees, and a welcome break from crowds and sightseeing.

From **Kalmar Castle,** follow signs for **Road E66** south. **Bicycle-route** signs for **Smedby** will take you parallel to the main road for about 1 km. Then turn **left** for **E66** and **Karlskrona** and **join E66** soon after. After about 8 km, veer **right** onto **Road 120** for **Långasjö.** Cycle kilometer after kilometer of gentle terrain, with only fern-covered forests and an occasional passing car for company.

Make the slight detour off Road 120 to pass through Långasjö. Be sure to stop at the small **tourist office** in town. If you need a room for the night, ask there. Continue on through town and turn **left** on **Road 124** to regain **Road 120** toward **Tingsryd.** We pulled off the road just past Ameboda to stake out a spot in the trees, sharing the cloudless night with mosquitoes, no-see-ums, and a host of stars.

## Ameboda to Hässleholm: 112 kilometers

Continue on Road 120 until just before **Tingsryd,** then merge with **Road 30** into town. You can stop at the **tourist office** before hopping back onto **Road 120** for **Ryd.** In **Urshult,** stop to peek inside the city church. It has a wonderful painted interior that's a pleasant surprise. Pedal on to **Ryd,** a small town with a glass factory and a music museum, then turn **left** onto **Road 119** to pass through gently rolling forestland for the remainder of the day.

**Lönsboda** has another fine church with beautiful light fixtures. Ride through **Glimåkra** and **Broby,** cross Road 20, and continue on Road 119 for **Hässleholm,** a midsize city with a handful of pleasant churches and parks. To find the **campground** before Hässleholm, turn **left** onto **Road 23.** Go across the overpass and turn **right** to circle onto **Road 21** east. You'll soon reach the signposted campground at **Ignaberga,** and you can visit the on-site limestone grottoes if you have the energy. We opted for dinner and hot showers instead.

If you need a room in the city, stay on **Road 119** into **Hässleholm** and look for signs for the **tourist office,** located in a modern building complex to the left of the road.

## Hässleholm to Helsingborg: 82 kilometers

Begin your last day of cycling in Sweden by leaving town on the busy **Road 21** through **Tyringe,** Perstorp, and Klippan. There's a wide shoulder most of the way, and there are several long, gradual hills. If you're fighting a persistent west wind, as we were, the going can be tough.

Abandon Road 21 about 3 km beyond **Kvidinge,** turning **left** for **Nord Vram.** Pedal up a gradual hill, then descend through forest to a T. Turn **right** toward **Astorp.** Continue on this road for **Gunnarstorp** (don't turn off for Astorp) and pass through Gunnarstorp. Then go **left** at the T. Turn **right** for **Hyllinge** soon after, pedal through the town, and follow signs for **Helsingborg.**

You'll come to an **overpass** and a ramp onto the **E4 freeway** for Helsingborg. Go **straight** for **Ödåkra** instead, and climb a hill to reach a **roundabout** and signs for a **bike route** into Helsingborg. Follow this marked route into town, staying with signs for the **center.**

Helsingborg has an attractive core, centered around its castle, its park, and its Santa Maria Kyrka. Climb to the castle keep for a fine view of the harbor, then descend to the church. Unimpressive on the outside, this lovely building has a Gothic-arched nave of dark red brick supported on massive pillars. Look for the carved pulpit, the crystal chandelier, and the fleet of fascinating hanging ships inside.

From the church, it's only a few blocks to the ferry terminal, and there are frequent 20-minute crossings to Helsingør, Denmark. You can spend the night in Helsingborg or ride across to seek lodgings in Helsingør, calling a last *hej-hej* to Sweden.

# Helsingør to Hillerød: 41 kilometers

The Helsingborg–Helsingør ferry lands in the shadow of **Kronborg Castle,** famed as the traditional home of Prince Hamlet. You can wander the grounds without charge or pay for a tour of the interior. Make the circuit of the castle and admire the view across the water to Sweden, then head **north** on the coast **Road 237** for **Hornbaek.** There's a large, noisy, and usually crowded campground just off Road 237 on the outskirts of Helsingør. It's rather expensive, and all it has going for it is its proximity to the ferry and the castle. There's a youth hostel in Helsingør as well.

Cycle along the coast, staring at sandy beaches and luxurious homes. Traffic can be heavy along the route, so try to ride early in the day before the sun-seekers are out and about. In **Hornbaek,** a bustling seaside town awash in shops and tourists, turn inland onto **Road 235** toward **Espergaerde.** Veer **right** just past **Horneby** for **Havreholm,** and ride through lovely rolling farmland on small, almost traffic-free roads.

Continue on through **Plejelt,** go **right** onto **Road 205,** then **left** toward **Tikøb.** Ride less than a kilometer and swing **right** for **Jonstrup** and **Fredensborg.** Cycle along the quiet shoreline of **Esrum Lake,** surrounded by undulating fields of grain, and catch an occasional glimpse of a thatch-roofed cottage or a flower-flooded garden.

Enter Fredensborg, turning **right** onto the **main road (A6),** then go **right** at the **traffic light** in town to coast down a shop-lined street to **Fredensborg Castle.** The magnificent park surrounding the spring and fall residence of Danish royalty is worth a visit in itself, and if you're looking for a picnic spot, look no farther. The palace is open to visitors only in July (from 1:00 to 5:00 P.M.), but you can admire it from without as you explore the park and gardens.

Return to **A6** and turn **right** to cycle a nice **bike path** beside the road for the final 10 km to **Hillerød.** Follow the signs into Hillerød and turn **right** for **Frederiksborg Slot.** If you want to camp, head for Dyrskuepladsen field on Blytaekkervej. Hillerød's **tourist office** is near the lakeside castle at Slotsgade 52. If you'd like some help through the tangle of bike paths on the way out of town, purchase an area bike-route map at the tourist office.

Leave yourself a few hours for a visit to Frederiksborg Castle. It's one of Denmark's most magnificent palaces. Not only is the building itself outstanding, but the National Historical Museum inside presents a fantastic blend of furniture, paintings, china, and crystal that will take you hours to examine.

## Hillerød to Lyngby/Copenhagen: 50 kilometers

We endured some frustrating wandering around, trying to find the best route out of Hillerød for Copenhagen, and road construction in the area added to our confusion. Decide on your own escape route with the help of the tourist-office map, or attempt to get on the **secondary road** paralleling **Road 19** to **Karlebo.**

Cycle past a large windmill at Karlebo and continue on through moderately hilly farmland to **Avderød.** Go **straight** toward **Kokkedal** and **Horshølm,** then angle **right** about 1 km outside of Avderød onto a larger road. Swing **right** again to get on **Road 229** for **Horshølm** after crossing the **E4 freeway.** Pedal along Road 229 for a few kilometers, then turn **left** for **Rungsted** and a return to the coast. The seaside **Road 152** has heavy traffic, but the route is scenic.

You can hop onto a **bike path** along the Copenhagen-bound train tracks if you prefer quieter riding. Watch for **bike-path signs** just before you reach **Road 152.** Cycle south through forest as you follow signs for **Klampenborg.**

There are several camping options in and around Copenhagen. We set up a base camp outside the city, then rode the train in for sightseeing. From **Skodsborg,** you can cycle inland 3 km on the **Naerum** road, then swing **left** after crossing **E4** to reach a well-marked campground. Tucked in between the freeway and the train tracks, it's noisy and unattractive, but it's only five minutes from the train station—very convenient for sightseeing in Copenhagen.

There's a second campground just off the Copenhagen-bound bike path about 2 km south of **Skodsborg** (also signed from Road 152). This popular and crowded spot has a pleasant setting next to Dyrehaven, an immense deer park. You'll need to backtrack the 2 km to Skodsborg to catch a train into the city, however.

From either campground, you'll have easy access to an extensive network of bike trails, and you can explore the nearby attractions without your panniers. For an enjoyable afternoon trek, follow signs for **Lyngby** on the gravel-surfaced bike ways. Lyngby (or Kongens

*Signs of spring in the Danish countryside*

Lyngby) has an old village centered around its twelfth-century church, but most of the city is glaringly modern. There's a youth hostel in Lyngby, if you're in the market.

Just north of town is the Frilandsmuseet, an open-air museum of Danish farm buildings and folklife. From Lyngby, continue on bike paths for **Klampenborg.** You can swing off to the left to explore the forest paths of Dyrehaven. Entry to the deer park is free, and the well-maintained paths are open to bicycles. Plan to enjoy a picnic near the royal hunting lodge, or stop for a visit to Bakken, Denmark's 400-year-old amusement park. If you're camping at one of the spots we've mentioned, make your ride a loop trip by cycling north through Dyrehaven and regaining the bike route along the train tracks at the northeast corner of the park.

Of course, all this suburb sightseeing will only increase your anticipation for Copenhagen. If you're ending your tour in the city, you'll probably cycle right into the center. Try to buy a detailed city map before you pedal in. There's an excellent Copenhagen cycling map available at tourist offices, and it's a valuable reference for the host of bike paths in the city, especially for the approach routes from Klampenborg and Lyngby.

If you need a room, head for the **tourist office** next to Tivoli Amusement Park on H. C. Andersen's Boulevard 22 (a few blocks from the central train station) and let the staff there do your legwork for you. Copenhagen has a handful of youth hostels, but expect lots of company. Ask about the Copenhagen Card while you're at the tourist office, too. It's a good bargain if you're using public transit or exploring many of Copenhagen's myriad attractions.

Read the first few pages of Tour No. 7 for additional information on Denmark and on Copenhagen, its lovely, lively capital.

# TOUR NO. 7

# FERRY TALES IN DENMARK
*Copenhagen, Denmark, to Kiel, Germany*

*Distance:* 266 kilometers (165 miles)
*Estimated time:* 6 riding days
*Best time to go:* Late May through early September
*Terrain:* Moderate hills; lots of pleasant, scenic cycling
*Connecting tours:* Tour No. 6

There are few European countries better suited for the vacationing cyclist than Denmark. The road system is excellent, with more than 46,000 km of secondary roads and a vast network of bike paths (please note that use of bicycle paths, when present, is mandatory in Denmark). The country is small and the land is green and gentle, with friendly hills that break the monotony but not the spirit.

You may find the Danish language to be frustratingly unpronounceable, but the Danes are superior linguists and you'll encounter many English speakers throughout your stay. People here are friendly and easygoing, and the Danes are blessed with a dry humor that will make your chance meetings a delight. We'll never forget the harried airline clerk at Copenhagen's Kastrup Airport who fielded our frantic inquiries as we faced a nationwide strike, a crippled airport, and only one vacant seat on the last flight out. "Don't worry," he told us with a malicious twinkle in his eyes, "if a standby seat doesn't open up before the plane takes off, one of you will speak excellent Danish by the time you meet again."

**CONNECTIONS.** If you're beginning your Danish tour in Copenhagen, you'll probably arrive at the immense Kastrup Airport south of the city. Kastrup is a small city in itself—with restaurants, shops, showers, and beds. It's served by frequent flights from the United States and Canada.

You might choose to lock your bicycle in a safe spot at the airport and hop a bus into the city center to do your map and accommodation hunting before you mount up to do battle with the city streets. Once you're equipped with a Copenhagen street map or one of the invaluable cycle maps available, your chances at a frustration-free introduction to this charming city will be much better. If you're cycling this tour as a continuation of Tour No. 6, you can pedal into Copenhagen on well-marked bike paths. Copenhagen also offers ferry connections to Malmö, Sweden.

**INFORMATION.** Write ahead to the Danish Tourist Board, 655 Third Avenue, 18th Floor, New York, New York 10017, for general information about Denmark. Request brochures on camping and on Copenhagen, and ask for their cycling pamphlet entitled *On a Bike in Denmark.* You'll probably want to supplement your knowledge of

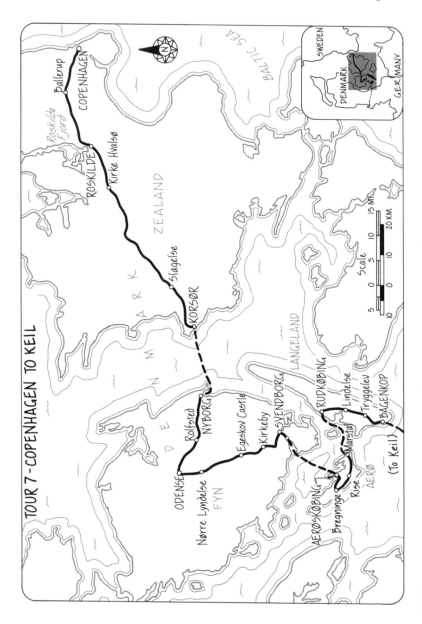

Denmark with a guidebook. *The Real Guide: Scandinavia*, the *Blue Guide Denmark*, and *Baedeker's Scandinavia* are three good options.

The Danish Cycle Federation (Dansk Cyklist Forbund), Kjeld Langes Gade 14, 1367 Copenhagen K, is a great source of specific information on cycling routes and regulations. Write ahead or stop in while you're visiting Copenhagen. We took this tour south toward Germany, as that country was our after-Denmark destination. If you plan to do some additional cycling in Denmark or the rest of Scandinavia instead, be sure to ask advice from someone at the Cycle Federation office. You might be interested in trying out Denmark's first national cycling route, a 240-km trip that traces the backbone of Jutland. If you think you might be doing some rail hopping during your stay in Denmark, stop by the train station to pick up a brochure on bike/train combinations (it's called *Cykler i tog*).

**MAPS.** You'll have many choices in this well-mapped country. Although special cyclists' maps are available, we opted for a superlative four-map series published by the Geodesic Institute. The 1:200,000 maps are easy to use and they show campgrounds, hostels, and a plethora of tourist sights.

**ACCOMMODATIONS.** Campgrounds in Denmark are excellent. They're clean, convenient, and well stocked with essentials like toilet paper and hot water. Coastal sites can be crowded and riotous with Tuborg-powered campers, however, and their prices are surprisingly high. Check the fees and the noise level before you drive your stakes. You'll need an International Camping Carnet or a Danish camping permit to camp here. Review Part I for more details. Camping on your own in Denmark (with permission) is legal but less than ideal. The small country is overrun with tourists in the summer, and beaches and forests take a beating as it is. *Always* ask permission before you pitch your tent outside a campground.

Denmark boasts more than 100 youth hostels, and inexpensive beds are also available in student sleep-ins and private homes. Local tourist offices can help you make arrangements, and they'll supply lots of free literature for your bedtime reading, too. Because of the popularity of cycling in Denmark, you'll seldom get blank looks from tourist-office workers when you ask for cycle maps or route suggestions.

**SUPPLIES.** Prices in Denmark are high, so prepare your budget for a shock. Camping, supermarket shopping, and cooking your own meals are good ways to ease the burden on your money pouch. Shopping hours in the country are generally Monday through Saturday until 5:30 or 6:00 P.M., with Saturday-afternoon shutdowns and all-day lockups on Sunday.

Denmark is world famous for key elements of its cuisine, and you'll enjoy sampling sweet Danish pastries, flavorful and pungent Danish cheeses, and robust Danish beers. Open-faced sandwiches called *smørrebrød* make wonderful picnic fare, and you can pile on toppings of fish, meat, cheese, or vegetables to design your own feast. One warning about Danish cheeses—unless you're hauling a refrigerator on your bike, buy them in small quantities. The aroma of a warm chunk of day-old *h'avarti* can knock your socks off!

There are several excellent bicycle shops in Copenhagen. Ask at the Danish Cycle Federation office for help with locating one. Once out of the Danish capital, you'll be able to find bicycle shops in almost every midsize town.

## Copenhagen to Roskilde: 45 kilometers

There are several hostels and campgrounds in and around Copenhagen where you can stay while you're sightseeing in this wonderful city. A large hostel at Sjaellandsbroen 55 is a short ride west of the airport. (Read the final paragraphs of Tour No. 6 for more information on lodgings around Copenhagen.)

There is one drawback to beginning your cycling tour in Copenhagen—the city is so delightful, you may not want to leave! But after an obligatory visit to the Little Mermaid (no, that doesn't mean a stop at the nearest video store), a leisurely afternoon spent sitting with the silver-haired grandmothers on the benches in Tivoli Amusement Park, long hours of wandering the city streets, and a few cool evenings spent listening to jazz at a Copenhagen cafe, perhaps you'll be ready to ride.

From **Tivoli Amusement Park,** follow **H. C. Andersen's Boulevard** northwest, crossing the canal on **Gyldenløvesgade** and continuing on **Aboulevard** and **Agade** (same street—different names) until you run into **Borups Allé.** Turn **left** onto the bike lane along this street and continue to **Frederikssundsvej.**

Go **left** here, riding through the districts of Brønshøj, Husum, and Herlev. Gain **Road 211** for **Ballerup** and go straight through an intersection with the road from Lyngby. Cycle into Ballerup, then turn **left** at the **first intersection.** Cross the railroad **tracks** and go **right** for **Smørumovre.** (If you're cycling from either of the campgrounds mentioned in Tour No. 6, you'll skirt to the north of Copenhagen proper and pedal through Lyngby, Bagsvaerd, and Hareskovby to join this route at Ballerup.)

From Smørumovre, follow signs for **Hove, Østrup, Gundsølille,** and **Store Valby,** cycling quiet secondary roads. We battled a tenacious headwind on this part of the ride, but hills are few and located mainly in the farmland beyond Smørumovre. After **Store Valby,** turn **right** for **Veddelev** to cross **Road A6** and reach a vast waterside campground. From this site, it's a short bike ride or a pleasant 3-km walk along Roskilde Fjord to reach the center of **Roskilde.**

If you're pedaling directly to the city to look for a room at the hostel

*Carved pews guard the shadowy corners of Roskilde Cathedral.*

or in a hotel, continue straight rather than turning off for Veddelev, and follow signs for the **city center**. Roskilde's **tourist office** is near the twin-spired cathedral.

You'll be delighted by the skulls, crosses, swords, and angels that compete for space on the royal tombs that fill the church. Don't miss the woodwork in the choir, either. The intricately carved scenes give a beautiful summary of Biblical history. If you're still game for sightseeing after visiting the cathedral and taking a walk beside the whitecap-studded fjord, venture inside Roskilde's Viking Ship Museum before calling it a day.

## Roskilde to Korsør: 84 kilometers

Follow the main road (**A6**) through Roskilde toward **Ringsted** and **Korsør.** Although there is an adequate-looking bike path beside the road, you'll do better to abandon the traffic noise for a secondary route through the green Danish countryside. On the edge of **Roskilde,** pass under the **A4 freeway,** and turn **right** onto the main road for **Holbaek** immediately after.

Go **left** about ½ km later onto a smaller road for **Lejre** and cycle through moderately hilly farmland past thatch-roofed houses and brilliant-hued rose gardens. The terrain becomes flatter as you pedal southwest throughout the day. From the **Lejre Road,** turn **left** at the sign for **Lejre ST** (station), cross the **train tracks,** and go **right** toward **Allerslev.** Come to a **T** and take the **bike path** next to the **school** to gain the road toward **Kisserup.**

In Kisserup, follow signs for **Kirke Hvalsø,** then angle **right** onto **Road 255** to pedal through Kirke Hvalsø. Stay on the lightly trafficked Road 255 for about 20 km, then turn **left** just before **Stenlille** onto **Road 57** toward **Sorø.** Leave Road 57 a short distance later, swinging **right** onto **Road 203** toward **Slagelse.** As you approach Slagelse, follow signs for **C. Slagelse** and the **center** (*centrum*). The city has a pleasant downtown and a handsome church. There are a campground and a hostel here, if you need a place to stay.

Look for signs for **Korsør Road 150** to take you out of town. Cross the **A1 freeway** several kilometers later, then veer **right** at **Vemmelev** toward **Forlev.** Go **straight** through Vemmelev, keeping the freeway on your right. Cross a road signed for Korsør, continuing straight on the secondary route beside the freeway through **Halseby** and on into **Korsør.** Turn **left** when the road hits a **T,** and pedal under **two overpasses** before swinging **right** to reach the train station and **ferry office.**

Buy your ferry ticket for the one-hour crossing to Nyborg. You'll have to ride a short distance to reach the ferry landing, then squeeze aboard with the passenger train that runs into the middle of the ship's ample belly.

There are campgrounds at both Korsør and Nyborg. Make sure you have enough daylight left after the ferry crossing to make the 2-km ride to Nyborg's campground.

## Nyborg to Odense: 33 kilometers

To reach Nyborg's campground, leave the **ferry harbor** and ride to a **T** with the main road. Turn **right** toward **Knudshoved,** then go **left** to cross **over the freeway** and follow campground signs to the jam-packed site. Hot showers, modern facilities, a small store, and lots of fellow campers await.

Retrace your route back into town from the campground (or turn left on the main road after leaving the ferry) and ride through **Nyborg** to where the **road branches.** Angle **right** toward **Road A8** and **Fåborg.** Come to a **junction** with A8 and go **left,** then turn **right** toward **Ferritslev** about 1 km later. Cycle through **Kullerup,** go past a turnoff for Pårup, then swing **right** at **Ellinge.** Stay right toward **Pårup** and go **left** for **Rolfsted** soon after. At Rolfsted turn **right** onto **Road 301** toward **Odense.**

Cycling is mellow throughout the day, with gentle hills and light traffic. Look for the wood-and-thatch country houses, the well-kept gardens, and the steeple-topped churches as you ride. The church at Fraugde is worth a visit if you can get inside. Beyond **Fraugde,** follow a **bike path** over the freeway, under a new road, and onto the **old road** beside the busy auto route. Follow the old road through a **small town** and then back onto the **main thoroughfare.**

Turn **left** at the **junction** toward **Neder Holluf,** then swing **right** onto a **bike path** and parallel the main road into **Odense.** Cross a small **creek** and go **left** for the **university** (*universitet*). You'll be cycling through a maze of bike paths around Odense's university. Many of the new paths were still unsigned when we wandered through. Keep the school buildings on your left and the busy main road off to the right as you ride. Pass the **campus entrance** and angle **right.** Turn **right** when the bike path runs into a **small road.** Follow the road to an intersection with **Road A9** and go **left** a short distance to reach a large campground on the edge of Odense.

The forest-bordered site at Hunderup Skov is immense, but it has good facilities and a well-stocked store. It's an easy 4-km walk to the center of Denmark's third-largest city from the campground. Take the footpath along the river and pass the city zoo and amusement park along the way. There are hotels and a youth hostel in Odense, if you need a room.

Odense's **tourist office** is well prepared to handle the crowds that arrive to pay homage to Hans Christian Andersen's hometown and to visit the fine museum the city maintains in his honor. Stop at the tourist office in the town hall on Vestergade, then continue on to H. C. Andersen's House, where a collection of letters, photographs, illustrations, and manuscripts tells the tale of the author's life.

Odense is a pretty city with many handsome homes, a handful of interesting churches, and a host of tantalizing byways. So park your bicycle and let your feet roam freely.

## Odense to Svendborg: 48 kilometers

Leave the campground (or the city center) by heading **south** on **Road A9.** Swing **right** for **Fåborg** just past the **campground,** and cross the train tracks. At the **roundabout,** follow a **bike sign** for

**Volderslev** to cross under **Road 43** and up and onto its shoulder. Cycle through flat fields of wheat and barley, riding to **Nørre Lyndelse,** then going **left** for **Lumby.** Turn onto the **next road** to the right, go **left** at the **T,** and continue on for **Freltofte.**

Follow signs for **Gestelev** and **Herringe.** Ride through Gestelev, cross under **Road 323,** and go **left** after crossing the **creek.** You'll spot a large manor house on the right as you turn **right,** bumping over the **train tracks** and pedaling along the signed route for **Rudme.** Enter **Volstrup** and turn **right** for **Egeskov Castle.** Road signs will direct you to the castle entrance. This wonderfully preserved moated castle, still a private residence, offers an on-site museum with collections of airplanes, cars, motorcycles, and carriages, and it has an extensive garden area for strolling.

If you're more interested in finding a scenic picnic spot than in museum going, turn right off the road from Volstrup just before the castle turnoff and walk out to a tall stone column in the field. You'll have a great view of the castle while you munch your lunch.

Continue from Egeskov Castle onto **Road A8** toward **Fåborg,** but veer **left** on the **small road** just before the **Egeskov Windmill.** Then join a **larger road** to pedal south toward **Stenstrup.** Cycle through Stenstrup and go **right** at **Kirkeby** toward **Egebjerg** and **Ollerup.** At the next intersection, continue **straight** for **Hvidkilde.** Pedal a quiet, narrow road through forests, then turn **left** onto **Road 44** for the final 5 km to **Svendborg.**

A **bike path** will lead you into town. Continue straight for the **city center,** bypassing a turnoff for Rudkøbing. Follow signs for the ferry and **harbor** (*havn*) to reach the small ferry landing. There are several crossings to Aerø per day.

If you have time to spare before departure, Svendborg is a spunky harbor town with narrow alleys and steep streets, half-timbered buildings, old churches, and a zoological museum. All are worth exploring. Those wishing to spend the night will find both a campground and youth hostel in Svendborg. The city **tourist office** is in the town square (*torvet*), not far from the train station.

## Aerøskøbing to Marstal: 26 kilometers

Aerø is a small Baltic island, one of the more than 500 islands that make up Denmark. Although Aerø's main industry is agriculture, tourism is a primary source of revenue, and the island is a favorite with vacationing Danes and Germans. The ferry lands at Aerøskøbing, Aerø's oldest town. Its medieval streets are lined with wooden houses with geranium-filled window boxes, and its shops are hung with fascinating metal signs (look for golden pretzels if you're hungry for bakery goods). Add Aerø's ever-present cobblestones to complete a delightful (albeit bumpy) journey back in time.

Follow **camping signs** to the west side of the city to reach the luxurious Aerøskøbing campground. With a television room, cooking facilities, washers and dryers, spacious bathrooms, and a seaside setting, the site is a treat. You'll see lots of other cyclists here. Explore the island's gentle hills and discover its striking scenery, and you'll realize why Aerø is so popular for bicycling.

There are several hotels in Aerøskøbing and there's a youth hostel 1 km from the center of town. Ask at the **tourist office** near the church on Aerøskøbing's main square for more information on the city and the island. You may want to set up a base camp for a few days and explore Aerø without your baggage. We've written up our own meandering Aerøskøbing-to-Marstal ride, and you can follow it to Marstal and yet another ferry, if you wish.

Leave **Aerøskøbing** on the secondary road **west** toward **Borgnaes.** (Turn right off the main road through town a few blocks past the school to gain the secondary road.) Stay to the right along the sea, with Aerø's windmill-studded backbone rising to your left and lovely vistas of the Baltic to your right. Pass through **Borgnaes** and turn **left** at the **T.** Then climb a **long, steady hill** to the ridgeline of the island and the small town of **Bregninge.** Take a look at Bregninge's thirteenth-century church and admire the thatch-roofed houses on the streets around it.

From Bregninge, follow Aerø's **main road** southeast toward **Marstal.** You'll notice an increase in cars and bicycles on this route, and you can exchange greetings with entire families of bike riders, trailer-pulling couples, and lone tourers as you ride. Views of the sea, the rolling fields, and the quaint towns make the journey enjoyable.

At **Rise,** another old church invites exploration; then you'll negotiate a couple of moderate hills just before Marstal. Marstal lacks the charm of Aerøskøbing, but it has attractions of its own—a fine maritime museum, a handsome church, lots of shops, and a campground and youth hostel, if you decide to stay.

Follow signs through Marstal to the **ferry landing** and join the throngs of cyclists awaiting the hour-long trip to **Rudkøbing.** There are several crossings per day.

## Rudkøbing to Bagenkop (and Kiel): 30 kilometers

The final leg of Tour No. 7 and your ride in Denmark takes you south on the long, skinny island of Langeland from Rudkøbing to Bagenkop. From Bagenkop, you can take a ferry to Kiel, Germany, and continue your cycling in a new country. If time restraints and plane reservations are tugging you back to **Copenhagen,** you may want to pedal north from Rudkøbing instead. Follow **Road 305 north** for 29 km to reach Langeland's tip, and board a **ferry** in **Lohals** for **Korsør.** In Korsør, you can make direct **train** connections to

Copenhagen, throwing bike and baggage aboard for the ride to Denmark's sparkling capital.

If you're riding on for **Bagenkop** and the ferry to Kiel, leave the **ferry dock** and turn **right** to walk through Rudkøbing's busy pedestrian core. Follow signs for the **campground** on the south edge of town and swing **right** on the **unmarked road** just past the site. Come to a **T** and turn **right,** then keep to the **left** for **Henninge** and pedal past a large manor house.

At Henninge, turn **right** onto **Road 305** and cycle on to **Lindelse,** where a large church dominates the town. On the **southern edge** of Lindelse, swing **left** for **Hennetved** and quiet countryside riding. Follow the road through Hennetved, go past a large **windmill** and **manor house,** and continue on through a sharp **right** turn. At the next **intersection,** go **left** and follow the signs to **Tryggelev.**

Turn **left** onto **Road 305,** then shoot **right** for **Kinderballe** and more lovely, lonely riding. Come to a **T** a few kilometers past Kinderballe. Go **right** and cycle along the coast to **Bagenkop.** There's a snazzy campground with lots of extras just outside Bagenkop or a smaller, cheaper, more convenient site a stone's throw from the ferry landing. If you're planning an early-morning departure for Germany, as we were, pass on the putt-putt and go for the somewhat dumpy ferry-side spot.

Buy your tickets at the **ferry terminal** near the dock. The Bagenkop–Kiel ferry makes the $2^{1}/_{2}$-hour crossing two or three times per day.

# TOUR NO. 8

# TO BELGIUM, LUXEMBOURG, AND BACK

*Köln to Trier, Germany*

*Distance:* 362 kilometers (225 miles)
*Estimated time:* 5 riding days
*Best time to go:* June, July, or September
*Terrain:* Some rugged areas with lots of long hills
*Connecting tours:* Tours No. 3, 7, and 9

This tour provides a pleasant blend of three European countries—Germany, Belgium, and Luxembourg. You'll hear lots of German spoken throughout your ride, and you'll see a strong French influence in Belgium and Luxembourg. Please refer back to Tour No. 3 for background information on Belgium, and scan ahead to Tour No. 9 for the data you'll need on Germany. We'll concern ourselves with the tiny land of Luxembourg in this introductory section.

Luxembourg is tucked comfortably in between its much larger neighbors to the east and west, and you'll need to observe carefully to fully appreciate its individuality. Much of the population is bilingual. French is the official language, Luxembourgeois is the common tongue, and German runs a close third.

Your sensitivity to the little country's hard-won independence will be appreciated by the locals, but the cosmopolitan Luxembourgers are unnervingly adept at dealing with the sometimes inept tourists who continually overrun their land. We were reminded of this native skill while ordering dinner in a restaurant in Luxembourg City. Struggling to use what we thought was the preferred language, we carefully ordered, *"Zwei Bier, bitte,"* in faltering German. "Two beers? Here you go," was the young waitress's deflating reply. So much for blending in.

**CONNECTIONS.** You can reach Köln and the start of this tour by bicycle from Amsterdam (end of Tour No. 3), from Kiel (end of Tour No. 7), or from assorted locations in Western Europe. On our first visit to the city, we pedaled from the northerly city of Kiel, passing through the enchanting towns of Lüneburg and Celle, then we swung west through the hill-studded Sauerland (not nearly so enchanting). And on our second trip to Köln, seven years later, we arrived from the south, via the fascinating Rhine River bike route. Train travel with bicycles is efficient and relatively hassle free in Germany, so if you fly into Munich or Frankfurt, you shouldn't have too much difficulty getting to Köln.

**INFORMATION.** Write to the Luxembourg National Tourist Office, 801 Second Avenue, New York, New York 10017, for preparatory information on Luxembourg. *The Real Guide: Holland, Belgium, and Luxembourg* or the *Blue Guide Belgium and Luxembourg* are two excellent guidebook options for your trip. Once in Luxembourg, make use of the extensive network of tourist offices (almost every city has one) to pick up local maps and English-language literature.

**MAPS.** You can buy Michelin maps at 1:200,000 for your ride in Belgium and Luxembourg, or use either the 1:300,000 N.V. Falkplan/CIB *Belgie-Belgique, Luxemburg-Luxembourg* or Rand McNally's

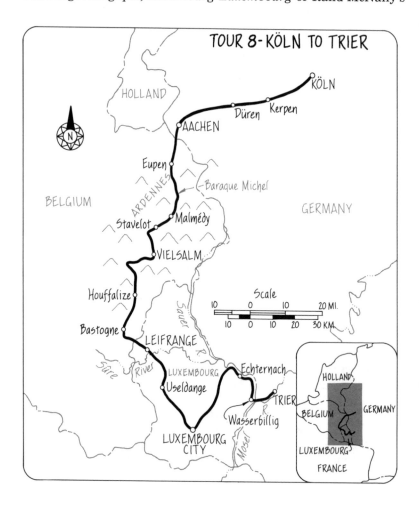

*Belgium, Luxembourg* map at 1:250,000 to get an overall look at the route from Aachen to the Luxembourg–German border. The latter map shows a multitude of campgrounds and youth hostels. Map options abound in Germany—from the expensive but excellent cyclists' maps to the 1:200,000 *Die Generalkarte,* also a great resource.

**ACCOMMODATIONS.** Luxembourg's hotel rooms, like Belgium's and Germany's, tend to be out of reach for the budget tourist. Make use of the country's 12 international youth hostels, or bring along a tent and choose among the many excellent campgrounds in the country. Please refer to the introductory material for Belgium and Germany to check on accommodation options in those countries.

**SUPPLIES.** Shopping hours in Luxembourg are similar to those followed by French shopkeepers, with all-day Sunday closures and Monday-morning shutdowns. You'll find widespread adherence to the two-hour lunch lockup, too. Belgian francs are accepted as currency in Luxembourg, although the country does have its own monetary system. Luxembourg's cuisine is a happy blend of French, Belgian, and German dishes, with a few regional specialties thrown in. Restaurants are expensive here, so do lots of supermarket shopping if you're on a budget.

## Köln to Aachen: 74 kilometers

Although Köln is a vast and modern German city, it's crisscrossed with bike paths and loaded with admirable architecture. You won't regret the hours you spend exploring here. Begin at Köln's *Dom,* one of the most fantastic Gothic cathedrals in Germany (if you arrive in the city by train, the central station is adjacent to the cathedral). Although virtually demolished during World War II, Köln's *Dom* has risen from the rubble to become the pride of the city once again. The museum next door will provide you with an inside look at how German technology is working to preserve this architectural treasure for future generations.

Stop in at Köln's **tourist office** (also near the cathedral) to obtain a city map and information on lodging options. Köln has youth hostels, pensions, and campgrounds to choose from. Be sure to ask for a pamphlet on Köln's churches while you're in the office, too.

From the west end of the **Deutzer Brücke** in Köln, continue west with signs for **Köln west.** An intermittent bike lane provides some insulation from the traffic, although it's a bit of a pain to follow. Look for the burnt-orange line painted on the pavement. At times, the "bike path" is no more than a crowded lane along the city sidewalks. Choose your poison....

Cross a **main ring road** and swing **left** at the next **major intersection** with signs for **Düren.** Go **right** not long afterward to gain

**Road 264** toward Düren. This route will take you all the way to Aachen, and you'll have bike paths (separate from traffic) or bike lanes (along the road) most of the way. The day's ride is primarily agricultural, flat, and unexciting.

"No Bike" signs along the main route (Road 264) will steer you off Road 264 on through the city centers of **Frechen** and **Kerpen,** then you'll rejoin **Road 264** toward **Düren.** Düren is a pleasant city, offering a potential resting spot for road-weary legs. Continue with signs

*A German cyclist is eager to talk of touring.*

for **Langerwehe,** a busy pottery town that marks the start of the rolling hills that lead to Aachen. Traffic picks up from Langerwehe, as a main road joins from Jülich to the north.

You'll endure seemingly unending city as you pedal on toward **Aachen** with **Road 264.** Traffic is thick and unpleasant, and scattered hills postpone your arrival at your goal. A final climb leads to your first view of Aachen, set in its mantle of hills. Descend toward the city from the ridgetop. Watch for signs for Aachen's municipal campground off to the right as you approach the city center. It's about 2 km from the cathedral and has a small camp store, good facilities, and lots of cyclists. The site fills up fast, so claim your spot before heading into the city for sightseeing. There's also a youth hostel in Aachen, if you're looking for an inexpensive bed.

Follow *Zentrum* signs to Aachen's cathedral, a wonderful conglomeration of architectural styles built around the nucleus of Charlemagne's ninth-century church. Visit the octagonal sanctuary with its tile-encrusted ceiling, stare at sturdy columns and a Gothic choir lit by rainbows of modern stained glass, and imagine the dreams of an emperor who once ruled most of Europe.

Aachen's *Rathaus* is a beautiful fourteenth-century building that looks out over the busy Market Square. Buy an ice cream cone in the square, watch the locals streaming into McDonald's, or invade the nearby **tourist office** for information on the city.

## Aachen to Vielsalm: 79 kilometers

Leave Aachen on **Road 264** southwest toward **Belgium.** Climb a **long, steady hill** outside of town (the road has a **bike path**) as you begin your assault on the foothills of the Ardennes. Pass the (probably unmanned) German **border station** and then turn **left** onto a secondary road for **Hergenrath.** Pedal through rolling green farmland on the route to Hergenrath and **Walhorn,** then join **Road N68** at **Kettenis.** Angle **right** on N68 for **Eupen,** and swing through Eupen's **center** to admire the town church and the cafe-lined streets.

Continue on N68 for **Malmédy.** You'll have a **13-km climb** as you pedal steadily upward toward **Baraque Michel,** at 675 meters one of the highest points in the Belgian Ardennes. The road attracts heavy tourist traffic, so hug the shoulder while you enjoy the views of lush hillsides and distant fields. From Baraque Michel, revel in a glorious **16-km descent** to Malmédy. A **bike lane** provides added breathing space.

Cruise through **Malmédy,** an attractive Belgian town, and pedal on for **Stavelot.** Climb a small hill, then descend into **Stavelot.** Leave N68 to cycle into the **city center.** You'll be jostled into wakefulness by the cobblestones of Stavelot's main street, and you can celebrate your first victory over the Ardennes with a cool beverage at a streetside cafe. If you need a room for the night, Stavelot is the last town of any size until Houffalize, 50 km farther on. Campgrounds are abundant in the area, so you can set your own schedule if you have a tent.

From Stavelot, return to **N68** and ride about 6 km before turning **left** (still with N68) for **Vielsalm** and **Luxembourg.** Cycle beside the **Salm River** to Vielsalm, a small town with a tidy campground (it's to the left of the road).

## Vielsalm to Leifrange: 67 kilometers

Pedal south on **N68** to **Salmchâteau.** From Salmchâteau, continue on **N68** for 4½ km and turn **right** onto **Road N878** for **Bovigny** and **Houffalize.** Then cycle 7 km to a junction with **Road N827** and continue on to **Houffalize,** an attractive town with many shops and lots of summer tourists. As you continue toward **Bastogne,** you'll begin to see roadside reminders of the battles that were fought in this part of Belgium during World War II.

Leave Houffalize on **Road N30** for **Bastogne,** passing an ancient tank on your way out of town. Climb a hefty hill and pedal through a challenging **17 km of dips and rolls** to reach Bastogne. Descend to the edge of the city and turn **left** for the **Mardasson War Memorial.** This striking modernistic monument and the slick on-site museum relate the story of the Battle of the Bulge. Your understanding of the region and its history will be greatly enhanced by the hours you spend here.

Bastogne itself is a touristy mix of traffic, hotels, and bars—a disappointing contrast to the simplicity and grace of the memorial. The city has a deluxe campground and a youth hostel, if you need a bed. Cycle **south** through Bastogne's **center** and swing **left** for **Lutremange** just before signs for Arlon lead onto the harrowing **Road N4** (don't take N4!). Pedal through **Lutremange** and continue through rolling terrain toward **Harlange.**

Climb a **steep hill** to reach a **small stone marker** announcing your entry into Luxembourg. Continue on to **Harlange,** with fine views of the fertile countryside, and pedal up another **large hill** before reaching a **junction** marked for **Luxembourg** (left 53 km) and Boulaide (right). Go **left** and descend a **long, steep hill** to a large reservoir formed by a dam on the Sûre River. Cycle along the reservoir's hilly **northern shore.** Cross a **small dam,** then climb a final hill to **Leifrange,** a pleasant village with a busy hillside campground.

## Leifrange to Luxembourg City: 65 kilometers

Continue along the main **waterside road** from Leifrange, climbing a **long hill** with vistas of the surrounding countryside. Turn **right** at the **T** for **Esch-sur-Sûre.** Reach the crest of the hill, then descend quickly to cross the reservoir on **another dam.** Go **right** beside the water for **Eschdorf,** then veer **left** to leave the reservoir on a **smaller road,** also signed for **Eschdorf.** Climb steeply, descend to an intersection, then **climb steeply** once more to reach the town.

In Eschdorf, turn **right** onto **Road N12** for **Luxembourg** and **Grosbous.** Pant through more rolling terrain as you stay **left** (still on N12) to reach Grosbous, then continue on through **Bettborn.** Angle **left** along the **Attert River** to **Useldange,** an interesting town with the remains of an old walled fortress. Turn **right** onto **Road N24** for **Noerdange,** then go **left** to rejoin **N12** toward **Luxembourg City.** Stay on N12 for the rest of the way as you negotiate an **exhausting series of hills** and ride through the heavy forests surrounding Luxembourg's capital.

Enjoy a **long descent** to the edge of the city. If you want to camp at the closest site to town, go **left** for **Echternach** onto a busy and exceedingly unpleasant **bypass road.** Follow signs for Echternach for about 3 km. You'll spot the hillside campground to the right off **Road N7.** It's crowded, noisy, and grim, but its closeness to the city and a crazy late-night card game with two Dutch bicyclists made it endurable for us.

Reach the **city center** by retracing your route along **N7** toward town and veering **left** to climb a **long hill** into the city core. Luxembourg City's fortified walls and stout turrets will mark your progress from the hillsides above. Arrive at a long pedestrian street (**Grand rue**) and go **left** past scores of glittering store windows. Walk to the **rue du Capucins,** then go **left** to reach the busy **Place d'Armes** and the city **tourist information** office. There's a **national tourist office** for Luxembourg at the main train station on the south end of town.

Luxembourg City offers a score of hotels and a youth hostel, if you need indoor accommodations. Get a walking map from the municipal tourist office, and let your urge to wander have free rein in this fascinating capital of fortifications, towers, and tourists. Then stop to quench your thirst at a cafe in the Place d'Armes. You can even order in English!

## Luxembourg City to Trier: 77 kilometers

Leave Luxembourg's center on the **Côte d'Eich,** and pedal **Road N7** toward **Echternach,** passing the campground and climbing a **long, gradual hill.** You'll have 15 km of main-road riding on **Road E29** with intermittent hills and steady traffic to **Junglinster.** Turn **left** for **Grundhof** just past Junglinster, leaving traffic and hills behind. Descend to ride beside a small river through a beautiful, cliff-enclosed valley, and share the scenery with dozens of energetic walkers wandering pathways through the trees.

Continue following signs to **Grundhof,** and turn **right** at the **T** just past Grundhof to cycle beside the **Sauer River** and begin your ride through countless acres of vineyards. A **bike path** will take you beside the main road for the 10 km to **Echternach.** Plan to stop for a picnic lunch and enjoy the sights and sounds in Echternach, a busy town of cobblestone streets and colorful buildings. Echternach's **tourist office** is near the Basilica.

If you'd like to spend a few more days in Luxembourg before crossing back into Germany, Echternach offers a youth hostel and two campgrounds. The small city makes an excellent stopping place, and you can forsake your bicycle for day hikes in the surrounding forests. The tourist office will supply information on trails, at your request.

Continue along the **west bank** of the Sauer River for the 19 km to **Wasserbillig.** Pedal the **bridge** spanning the Sauer to cross the **border** into Germany. The beautiful terraced vineyards of the Mosel River will soothe your senses as you ride along the **north shore of the Mosel** on **Road 49** for **Trier.** Look for a **bike path** along the river to take you into Trier.

You'll pass a handful of campgrounds on your way into Trier. Although the riverside campsites are often crowded, the pleasant setting is worth the close quarters. If you do camp, you'll find lots of cyclists to share stories with in this extremely popular cycling area. To continue into Trier on foot, follow the riverside bike path to **Römer Brücke** and climb the stairs to walk across the bridge into the city. If you're pedaling into town, return to **Road 49** and turn **right** for **Trier's center** to cycle across the bridge.

Once the capital of the Western Roman Empire, Trier is Germany's oldest city. It offers Roman monuments such as the Emperor's baths and the dark gateway called the Porta Nigra, and it boasts Germany's earliest Christian church, Trier Cathedral. The **tourist information** office is near the Porta Nigra. Take **Karl Marx Strasse** toward the *Hauptmarkt* from Römer Brücke. Ask at the office for information on the Mosel Valley, cycling, camping, wine tasting, or anything else you're interested in.

A youth hostel and several pensions provide inexpensive lodging options in the city, in addition to the assorted campgrounds on the perimeter. If you have time, put this tour together with Tour No. 9 and enjoy another five days of delightful German cycling on the Mosel and the Rhine. You may want to invest in a good bike-route map here, as the Mosel and Rhine are both traced by long-distance cycle paths.

# TOUR NO. 9

# RHINE, WINE, AND TOURISTS
### Trier to Bingen, Germany

*Distance:* 253 kilometers (157 miles)
*Estimated time:* 5 riding days
*Best time to go:* June, July, or September
*Terrain:* Mostly flat with some gently rolling hills
*Connecting tours:* Tours No. 8 and 10

On this superlative ride, you'll pedal from the ancient Roman city of Trier along the vine-lined Mosel River to Koblenz and the legendary Rhine. Then you'll cycle past castle and vineyards galore as you continue on to Bingen through the beautiful Valley of the Rhine. Throughout the tour, you'll be treated to an abundance of well-signed and well-maintained bike paths, the product of the Germans' affluence, industry, and infatuation with bicycle touring. And you'll share your way with bike tourers from throughout the world, drawn to this enchanting river ride by the castles, vineyards, and famous towns that enhance the route.

Germany, despite its image as a European industrial superpower, its large population, and its diesel-powered fleets of flying Mercedes, is a delight for the cycle tourist. Secondary roads are well maintained and direct (however, they usually come with a hefty share of traffic). The good news is that Germans have gone crazy for bike touring in the past few years, and the popularity of the sport has resulted in widespread construction of long-distance bike routes. Bike paths currently trace the Mosel River, the Rhine River, and the Danube River, to name a few. You'll have more cycling options than you know what to do with in this attraction-packed land. German drivers are usually courteous to cyclists, although the national fondness for raw speed can be downright terrifying at times. And, since 1945, Germany has swept away the rubble of World War II to reveal a treasure of matchless architecture, charming towns, and lovely countryside.

Many bike tourers are eager to explore Germany's new territory—the former East Germany. We were, too, when we returned to Germany with our bicycles in 1991. However, reports from those who had been there were mixed, often filled with tales of mile after mile of cobblestone roads, rough pavement, bleak urban areas, and devastated countryside. We decided to give the industrious Germans a few years to work their magic on the new territories to the east before we visit, choosing to explore a bit of Hungary and Czechoslovakia instead (see Tours No. 12 and 13).

Look beyond the seeming sternness of the Germans you meet and you'll find the people of this land possess a generous hospitality, a warm humor, and a stimulating interest in the world around them. Germans are some of Europe's greatest travelers, and you'll encounter German tourists in every European country you visit. To meet the Germans at home, though, it's best to do your cycling here at either end of the summer holidays. School and industrial vacations deplete the native population in August, and incoming flights replace the locals with scores of North American tourists.

**CONNECTIONS.** You can reach Trier and the start of this tour by cycling Tour No. 8 and pedaling here from Köln, or you can arrive by train instead. Train travel with bicycles is efficient and relatively hassle free in Germany, so if you fly into Munich or Frankfurt, you shouldn't have too much difficulty getting to Trier. If the train you choose has a baggage car (*Gepäckwagen*), your bicycle will accompany you. Otherwise, you'll need to send it a few days in advance.

**INFORMATION.** German tourist offices (*Verkehrsamt*) are good sources of free literature and city maps. They're usually located near the town church (*Kirche*), the city cathedral (*Dom*), or the main train station (*Hauptbahnhof*). Write in advance to the German National Tourist Office, 747 Third Avenue, 33rd Floor, New York, New York 10017, for preparatory reading. Be sure to let them know you're particularly interested in cycling. Don't neglect to take along a good guidebook to supplement the tourist-office offerings, too. Try Michelin's *Green Guide Germany; Let's Go: Germany, Austria, and Luxembourg;* or *The Real Guide: Germany.*

**MAPS.** Map options abound in Germany—from the expensive but excellent cyclists' maps to the 1:200,000 *Die Generalkarte,* also a great resource. If you have the Deutschmarks to spare, specialized bicycle maps would probably serve you best on this tour, as you'll be negotiating miles and miles of bike paths on the way to Bingen. The bookstores in Trier should be filled with all the map varieties you'll need.

**ACCOMMODATIONS.** Camping in Germany is convenient and comfortable. There are scores of sites, and most large cities have one or more municipal campgrounds. Locations vary—some are close to town and tourist/cyclist friendly, while others are planted near motorways and obviously designed with the automobile traveler in mind. Avoid lakeside and seaside spots whenever possible, however, as these are often expensive, crowded, and noisy. German campgrounds aren't cheap, and you'll sometimes have to pay camping "extras," such as city taxes, shower charges, or an occasional fee for your bicycle. Freelance camping is illegal in this country committed to environmental preservation.

Youth hostels are a source of national pride in Germany, and there are hundreds of them throughout the land. We were nearly always eagerly directed to the youth hostel when we stopped in a German town, cheered on by robust gentlemen and sparkling-eyed women who waggled their walking sticks vaguely upward and muttered, "*Jugendherberge*," with far-away looks in their eyes. However, though plentiful and inexpensive, German hostels are often overrun with noisy teens, and they're invariably at the top of steep hills—never a welcome feature at the end of a long cycling day.

Rooms in pensions and hotels vary in price. You'll probably need help at the tourist offices to locate unfilled or less-expensive ones. Watch for *Zimmer Frei* signs in private homes as another option (however, one-night boarders are sometimes turned away from these).

**SUPPLIES.** Shopping hours in Germany are generally from 8:00 A.M. to 6:30 P.M. on weekdays (with some afternoon shutdowns in small villages) and from 8:00 A.M. to 1:00 or 2:00 P.M. on Saturdays. Some stores close for an hour or two at noon. Don't count on any stores being open on Sundays. Grocery prices in Germany are comparable to those in the United States, perhaps a little higher with a weak dollar. Prepared food prices skyrocket, so stick with basics such as meat, cheese, and bread.

German food is wonderful fare for a famished biker. Picnic lunches of dark rye bread, cheese, and salami will fuel your legs until the 4:00 P.M. ritual of coffee and cake (*Kaffee und Kuchen*) makes you consider

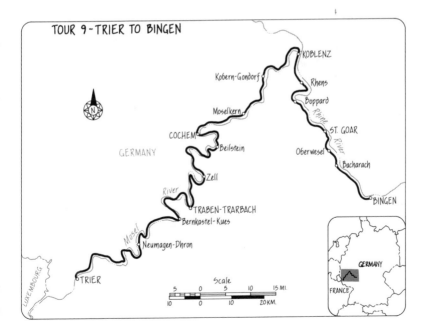

applying for German citizenship. And a dinner of *Kraut* and *Wurst* accompanied by strong German coffee or a bottle of local beer (*Bier*) or wine is a joy at the end of a tough riding day.

Bicycle shops abound in Germany, and with the recent soaring popularity of bike touring, excellent touring gear is readily available. Expect to pay considerably more for equipment and replacement parts than you do at home, however.

## Trier to Traben-Trarbach: 85 kilometers

From Trier, you'll have three lovely, leisurely days of cycling as you trace the winding route of the Mosel River on its journey to the Rhine. Set your own pace and stop often to explore the dozens of picturesque towns along the way. We've suggested cycling days and listed some of our favorite spots, but the region is so full of charm, you'll undoubtedly have your own list of favorites when you're through. Campgrounds are plentiful on both the Mosel and the Rhine, so you'll have lots of flexibility if you have a tent.

Please refer back to the final riding day of Tour No. 8 for information on Trier. There's a riverside **bike route** on the **Mosel's north bank** as you leave Trier for **Schweich**. Watch for **Mosel Radweg** signs as you ride. If you do happen to lose your way on occasion, don't hesitate to ask the locals for help. They're accustomed to dealing with confused cyclists. Your main reference point as you travel along the river will be **Road 53**. There are **bike lanes** on some sections of the road and the riding is not too bad, despite heavy tourist traffic. But be sure to make use of the off-road bike route whenever possible. It's infinitely more pleasant.

Because German bike-route construction has been proceeding in leaps and bounds in recent years, and because we haven't cycled this leg of the Mosel between Trier and Koblenz recently enough to write the bike route up in detail, we'll have to let you rely on bike-route signs and your map and simply tell you a bit about the terrain, scenery, and towns along the way. The Mosel route is well signed and there are lots of cyclists following it, so your route-finding difficulties should be few.

Cycling is pleasant once you escape the development of Trier and its suburbs. Enjoy solitary riding beside the Mosel after **Schweich,** and pass under two bridges before **Ensch.** Just past Ensch, veer **right** to cross the Mosel, then go **left** for **Köwerich** along a wonderful secondary road on the river's **southern shore.** Stay on the south side of the Mosel as you pass through Köwerich, round a long bend, and cycle on to **Neumagen-Dhron. Road 53** crosses the Mosel to join you in this pretty town of flowers and wine presses.

Continue through **Nieder-Emmel,** then follow signs for **Minheim**

*Vineyards, castles, and picturesque towns line the Mosel River beyond Trier.*

across the **bridge** spanning the Mosel. You'll lose the traffic again as you play hide-and-seek with Road 53, pedaling through **Kesten** and on to **Lieser.** Stroll through Lieser and pass beautiful stone houses with flower-dripping window boxes on your way to the town square. A cheery fountain, a trim church, and the friendly smiles of women on their morning shopping rounds will greet you in the town.

Continue along the river to **Bernkastel-Kues,** and change sides with **Road 53** once more. Take an hour to explore the fairy-tale town of Bernkastel-Kues. Tucked beneath a castle ruin, it's full of tantalizing streets, enchanting houses, and unique metal signs—all of them sure to drastically deplete your film supply. Save some shots for the overwhelming *Hauptplatz.* With its sparkling central fountain and ornate *Rathaus,* the *Hauptplatz's* charm transcends the milling crowds that prowl its shops for postcards.

There's a **tourist office** in Berkastel-Kues at Gestade 5, along the river, and there's a hilltop youth hostel if you want to spend the night. Leave town by cycling along the Mosel toward **Zeltingen,** and continue on to **Kindel.** Cross to the **north bank** and rejoin **Road 53.** Ride through **Kröv** and pedal on to **Traben-Trarbach.** The city **tourist office** is on the right, inside the *Rathaus* at 22 Bahnstrasse. Look for it just before you turn right to cross the **Mosel** on Road 53. There are several pensions and a youth hostel in this twin town that sits astride the Mosel. The surrounding vineyards and the ruined Grevenburg Castle increase its appeal as a stopping spot.

## Traben-Trarbach to Cochem: 49 kilometers

Cycle onward to **Enkirch** and take a few minutes to walk your bicycle through the center of town. Picturesque houses, mazelike streets, and air filled with the fragrance of freshly baked bread will make you want to linger. Continue along the Mosel's winding shoreline for the 11 km to **Zell,** another small town with streets that beg for exploration. Abandon the main road before Zell, staying on the **south bank** as the road recrosses to the north. There's a campground on the north bank of the river about 1 km from Zell's center.

From Zell, cycle on a quiet **secondary road** to **Neef.** Cross the **Mosel** to join the main road (now **Road 49**) just past Neef. Ride through **Ediger,** a lively tourist town with a busy waterfront, then pedal on to **Nehren** and forsake Road 49 as you cross the **Mosel** and ride toward **Beilstein.** You'll be delighted by this miniature town, squeezed in between the river and its hillside church. Burg Metternich, a picturesque castle ruin, dominates the valley from the ridge above.

Beilstein's **tourist office** is near the stairs to the Karmelitenkirche. Climb the city's steep, narrow streets for a peek inside the church. There's a fine view from the courtyard in front, and the interior offers handsome woodwork and decorative painting.

From Beilstein, continue on the Mosel's **south shore,** and lose much of the traffic as you pedal the final 8 km to **Cochem.** Recross the river when you reach the city. Cochem is one of the loveliest of the Mosel towns. The view of the city from the **bridge** into town is the stuff that travel posters are made of. A colorful riverside park, a central core of jumbled houses and church towers, a near-perfect castle perched on one hill, a ruined fortress on another—Cochem is a gem.

Walk your bicycle through the crowded streets to the chaotic town square, where a bright pink *Rathaus* is one of the more reserved buildings overlooking the festive scene. Cochem's **tourist office** can help you locate a room in a pension or hotel. There's a youth hostel across the bridge in Cond, and several campgrounds dot the shoreline beyond the city.

## Cochem to Koblenz: 50 kilometers

Take **Road 49** out of Cochem, with the Mosel on your right, and pedal to **Karden,** where Road 49 crosses the river to the south shore. Stay on the north bank, following **Road 416** to **Moselkern.** There's a large riverside campground in Moselkern where you can spend the night if you'd like to make the 5-km hike into the hills above town to visit **Burg Eltz.** It's a pleasant climb on a well-marked trail to reach the secluded castle. Burg Eltz is a rare example of an unspoiled Mosel fortress—because of its isolated position, it was never taken in a siege.

Continue along **Road 416** to **Kobern-Gondorf** and turn **into town** to parallel the main road and the train tracks. The ridgetop ruins and green vineyards above the city add to its charm. At the **end of town,** hop onto a **small road** between the tracks and the vines, and enjoy quiet riding until rejoining **Road 416** at **Winningen.** There's an excellent **bike lane** along Road 416 for much of the remaining 8 km to **Koblenz.**

If you're hoping to camp in Koblenz, the city's campground is signed from the bike route as it enters town. Instead of crossing the Mosel on the **Balduinbrücke** (the main Rhine route toward the south), follow camping signs to the sprawling campground at the confluence of the Rhine and Mosel rivers. You can erect your tent with a view of the city's Deutsches Eck and the Ehrenbreitstein Fortress. (The fortress holds Koblenz's youth hostel.)

To find the city **tourist office** across from the *Hauptbahnhof,* stay with the bike route as it crosses the Mosel on Balduinbrücke, then follow **Hohenfelder Strasse** and stay beside the train tracks to reach the train station. Pick up a map of Koblenz, information on the city, and some reading material for your journey up the Rhine at the information office.

## Koblenz to St. Goar: 38 kilometers

Your route south along the Rhine, like the route along the Mosel, is traced by an excellent bike-path system. You'll have lots of riding companions as you journey south—in fact, weekends can get downright crowded on the riverside pathways. One disadvantage of the Rhine bike route is that it skips some of the region's attractions (i.e., towns and castles) in favor of quiet shoreline cycling. Stay familiar with your map and your tourist literature. You may want to abandon the route to add in some sightseeing on occasion.

From Koblenz's **Balduinbrücke,** pedal to the **west bank** of the

Rhine and follow the **bike path south** along the riverside parkway. Long-distance **bike-route signs** call out **Rhens** along this portion of the ride. (Watch out for one errant bike path that leads to the left across a small harbor/inlet.) You'll leave the parkway and emerge onto **Hohenzollernstrasse.** Go **left** here and gain **Jahnstrasse** (signed for *Stadion*). Cycle Jahnstrasse to a **sign** for the **bike route** that leads onto an unpaved path through the trees. From here, you'll gain a **bike path** between the train tracks and the Rhine and continue south.

Watch for the **Lahneck Tower** on the opposite shore of the Rhine as you draw away from Koblenz. The disadvantage of the bike route here is that it bypasses Stolzenfels Castle and Rhens with its lovely town core. The advantage is that it also bypasses the terrifying traffic on Road 9. Choose for yourself which you prefer. Stay with **bike signs** as you pedal onward on small roads, then a (sometimes bumpy but usually paved) waterfront route.

Look for the grandiose **Marksburg Castle** on the ridgetop across the Rhine as you pedal past **Rhens** (a detour from the bike route) and continue with your riverside route signed for **Boppard.** Marksburg is unique among Rhine castles because it was never taken in a siege— quite an accomplishment in this war-torn region. Stay on the **bike path** through **Spay,** then hop onto a **bike lane** beside the main road until you arrive in **Boppard.**

You can swing down onto the colorful **riverfront promenade** as you pass through Boppard. The promenade is heavily signed with **"No Bike"** signs (a round sign with a red border around a bicycle), so you'll need to walk this section. Push your bicycle along Boppard's crowded, colorful Rhine Promenade and absorb the atmosphere of this perky riverside town. Hundreds of strolling tourists will join the parade, as Boppard is a major stopping point for Rhine tour boats.

Bike signs for **St. Goar** take over after Boppard. Return to **Road 9** as you lose the bike lane for a while. Enter one of the most scenic stretches of the Rhine Valley south of Boppard. The **Hostile Brothers Castles,** the **Mouse Castle** (Burg Maus), and **St. Goarhausen** beneath its castle called the Cat (Burg Katz) will delight you from the opposite shore. Stay on Road 9 until the town of **St. Goar,** where the square, flag-bedecked ruin of Burg Rheinfels is rooted in the ridgetop.

If you're camping, you'll have a couple of options near St. Goar. You can turn right at the campground turnoff just before town, and climb gently for about 1 km to reach a secluded, streamside site. From the campground here, you can take off on a small trail up the hill to make the 20-minute assault on Burg Rheinfels. Pay the reasonable entry fee and explore the castle's ruined walls and turrets, visit the small castle museum, and enjoy a fantastic view of the castle-rich Rhine Valley.

There's also a riverside campground just south of St. Goar, but its prime location contributes to often crowded conditions. If you're looking for a bed, St. Goar offers a youth hostel and a few hotels to choose from. The town itself is a pleasant spot for an evening stroll. Join the tourists who prowl the streets, peering in restaurant windows and studiously spinning the scores of postcard racks.

## St. Goar to Bingen: 31 kilometers

There's a **bike lane** along the main road (on the river side) as you pass through St. Goar. It's rideable through here, but the lane narrows as you pass the legendary **Loreley** rock. You may find it easier to simply abandon the bike lane and ride with traffic for a while. Turn off the main road to cycle through **Oberwesel,** a midsize town with two large churches, 18 watchtowers, and a castle. There's a youth hostel in town as well. Stop to explore the Church of Our Lady on the south end of Oberwesel. A lovely painted ceiling and several handsome stone carvings make the stop worthwhile.

Pedal on with **bike signs** for **Bingen** as you regain a **wide, lined bike route** on the river side of the road. Pleasant cycling follows. Look for the town of Kaub on the opposite shore, with the ruin of **Gutenfels** Castle guarding the hill above it. A little farther on, **Pfalz** Castle sits squarely in the center of the river, its once-mighty turreted walls now claiming tribute only from the tour boats that pause to drop off visitors.

Turn off the bike route at **Bacharach** and pedal through the town, stopping to admire the half-timbered houses on the main square. Climb a rough path to Burg Stahleck (home of a youth hostel), visit the city church, or stop to marvel at the Gothic Chapel of St. Werner. Bacharach has a great riverside campground, if you decide to linger. The city **tourist office** is in the *Rathaus,* and the helpful staff will load your packs with English-language literature on the town and its surroundings.

Pedal on toward **Bingen** with the **bike route along Road 9.** You'll be facing traffic in this section, so it's not ideal. However, there's a good bikeway right along the Rhine shore from **Niederheimbach** onward. You'll need to watch for a signed **bike turn** as you're riding south through Niederheimbach, then dive under the **train tracks** to gain the **paved route.** The absence of traffic and fine views of the opposite bank make the cycling pleasant; however, frequent trains and noisy boats make it something less than serene.

Pass beneath three castles as you pedal on. **Sooneck, Reichenstein,** and **Rheinstein** are all open to tours, but a visit to any of the three will mean a departure from the bikeway and a hefty climb. The **Mouse Tower** (Mäuseturm) on a small island in the Rhine marks your arrival in Bingen, and you'll see the Ehrenfels ruin on the opposite shore, surrounded by the vineyard-covered hillsides stretching down to Rüdesheim.

Enter **Bingen,** a very long and very busy city. The bike route kind of fizzles here, although there are some bike lanes along the road. Bingen's campground is on the far end of the city, well signed from the road through town. If you'd like to visit Rüdesheim, the popular wine town just across the Rhine, you can take one of the frequent ferries crossing the river from Bingen. Rüdesheim has a campground, a youth hostel, and several hotels.

If you'll be cycling from Bingen to Heidelberg to continue with Tour No. 10 and you'd like a break from river riding for a time, we suggest you pedal **south** through **Wörrstadt, Westhofen, Worms, Freinsheim,** and **Speyer,** then swing northeast for **Heidelberg.** The Rhine bike route continues on toward **Mainz** from Bingen. If you'd like to see even more of this mighty river, you could follow the Rhine all the way to where the Neckar joins it (in Mannheim), then swing up the Neckar toward Heidelberg from there. Or you can simply hop a train in Bingen and ride the rails to Heidelberg. If Bingen marks the end of your European cycling trip, Frankfurt's busy international airport is a short train trip east.

*A tidy German campground rolls out the "welcome wagon."*

# ROMANTIC ROAMING

*Heidelberg to Munich, Germany*

*Distance:* 449 kilometers (279 miles)
*Estimated time:* 7 riding days
*Best time to go:* June, July, or September
*Terrain:* Lots of easy river riding sprinkled with gentle hills
*Connecting tours:* Tours No. 9, 11, and 13

If you're looking for an intensive, two-week introduction to Germany, with gentle terrain, lovely scenery, and enchanting cities, this tour is hard to beat. You'll see three of Germany's best-loved cities on this tour—Heidelberg, Rothenburg ob der Tauber, and Munich. Sure, you'll also see lots of fellow tourists along the way, but you'll share their delight in the sights, the sounds, and the tastes of the Neckar Valley, the Romantic Road (Romantische Strasse), and beautiful Bavaria.

Combine this ride with the ones described in Tours No. 9 or 13 and you'll get a better look at Germany than most short-term travelers ever dream of. Please read the introductory material for Tour No. 9 to prepare for your ride in Germany.

**CONNECTIONS.** Heidelberg doesn't have an airport, but it's easily accessible by train from Frankfurt, Munich, and other cities with international air connections. Refer to the final paragraph of Tour No. 9 for information on cycling to Heidelberg from Bingen. If you'd like to tag this tour onto our ride from Prague to Frankfurt (Tour No. 13), you can either turn south along the Tauber River from Wertheim or ride the rails from Frankfurt, thus avoiding an urban/industrial area that can be a traffic nightmare.

**MAPS.** Please refer to maps information provided in the introduction to Tour No. 9.

**ACCOMMODATIONS.** Check the "Accommodations" section in the introduction to Tour No. 9.

**SUPPLIES.** Look for details on shopping hours, food, and bike supplies in the introduction to Tour No. 9.

## Heidelberg to Bad Wimpfen: 75 kilometers

Heidelberg, on the banks of the Neckar River, is a city for the lover of learning and history. Huddled beneath a mighty hilltop fortress,

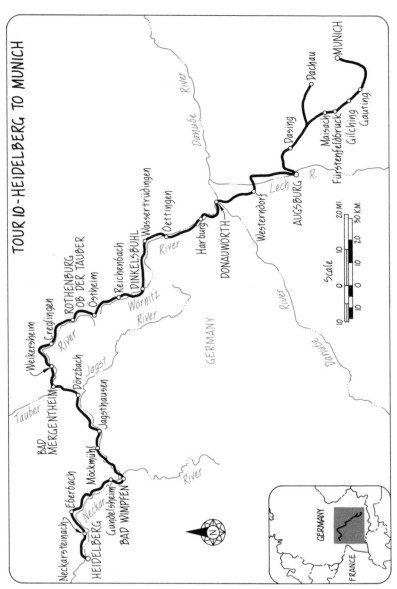

TOUR 10—HEIDELBERG TO MUNICH

honored with the oldest university in Germany, Heidelberg has both
an exquisite setting and an irresistible charm. As you explore the
city's streets and museums or climb to the ramparts of its magnificent
castle, your admiration will continue to grow. Try to block out the
chatter of the tourist crowds you'll rub shoulders with, and don't lose
heart over the torrents of English and Japanese you'll hear—Heidelberg is special—and the word is out.

As a tourist, you'll be well looked after in Heidelberg. Stock up on English-language literature and get a city map at the **tourist office** next to the train station. Be sure to ask about cycle routes in the Neckar Valley while you're at the office, too. There are dozens of hotels near the station, and you can get a list of addresses and prices from the tourist-office staff. Heidelberg has a youth hostel and a couple of campgrounds (upriver from the city, on both sides of the Neckar), for those in search of budget lodgings.

Plan to spend a day or two exploring Heidelberg. Climb to the castle and enjoy the view of red tile roofs around the Gothic Church of the Holy Spirit. Then stroll along the Philosopher's Way (Philosophenweg) on the Neckar's opposite shore to get a postcard look at the river city beneath its fortress. If the crowds begin to get you down, look forward to the riding days ahead, for Heidelberg is not an end but a beginning—a gateway to the Neckar Valley and the Romantic Road.

Leave Heidelberg's **center** by crossing one of the **Neckar bridges** to gain the river's **north shore.** Cycle **east** on the main road, paralleling the river toward **Neckarsteinach.** You'll have flat riding and fairly heavy traffic for most of the ride to **Bad Wimpfen** as you follow the river's winding course. Keep a sharp eye out for bike-path opportunities. Although bike lanes were scattered and inadequate when we cycled this river, it's only a matter of time before the cycle-happy Germans construct a long-distance cycle route through this scenic valley.

Pass a riverside campground about 7 km from Heidelberg and continue on to where **Road 37** crosses the Neckar to add more cars to the north-shore route. Watch for a **bike-path sign** for **Neckarsteinach,** and gain a **paved riverside lane** that provides a pleasant break from traffic. Rejoin the **main road** just before **Neckarsteinach,** a small river town that boast four castles and an attractive city center. There's a good **bike lane** along **Road 37** for most of the ride to **Hirschhorn.**

Swing **under Road 37** just before **Hirschhorn.** The main road crosses the river and shoots into a tunnel here, lopping off one of the Neckar's many loops, but you'll take the **secondary route** and cycle through **Hirschhorn,** a midsize town with a tourist office and the obligatory castle. Follow a well-signed **bike route** for **Eberbach** from Hirschhorn, crossing a **bridge** above the Neckar and turning **left** along the **south shore.** Ride on a small road to the end of town, then gain a **walking/biking path** toward Eberbach.

You may have a bit of rough going if the path still has the gravel surface we encountered, but the solitude and scenery are worth the rattles. If you'd prefer faster, smoother cycling on **Road 37,** you can **recross the river** when the shortcut road pops out of its tunnel. There's a wide **bike lane** along Road 37 for most of the remaining kilometers to Eberbach.

From Eberbach, follow **Road 37** through **Lindach, Neckar-**

**gerach,** and **Binau,** passing Zwingenberg Castle along the way. Go **right** to cross the Neckar into **Obrigheim,** then pedal along the **secondary road** toward **Hassmersheim** and **Bad Wimpfen.** On the opposite shore, its tall round tower standing proudly atop a vine-covered hillside, is **Hornberg Castle,** one of the oldest and most striking of the Neckar fortresses.

Ride through Hassmersheim, staying with the signs for **Bad Wimpfen,** and continue on to **Neckarmühlbach.** You can make the short sidetrip to tour the medieval museum in **Guttenberg** if you have the time. The keep offers a fine view of the Neckar Valley. To reach **Gundelsheim** (across the Neckar on Road 27) and a pleasant riverside campground, continue on from Neckarmühlbach and turn **left** to **cross the river** and gain **Road 27.** Go left again to find the well-equipped campground.

Gundelsheim is worth a visit, and it's just a short walk from the campground to the city center. With its old walls and towers, its renovated castle (now an old folks' home), its humble church, and its half-timbered houses hung with flower boxes, this small city is one of the hidden delights of the Neckar Valley.

You may want to cycle on to **Bad Wimpfen** if you're hunting for a room. The city offers a youth hostel and a handful of pensions. Recross the Neckar on the **Gundelsheim bridge** and ride the 7 km along the river's **left bank** to reach the ridgetop town. The brief uphill push

*Heidelberg, awash in charm and tour groups, stands beside the Neckar River.*

won't be fun if you're arriving at the end of a long cycling day. But Bad Wimpfen will charm you out of your weariness with its colorful houses, enchanting streets, and ruined palace.

Be sure to stop at the **tourist office** in the *Rathaus* (across from Stadtkirche) to get a map and an English walking tour of the city. The talkative gentleman behind the desk loaded us down with more literature than we could carry.

# Bad Wimpfen to Bad Mergentheim: 75 kilometers

We camped at Gundelsheim, made a day trip into Bad Wimpfen, then rode on toward our rendezvous with Rothenburg by heading south along **Road 27** from Gundelsheim. At **Offenau,** turn **left** for **Duttenburg.** Ride through Duttenburg and go **right** at the **T** just past town. Cross the **Jagst River** and climb a small hill past a tumbledown **castle.** Veer **left** for **Jagsthausen** at the next intersection.

If you're riding from Bad Wimpfen, you can reach the same spot in the following way. Leave the **city center** by descending to the banks of the **Neckar.** Cross the river and gain **Road 27** for **Bad Friedrichshall** and **Heilbronn,** cross the **Jagst River** and the train tracks, then go **left** onto a **secondary road** toward **Möckmühl** and **Jagsthausen.**

You'll be riding in the quiet Jagst Valley now, enjoying peaceful roads and moderate hills as you follow a snakelike path northeast toward Bad Mergentheim and your introduction to the Romantic Road. Pedal through **Untergriesheim** and **Herbolzheim.** Play hopscotch with the river and train tracks as you follow signs for **Jagsthausen.**

Make the short sidetrip to cycle through the center of **Neudenau** (turn **left** after crossing the **bridge** below town). The attractive old houses on the *Marktplatz* and the friendly smiles of the men who linger in the square make the detour worthwhile. Return to the **main road** and continue past **Siglingen** and on to the handsome belfry and tower at **Möckmühl.**

In Möckmühl, turn **right** for **Jagsthausen** and follow the river's contortions to **Götzenburg Castle,** just outside Jagsthausen. If you feel like a splurge, spend the night at this restored castle/hotel or catch an open-air play in its courtyard on a summer night. Ride on along the river to **Schöntal** (6 km from Jagsthausen). An immense Cistercian abbey engulfs the town. Be sure to visit the abbey church for a closeup look at baroque gone wild. If the alabaster carvings, glittering gilts, and painted ceilings don't give you indigestion, pause for a picnic lunch on the abbey grounds.

From Schöntal, ride another 16 km to **Dörzbach,** then go **left** on **Road 19** and bid the Jagst Valley *auf Wiedersehen*. Make the **long,**

**gradual climb** to the plateau above. Traffic is heavier on Road 19, so ride carefully. You'll have about 8 km of uphill pedaling before the **6-km descent** into **Bad Mergentheim.** There's a marked campground to the right, on the road to Wachbach, if you want to camp before the city.

Sprawling on the banks of the Tauber River, Bad Mergentheim marks your arrival on the Romantic Road. The city has a castle dating back to 1565, a beautiful surrounding park, and several pensions and hotels. Check at the **tourist office** in the *Marktplatz* for help with lodgings, and inquire about the long-distance bike route (*Taubertal Radweg*) that traces the Tauber River.

## Bad Mergentheim to Rothenburg ob der Tauber: 50 kilometers

The main road between Bad Mergentheim and Rothenburg follows the vineyard-dotted course of the **Tauber River.** The scenery is pleasant and the small towns are a treat, but the heavy traffic on the narrow **Romantische Strasse** is enough to make the romantic spirit of any cyclist run for cover.

Luckily, the bike route known as the *Taubertal Radweg* (Tauber Valley bikeway) or the *Liebliches Taubertal* runs beside the Tauber River from Wertheim in the north all the way to Rothenburg. Unless you're in a great hurry to cover ground, this is the route you'll want to follow from Bad Mergentheim. The path is well marked by **signs with bike logos,** and the local populace is accustomed to helping disoriented cyclists find their way. Tourist offices in the area stock maps of the route. Be sure to have one in your grasp as you set out.

Look for the **bike-route signs** as you leave **Bad Mergentheim** along **Road B19,** then angle **right** at **Igersheim** (hostel nearby) to follow the **Tauber River** south. **Weikersheim** is a colorful town built around a sixteenth-century castle. If you're fortunate enough to arrive during a weekend festival, you can spend a delightful afternoon listening to an "oompah" band and wrestling with enormous pretzels while ruddy-cheeked Germans sing and dance around you.

Continue along the **left bank** of the Tauber to **Bieberehren,** then join the **main road** for a short distance. The gently rolling terrain is sprinkled with orchards, vineyards, and thin forests. **Creglingen** is an attractive Tauber town. You can make a short sidetrip (about 3¹/₂ km) from Creglingen to visit the **Chapel of Our Lord** (Herrgottskirche). An amazing altarpiece by the greatest of German woodcarvers, Tilman Riemenschneider, is housed in the chapel.

Pedal beside the **river,** then cross it to join the **main road** once again at **Tauberzell** before pedaling the final 9 km to **Rothenburg.** You'll see fuzzy splotches of white grazing on the verdant hillsides as you cycle through a deep, rolling valley toward the city. The **campground** at **Detwang,** about 2 km from Rothenburg's center, makes a great base for exploring the famous town. It's a pleasant walk into Rothenburg from the large, riverside site, and you'll share your tent space with travelers from dozens of countries. The campground has a well-stocked store and good facilities, and it's a two-minute walk to Detwang's church, where another carved altarpiece by Riemenschneider awaits.

If you're looking for a room, continue into Rothenburg, climbing a hill to reach the matchless city on a ridge above the Tauber. Head for the **tourist office** near the *Rathaus* to gather maps and pamphlets for your sightseeing in the town. There are two hostels and several pensions in Rothenburg. Like Heidelberg, Rothenburg must contend with the side effects of fame. Thousands of tourists fill its streets on every summer day. But who can blame them? Rothenburg is one of a kind.

Invest an entire day in wandering the city streets, marveling at the carved altarpiece in St. James's Church (a Riemenschneider, of course) or making the harrowing climb to the top of the *Rathaus* tower. Wait in the *Marktplatz* for the clock to strike 12:00, and watch the figures in the Ratstrinkstube clock perform their famous ritual. Shop at one of the stores outside the old town, and walk to the Burggarten beside the city walls to enjoy a picnic lunch while you watch the timeless Tauber wind through the valley below.

# Rothenburg ob der Tauber to Dinkelsbühl: 45 kilometers

From the **campground,** follow the small road through **Detwang** along the river's edge. Avoid the climb to Rothenburg by turning **right** just outside Detwang to **cross the Tauber,** then take the **first left** beside the water. You'll have a terrific view of the city's famous skyline as you pass Topplerschlösschen, an old tower/house. Continue on to cross the river on **Doppelbrücke,** an ancient two-tiered bridge. Turn **right** after the bridge, then **recross the Tauber** a short distance later. Veer **left** onto a **small road** beside the river. You may have a short stretch of unpaved cycling along the way.

Reach an **intersection** with **Road 25** for **Dinkelsbühl.** If you're coming from Rothenburg's center, you'll join the route here. **Cross Road 25** and gain the road toward **Gebsattel.** Cycle through Gebsattel and **Bockenfeld,** passing through quiet farmland on silent roads. Go **left** at the **T** in **Diebach,** then take the **next right** (it was unmarked when we were there). You'll see signs for **Östheim** as you cycle out of town.

Veer **left** onto **Road 25** in Östheim and endure about 5 km of

*The streets of Rothenburg ob der Tauber delight from every angle.*

unpleasant riding as you climb the day's only hill on a narrow, winding stretch of main road. Cross the **freeway** and turn **right** for **Wörnitz,** forsaking Road 25 once more. In **Wörnitz,** go **right** for **Schnelldorf,** then veer **left** one block later for **Ulrichshausen.** Reach a **T** and go **right** for **Ulrichshausen,** then swing **left** for **Waldhausen.**

Cycle through Waldhausen and ride on to **Zischendorf.** Go **right** for **Zumhaus,** then turn **left** at the **T** for **Ungetsheim.** Cross **under** the **A6 freeway** and pedal to **Reichenbach. Cross Road 14,** continuing straight for **Mosbach.** From Mosbach, follow signs for **Schopfloch** and ride past the midsize town (on the left across the Wörnitz River). Go straight at the **junction** to stay on a **small road** along the west bank of the Wörnitz for the final 6 km into **Dinkelsbühl.**

Enter at the north gate (Rothenburger Tor) of the small walled city, and immerse yourself in tantalizing streets filled with half-timbered houses, amusing metal signs, and kaleidoscopic colors. Dinkelsbühl is a scaled-down Rothenburg—with a few less tourists and a less impressive silhouette, but a healthy dose of small-town charm. Go straight on **Martin Luther Strasse** from the Rothenburger Tor to reach the **tourist office** (it's on the right, across from the church). There's a youth hostel in Dinkelsbühl, and there are several pensions and hotels.

To reach the campground on the edge of town, leave Dinkelsbühl via the Wörnitz Tor (go left off Martin Luther Strasse just past the church), cross the river and turn left on Road 25 toward Feuchtwangen. Go right just past the train tracks and follow signs to the campground (about 3 km from the city center). Dinkelsbühl's campground is one of the cleanest, most modern sites you'll find in Germany, with great hot showers, heated bathrooms, and hot water for dishwashing. Check in at the office before you put up your tent, as some areas are reserved for trailers. From the campground's upper slopes, there's a fine view of the floodlit city walls at night.

## Dinkelsbühl to Donauwörth: 70 kilometers

Leave Dinkelsbühl on **Road 25** toward **Nördlingen.** You can pedal the Romantic Road a little longer by following Road 25 south for the 31 km to Nördlingen, another walled city of ancient gateways and stout towers. We opted for a quiet ride toward Donauwörth instead, enjoying the Bavarian countryside along the way.

Swing **left** off **Road 25** just outside Dinkelsbühl, following signs for **Wassertrüdingen.** Pass through gentle hills and descend to **Wittelshofen.** Continue on through farmland and small villages toward **Wassertrüdingen,** then follow signs for **Oettingen.** With its riverside setting, old buildings, and traces of a city wall, Oettingen is a town worth diving into. Swing **right** onto **Road 466** just before town, and go **left** for **Munningen** as you pedal away.

Cycle the quiet secondary road through Munningen, **We-Fessenheim,** and on to Ha-Heroldingen. Veer **left** on the far edge of **Ha-Heroldingen,** and climb a hill past **Ronheim.** You'll have a fine view of Harburg's castle from here. Follow the road along the **Wörnitz River** into **Harburg,** and take the old **bridge** into the heart of town.

Turn **left** to cycle through the **city center,** then recross the Wörnitz at the **second bridge.**

Go **right** and pedal toward **Brünsee.** Climb a slight hill to ride through Brünsee, and continue along the Wörnitz Valley to **Ha-Ebermergen, crossing Road 25** along the way. Turn **left** in **Ha-Ebermergen,** then go **left** again for **Wörmitzstein.** Turn **right** at the **T** in Wörmitzstein, cross the **train tracks,** and go **left** for **Riedlingen** and **Donauwörth.**

Climb a **steep hill,** then descend into **Riedlingen,** with Donauwörth spreading up the hillside beyond. Pedal through town, keeping the train tracks on your right. Then cross **under the tracks** and join **Road 16** to ride into Donauwörth's center. You'll get your first look at the Danube (Donau) River in this midsize city overlooked by its Holy Cross Church.

Be sure to make the short trek up the hillside to this wonderful baroque building. Its interior is a visual extravaganza of colorful ceiling murals, elaborate stuccoes, and ornate gilt altars. Don't miss the richly attired skeletons resting peacefully in their glass coffins around the sanctuary.

Donauwörth has a youth hostel and pensions if you're looking for a less permanent spot to rest your bones. Check at the city **tourist office** in the *Rathaus*. If you're not bound and determined to visit Augsburg and Munich this time around, you might consider hopping on the **Danube bike route** here. You can trace the long-distance cycle route and the river all the way to Passau and the Austrian border, then hook up with our Tours No. 11 and 12 for a riverside ride to Vienna and Budapest.

## Donauwörth to Augsburg: 48 kilometers

Leave Donauwörth on **Road 16** toward **Neuburg,** crossing the **Danube River** and going **right** for **Wertingen** and **Mertingen** soon after. Ride through Mertingen and continue on to **Nordendorf.** Then turn **right** for **Blankenburg.** When the road **branches,** take the **small road** to the **left** to ride along a pretty valley toward **Westerndorf.** Angle **left** to enter Westerndorf, and cross **under Road 2.** Cycle on to **Ostendorf.**

Go **right** for **Thierhaupten,** then swing **left** beyond **Waltershofen** at a **second sign** for Thierhaupten. Cross the **Lech River** and take a **small road** to the **right** when the main road angles left. Cycle into **Thierhaupten** and go **right,** riding through **Bach** and **Sand** on the way to **Mühlhausen.**

As you continue south throughout the day, pedaling deeper into the heart of Bavaria, you'll notice the gradually changing architecture—bulb-towered churches and finely crafted homes—and you'll be greeted with the traditional Bavarian *"Grüss Gott"* as you pass women in bright embroidered blouses and men in supple *Lederhosen.*

In **Mühlhausen,** veer **right** for **Augsburg.** You'll pass a selection of campgrounds in quick succession. We stayed at the second one (on the right), and we were delighted by its grassy setting and well-kept facilities. Use this spot as your base and make the 8-km ride into Augsburg without your bags.

To pedal into Augsburg, ride along the busy main road from the **second campground** and turn **right** at the **bike-path sign** a short distance later. Cycle along a **small road** that veers southwest and leads onto a **second road** running west toward **Gersthofen.** Go **right** on this road, then turn **left** onto **Neuburger Strasse.** Cross **over the A8 freeway,** pedal through busy suburbs, and cross the **Lech River.**

Enter Augsburg's core at the **Jakobertor Gate.** Augsburg's **tourist office** is on the opposite side of town at Bahnhofstrasse 7, near the main train station. Go straight on **Jakoberstrasse** from the gate, and continue onto **Pilgerhausstrasse** past the *Rathaus* (on the left) and the *Dom* (on the right) to **Schaezlerstrasse,** where you'll turn **left.**

There are several pensions and a youth hostel in Augsburg, and this 2,000-year-old city (founded by Caesar Augustus in 15 B.C.) offers much for the sightseer. The beautiful medieval *Rathaus,* the *Dom,* and the city's many churches will take you hours to explore. Wander the alleyways of the Fuggerei or stroll Maximilianstrasse as you make your way from place to place.

## Augsburg to Munich: 86 kilometers

You may want to consider loading your bike and baggage aboard a train in Augsburg to make the short rail trip into Germany's mighty Bavarian city, Munich. If you don't like dealing with big-city traffic, a train ride could save you some stomach-churning miles. But Munich is crisscrossed with excellent bike paths, and you can hook onto the network from many points outside the city, so riding in really shouldn't be too harrowing.

We were fortunate enough to have a friend who lives in a small community south of Munich, so we didn't have to brave the city center with our bicycles. We'll describe our end-around route, with some suggestions for direct riding routes into the city core. Whatever your destination, plan on a tough day of cycling as you set out from Augsburg, with traffic and hills aplenty.

If you're departing **Augsburg** from the campground outside town, turn right on the main road as you leave the campground entrance. Take the left for Dickelsmoore at the first street light past the airport. Parallel the A8 freeway, riding through Derching and angling right for Haberskirchen and Dasing. Go by a freeway underpass, climb a short, steep hill, and go right to cross over the freeway and enter **Haberskirchen.**

If you're leaving from Augsburg's center, retrace your route out of the city via the Jakobertor Gate and turn right off Neuburger Strasse for Friedberg after crossing the Lech River. Veer left for Stätzling soon after, and continue on to **Haberskirchen** from there.

Follow signs for **Dasing** from Haberskirchen. In Dasing, go **left** onto **Road 300,** cross the **train tracks,** and then turn **right** for **Harthausen.** Play "connect the dots" from one Bavarian village to another, staying on small roads through rolling forest and farmland. Watch for the onion-bulbed churches, the beautifully carved balconies, and the painted walls of homes and churches as you ride.

If you want to approach Munich **from the north** rather than the south, turn **left** just outside of **Dasing.** Ride through **St. Franziskus, Burgadelzhausen,** and **Ebertshausen,** pedaling southeast. Veer east at **Einsbach** to pedal the final 12 km to **Dachau.** You can visit the concentration camp memorial and museum at Dachau, then work your way south to the outskirts of Munich. There are excellent **bike paths** around the **Olympic Park** in the northwest quarter of Munich, and they'll lead you into the city center on preferred bike routes. The total distance for this ride into Munich is about 75 km.

To follow the **southerly approach** to Munich, ride for **Harthausen** from Dasing. Turn **right** for **Rinnenthal** in Harthausen, and pedal on to **Eurasburg, Hergertswiesen, Weyhern, Aufkirchen,** and **Maisach.** Reach a T just before **Maisach** and turn **right** for **Fürstenfeldbruck.** In Fürstenfeldbruck, a busy Bavarian town on the Amper River, go **left** onto **Road 2** for **Munich** (München). Cross the **Amper River** and continue out of the city on **Road 2,** climbing a **long hill.**

Veer **right** for **Starnberg** 5 km past Fürstenfeldbruck, and follow signs for Starnberg through **Alling** and **Gilching.** Pass the **A96 freeway** and go **left** 4 km later for **Gauting.** From Gauting, follow signs for **Buchendorf** and continue on to a **T,** then go **left** to parallel the **A95 freeway.** Cross **under the freeway** and go **right** at a **second T.** Then reach a junction with **Road 11** for Munich.

When you join Road 11, you'll be within a few kilometers of both the youth hostel in Pullach (to the south) and the campground and youth house in Thalkirchen (to the north). Both have good train connections for sightseeing in Munich. There is also a **bike route** into the city along **Road 11.**

Munich is big and beautiful and as captivating as Bavaria itself. Pick up a guidebook for the city or collect an armload of literature and a city map at the **tourist office** in the main train station. Then join the crowds who linger in "Munich's living room," the Marienplatz, and plan your sightseeing strategy while you await the fanciful *Glocken-spiel*.

Be forewarned—Munich goes wild during the two weeks of *Oktoberfest* from late September to early October, so plan to avoid (or seek out) the mayhem, according to your personal pleasure. Even without the added spirit that *Oktoberfest* brings, Munich will surely capture your heart with its world-class museums, its overwhelming churches, its rich Bavarian culture, and its irresistible charm.

If you're game for more pedaling from here, pick up the start of Tour No. 11 in Salzburg, Austria, by cycling east from Munich with a stop at the beautiful Bavarian Chiemsee along the way. The ride is hilly and scenic, and provides a wonderful opportunity to bid a leisurely *"Grüss Gott"* to the friendly folk of Bavaria.

# TOUR NO. 11

# IN TUNE WITH THE DANUBE
### *Salzburg to Vienna, Austria*

*Distance:* 474 kilometers (295 miles)
*Estimated time:* 8 riding days
*Best time to go:* June, July, or September
*Terrain:* Relatively easy with a few tough hills
*Connecting tours:* Tours No. 10 and 12

If you're looking for a superb week and a half of riding, with lovely scenery, gentle terrain, and visits to two of the most stimulating cities northern Europe has to offer, consider this ride between Salzburg and Vienna. You'll follow first the Salzach, then the Inn River north to Passau, Germany, then you'll ride along the banks of the Danube, viewing vineyards, castles, and abbeys along the way. And you'll finish the tour in Vienna, an extraordinary city rich in architecture, history, and culture.

Austria offers much to the cyclist—friendly people, beautiful buildings, delicious food, and pleasant scenery. The neat thing is, this "river ride" to Vienna has been discovered in recent years and transformed into a well-signed, well-maintained, and exceedingly popular long-distance bicycle route. You won't believe the "red carpet" treatment you'll receive along the way. Special bike-path signposts indicate hotels, bike shops, and restaurants, all for the benefit of tourers passing through. There are even tourist offices set up beside the off-road bike lanes, established exclusively for the benefit of tourists seeing Austria by bike.

When you are on the road, you'll find Austrian thoroughfares to be well maintained, if somewhat busy. And you'll also discover that Austrian drivers generally temper their European fondness for blazing speed with a welcome courtesy toward cyclists. Work on your German-language civilities while you're pedaling each day—a *"Grüss Gott"* and a *"danke"* will take you far in this Catholic and somewhat formal land.

**CONNECTIONS.** Salzburg is served by the Vienna–Salzburg railway line (a good option if you'll be flying in and out of Vienna, where this tour ends). And Salzburg boasts its own international airport, too. If you're cycling our Tour No. 10 from Heidelberg to Munich, Germany, you can reach Salzburg with a gently hilly ride across Bavaria or a quick train hop from Munich. By all means, tack our Danube ride from Vienna to Budapest (Tour No. 12) onto this tour to get a look at Hungary as well.

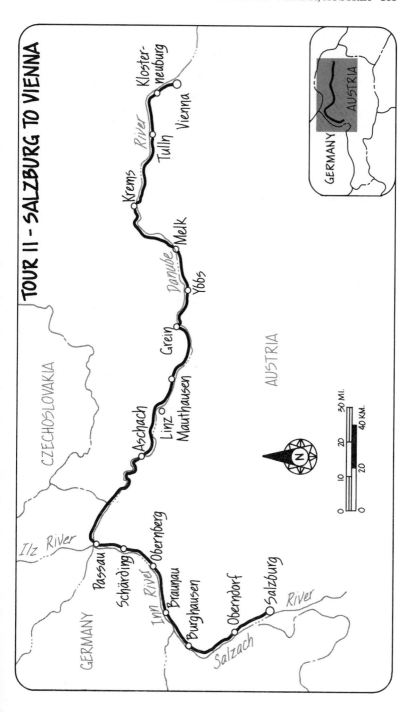

TOUR II – SALZBURG TO VIENNA

**INFORMATION.** Write in advance to the Austrian National Tourist Office, 500 Fifth Avenue, #2009-2022, New York, New York 10110, for information on cycling, camping, hotels, shopping, and so forth. If you want an *intellectual* taste of Austria, save some pastry money for a guidebook. Michelin's *Green Guide Austria* provides extensive coverage of Salzburg, Vienna, and the Danube Valley. The *Blue Guide Austria* is another straight-facts option. For a blend of light historical coverage and much-needed tourist advice, turn to *Let's Go: Germany, Austria, and Switzerland.* Take advantage of the Austrian tourist offices (called *Verkehrsbamt* or *Verkehrsverein*), too. They'll load you down with plenty of free English-language literature.

**MAPS.** Because almost every kilometer of your ride to Vienna will be on an established long-distance bike route, Austria is one country where purchasing special bicycle maps is undoubtedly worth the extra schillings. For your ride along the Danube, look for Map No. 151 of the superlative *Donauradweg* series published by Kompass. It covers the route from Regensburg, Germany, to Hainburg, Austria, at 1:125,000 scale. For the ride from Salzburg to Passau, we relied on standard 1:200,000 road maps to get us to Hochburg-Ach, then picked up a great little tourist-office map called *Bayerisch-Oberösterreichischer Rad- und Wanderführer* to lead us on to Passau. (Both bike maps we've listed have loads of accompanying text in German, so you'll be in great shape if you can read the language.)

**ACCOMMODATIONS.** Living costs in Austria are similar to those in Germany, fitting neatly between the high prices of Scandinavia and the economy of Greece and Portugal. Austria's campgrounds are probably your best accommodation bargain, and there are loads of them along the Danube. They're generally well run and moderately priced.

Austrian hotel rooms can be expensive. If you're not camping, hunt for small pensions, student-oriented lodgings, or rooms in private homes (*Zimmer Frei*). Youth hostels are another good low-budget option.

**SUPPLIES.** Shops in Austria close on Saturday afternoons and Sundays. In smaller towns, you may have difficulty finding groceries during the lunch break (12:30 to 1:30 P.M.), and you'll want to watch out for scattered weekday-afternoon closures (often a Wednesday or Thursday). We once had to rely on a "supper" of bread and marmalade after a 60-km day when we pedaled blindly into a "stores-closed" zone on a Wednesday afternoon.

While in Austria, be sure to sample some of the local specialties. Try a hearty meal of Viennese filet of veal (*Wiener Schnitzel*) or dig into a plateful of deliciously prepared potatoes (*Kartoffeln*). As in Germany, the Austrian tradition of a late-afternoon snack with a cup of coffee (*Kaffe und Kuchen*) will fuel your sweet tooth with goodies like chocolatey *Sachertorte,* delectable *Linzertorte,* and a vast array of other bakery items. Duck into a *Konditorei* and indulge!

Cycling is popular in Austria, and you'll find loads of bicycle shops along this heavily toured route. Expect to pay considerably more for equipment than you do at home, however.

## Salzburg to Braunau: 78 kilometers

Salzburg has several strategically placed **tourist information** offices (train station, Mozartplatz, and main roads into town). They'll provide you with a city map and lots of literature. Be sure to ask about the bike path along the Salzach River, too.

If you visit during Salzburg's summer music festival (late July and August), expect to scramble for accommodations in this exceedingly popular city. You'll find several youth hostels to choose from, as well as some dormitory lodgings open in the summer months. The closest campground to the downtown core (Stadtcamping Salzburg) is on Bayerhamerstrasse near the train station (*Bahnhof*). It's certainly convenient, but it's less than luxurious and has a strong potential for bedlam during the height of tourist season. If you don't mind "commuting" for your sightseeing, check out one of the campgrounds a little farther from the core.

Make your way to Salzburg's center, fortifying yourself with a nibble or two of Mozart chocolate along the way, and dive inside the massive Salzburg Cathedral (*Dom*). Make yourself dizzy staring at the fantastic central dome, then go outside to watch a giant-sized chess game in the busy Kapitelplatz nearby. Climb the hill to Hohensalzburg, joining hordes of ice cream–toting tourists, and explore the massive fort that runs a close second to Mozart as the city's most recognized trademark.

If you'd like to take a short day trip on your bicycle while you're visiting Salzburg, pedal around the east flank of Hohensalzburg's hill and cycle south from the city on Hellbruner Allee for the 20-minute ride to Schloss Hellbrunn, an irreverent bishop's palace with fountain-filled gardens. Perhaps the best thing about Salzburg are its lively streets. Take your city map and your camera and explore the town on foot. You'll find gardens and churches, street artists and ice-cream vendors, narrow alleyways and shop windows galore—in short, a symphony for the eyes that will keep your feet tapping for hours.

After you've satisfied your tourist appetite on Salzburg's sights and specialties, it'll be time to abandon the city for your ride toward Vienna. We took off from the campground near the train station, so we'll give you cycling directions from there. However, our ride took us on the unpleasant Road 156, and we found out (later) that there is a recently completed **bike route along the banks of the Salzach River** that departs right from the **city core.** We recommend you try following this route instead. Look for **bike-route signs** on the **right bank** of the Salzach River near Salzburg's **Staatsbrücke.**

If you don't take the bike route, start from Salzburg's **train station,** and take **Kaiserschutzenstrasse** to **Plainstrasse.** Turn **right** and follow Plainstrasse across the **train tracks,** then take the first **left** onto **Schillerstrasse.** Go **left** at the **T** onto **Road 156** (unsigned) for **Oberndorf** and **Braunau.** The road is wide, but it's also busy with city traffic.

If you do choose the road route rather than the signed bike route as you're leaving Salzburg, you can get on the Salzach bikeway at **Oberndorf.** When the **main road** makes a **sharp turn to the right**

*Cyclists enjoy special treatment on the bike route between Salzburg and Vienna.*

in Oberndorf, watch for a **green bike-route sign.** Carefully **cross** the main road to gain the bikeway. Wonderful quiet cycling along the Salzach River follows. You'll see signs for the ***Naturelebnisweg Inn-Salzach*** throughout your ride, and you'll have lots of fellow tourers (mostly visiting Germans) for company.

Although much of the riverside route is unpaved, the surface is adequate for touring-width tires. You should be aware of one thing, however—because you'll be tracing the riverbank much of the time, you will miss out on some of the small towns and farms that characterize the region. If you get bored with trees and water after a time, simply abandon the bike route and the river for some asphalt miles and a change of scenery.

The bike route will dump you onto a **small paved road** when you reach the **bridge** to **Tittmoning. Climb steeply** through trees for about 1 km (the route is signed for **Ach**), then enjoy more level riding before the wonderful descent to **Burghausen.** (The signed bike route swings off to the left as another road joins at Holzgassen, but it's quicker and more enjoyable to sail downhill to Burghausen with the main road.)

Cross the Salzach to enter **Germany** at Burghausen. Then follow the road along the river to find the city's attractive main square (*Hauptplatz*). The **tourist office** is on the right in the town hall (*Rathaus*). Burghausen's castle stretches along the ridge above the city, its long walls overlooking the thousand-year-old town where Napoleon crossed the Salzach in 1809. You can push up the hill to the fortress for a fine view of the city, the river, and the Wöhrsee, but it's probably worth the climb only if you're hunting for a special picnic spot.

Leave the *Hauptplatz* and ride toward the river. Cross a **bridge** spanning the Salzach and reenter **Austria** (Österreich). At the **main road** beyond the bridge, turn **left** for **Braunau** and climb a **steep hill.** Continue following signs for Braunau through gentle terrain on a well-surfaced road.

We "bit" the first time the signed bike route abandoned the paved road, and we grumbled through a wild goose chase down to the river and back up the hill that added about 4 km and plenty of climbing to the asphalt route. However, the **second time** the bike route swings away from the road (near the confluence of the Salzach and the Inn), you may want to follow it. You'll enjoy a riverside entry into Braunau with this path.

We kept with the main road to Braunau, primarily because we were looking for the city's campground. It's signed from the road, and it's a very pleasant site, not far from the city center. With its lively main street, its handsome church, and its grocery stores stocked with pretzels, *Wurst*, mustard, and *Bier,* Braunau will ensure your visit is a pleasant one. If you need a bed, you'll be able to find a pension in the small city core.

# Braunau to Passau: 65 kilometers

From the **bridge** across the **Inn** in downtown Braunau, continue downstream with the road beside the river. Follow **bike-route signs** to the **right,** then go **left** at the **next intersection.** Stay with signs for the bike route as you veer **left** off this street to gain a **gravel path** beside the river. (This may change, as bike-lane construction was underway when we visited in 1991.)

Pedal on to **Hagenau** and go **left** to gain a **paved road** here. **Abandon the bike route** when it leaves the roadway once again, and **stay with the paved road** to **Bogenhofen.** Swing **left** for **Mining** and **Mühlheim** in Bogenhofen, and relish pleasant, easy cycling as you continue east. In **Mühlheim,** stay with signs for **Kirchdorf** (ignoring the bike route once again), and veer **left** for **Kirchdorf** to gain a smaller road toward the river.

You'll **return to the bike route** in Kirchdorf, angling **left** with signs for **Katzenbergleithen.** Pedal a small road toward Obernberg, and **leave the bike route** to ascend a **short, steep hill** to **Road 142.** Go **left** here to pedal into **Obernberg,** entering through an attractive town gate and arriving at the colorful town square (*Marktplatz*). A chortling fountain, a bulb-belfried church, and the painted façades of the surrounding houses make the scene remarkable. There's a nearby **tourist office,** if you're in quest of the city campground, indoor lodgings, or additional information on the town.

Continue through the *Marktplatz,* departing via a second **gateway,** and stay with the **main road** through **Reichersberg.** Note the large monastery complex that rules this town. The signed bike route alternately follows and abandons the main road. Stay with the bike signs if you have the time and patience, or simply pedal the main road if you don't. **Road 142** becomes **Road 137** just after **Suben,** and you'll pick up stretches of paralleling bike path for portions of the increasingly busy route.

As you approach **Schärding,** follow signs for the **center** to find the busy city's attractive main plaza lined with painted houses. If you want to shop before Passau, this is the place to do it. Wander through the town square and **descend** toward the **Inn River,** keeping an eye out for a **bike-route sign** directing you to the **left** toward **Wernstein.** You'll keep with the signed bike route from here to **Passau.**

Between Schärding and Wernstein, the route follows a paved roadway through gentle hills, then you'll gain a **carless gravel path** beside the river the remainder of the way to Passau. Only the busy train tracks beside the bike route will disrupt the silence and solitude of your ride. You'll see the hilltop high-rise apartment buildings of Passau long before you reach the city core, crossing into **Germany** along the way.

Enter the suburbs of the city and swing **left** onto the auto **bridge** across the **Inn.** Just after crossing, veer **right** to **walk your bicycle** through a short auto **tunnel** and emerge at the rear of Passau's *Dom*. The richly decorated cathedral is a baroque jewel set among the city's many glittering churches. Passau has attractive streets, personable buildings, and the pretty waterfront setting of a town where three rivers (the Danube, the Inn, and the Ilz) come together. You can easily spend a day here, wandering the avenues, picnicking on the riverbanks, and climbing to the hilltop castle for a tremendous view of the city.

You'll find Passau's **tourist office** near the train station at the Nibelungenhalle. Pick up a city map and information on lodgings at the desk. Passau offers a handful of hotels and a hilltop youth hostel tucked inside the city fortress (you won't like the incline after a long day's ride).

If you're planning to camp in Passau, you're in for a treat. The city's tents-only campground is set right on the banks of the Ilz River. It's secluded, tiny, and inexpensive. To find it, cross the Danube (Donau) River from the bridge near the *Rathaus* and turn right on Angerstrasse. Cycle through a tunnel just before the Ilz River, cross the river, then turn left and go left again, recrossing the Ilz. To the right, on Halser Strasse, a campground sign will beckon you along the river and up a residential street to a delightful tent spot beside the water.

One more note—if you're running late or running out of gas by the time you hit Passau, there are many passenger ferries that ply the waters of the Danube between here and Vienna. Bikes are allowed, fares are reasonable, and the scenery is grand. Check on times and fees at the ferry office on the right bank of the Danube.

## Passau to Aschach: 67 kilometers

From Passau's **center,** cross the Danube on the **bridge** near the *Rathaus* and go **right** for **Obernzell.** Cycle along the **left (north) bank** of the Danube as you follow a signed **bike route** beside the road. Enjoy flat and effortless cycling with plenty of traffic. You'll lose the bike lane after a time, then hug the shoulder to **Obernzell.**

In Obernzell, swing **right** for **Gottsdorf** to gain a much quieter road beside the river. Cross the **Austrian–German border** soon after. Pedal this pleasant route past the Danube dam at Jochenstein, then watch for a turn to the **right** signed *Radweg zur Grenze.* Swing down to the right to cruise through the small community at Jochenstein (if you start uphill with the main road, you missed your turn). Then gain a **cycle route** beside the river to continue downstream.

If you're riding in the summer months, you should have scores of other cyclists for company. As you continue with the Danube, you'll pass many small ferry landings that present opportunities for cyclists to cross to the opposite shore. Fees are minimal, and most of the ferries run from April to October. Because we were very heavily loaded (and had a bike trailer and a toddler in tow) on our most recent journey down the Danube, we shunned the small ferry crossings and opted for auto bridges instead. You can choose your route according to personal preference.

We crossed the Danube on the **bridge** before **Wesenufer,** a pleasant Austrian village, then we climbed with the road away from town. There's a **signed bike route** along the road, but traffic is fairly steady. This secondary route joins the main Danube cycle path as it crosses the river at Schlögen. (If you're not adverse to a boat ride and a small fee, a better option would probably be to stay on the **left bank** of the Danube, following the signed cycle route to the **Au/Schlögen ferry,** then crossing the river to the **right bank** here.)

From **Schlögen,** bask in blissful cycling on a **paved riverside route.** This is really wonderful, and you'll be able to enjoy the Danube and its river traffic (barges, ferry boats, and floating swans) without worrying about heavy auto traffic along the way. There are several campgrounds scattered along this section of the river, and the *Gasthäuser,* pensions, and inns near the route garner much of their business from cycle tourists. However, there are few shopping opportunities between Wesenufer and Aschach. So keep this in mind if you're cooking for yourself.

There's a deluxe (and expensive) riverside campground set right on the cycle route about 7 km short of Aschach. In the summer months, its tent area is crammed with bike tourers. If you decide to pitch it here, look for a sheltered spot. Sudden Danube storms sometimes race down the river from Passau, with heavy winds that can flatten a tent in seconds.

Continue along the peaceful and shaded **bike path** to **Aschach,** a lively Danube town with a good selection of indoor accommodations and a handful of grocery stores. Bike tourers are very welcome here. In fact, you might get the feeling that the little city's business owners are seeing a pile of Schillings pedaling your bicycle through town—not just another tired tourist.

## Aschach to Linz: 28 kilometers

You'll have two options for your ride from Aschach. If you don't mind another ferry crossing, stay on the **right bank** of the Danube with a level, quiet **bike path.** Pass another Danube **dam,** and hop the **bike ferry** across the river to **Ottensheim.** If you'd just as soon skip another ferry ride, cross to the Danube's **left bank** with the **bridge** from Aschach. Signs for the ***Donau Radweg*** will lead you across the bridge, then onward on a zigzagging path through cornfields and farmland toward **Ottensheim.** This route is somewhat difficult to follow but quite pleasant, and you'll approach the city via a riverside **bike path** that's wonderfully secluded.

The left-bank route branches before the **Danube dam.** Swing **left** for **Ottensheim** to cycle into the attractive town. Ottensheim is another city "geared" for bike tourers. You'll find bicycle-oriented merchants everywhere, and the town will welcome you with open arms.

To pedal on toward **Linz,** you can either follow the **bike lane** along the **north side** of the busy **Road 127** or recross to the Danube's **right bank** and pedal on a **smaller, quieter road** toward Linz. If you're entering the city from the left bank, you'll cross the Danube on a large **bridge** and continue **straight** to reach Linz's ***Hauptplatz.*** The city **tourist office** is located in this expansive central square.

Pick up a map of the city (ask for the great Linz cycle map) and request the English-language pamphlet, *Danube Cycle Track,* while you're there. You can gather information on lodgings at the tourist office, too. Linz offers three youth hostels and scores of hotels. Read the first paragraph of our ride to Grein for directions to Linz's cyclists' campground. You'll find excellent bike shops, interesting streets, and lots of activity in this large city. Check out the sixteenth-century *Landhaus* and the baroque Former Cathedral (*Alter Dom*) while you're exploring.

## Linz to Grein: 60 kilometers

From Linz's ***Hauptplatz,*** retrace your route to the **left bank** of the Danube and get on the signed **cycle route** toward **Grein.** You'll work your way out of the city, pedaling a parkway along the Danube shore, and arrive at Linz's **cyclists' campground** beside the Pleschinger Badesee about 6 km from the city center. Continue with the **riverside bike path,** finally swinging onto auto roads at **Abwinden.** (If you're up for a detour, you can cross the Danube on the dam near Abwinden and leave the river to visit the remarkable Abbey of St. Florian. St. Florian is one of the patron saints of Austria, and he's pictured on or in nearly every Austrian church you'll cycle past.)

Pedal roads and bike paths through **Gusen, Langenstein,** and on to **Mauthausen.** Once the site of a Nazi concentration camp (tours available), Mauthausen is now a pleasant village with several attractive buildings. Regain your **riverside bike path** after Mauthausen, and ride onward to **Au,** where a delightful campground awaits passing cyclists.

Keep with the **bike path** from Au, and enjoy quiet, level cycling toward **Mitterkirchen.** We got lost in the cornfields trying to stay with the bike route south of Mitterkirchen, so it's probably best to simply follow **bike signs** for **Mitterkirchen,** keeping **left** when the route splits just after a pathside **information office,** then pedal through the city on paved roads.  Veer **right** with the **signed bike route** for **Grein** as you leave town.

Follow small roads through **Mettensdorf** and **Eizendorf,** then regain the **riverside bike path** once more. You will be dumped unceremoniously onto the less-than-idyllic **Road 3** at **Dornach.** Pedal on toward **Grein,** passing another Donau **bridge** as you approach the city. You can escape Road 3 for the final kilometer into Grein by hopping onto an **off-road bike lane** on the left side of the road.

Grein boasts a convenient and inexpensive municipal campground, as well as a handful of pensions. Set off on foot to view the small town's church and hilltop castle. If you're a fan of the theater, don't miss a visit to the "oldest town theater in Austria." It shares a building with Grein's **tourist office.** And be sure to venture outside after dark to catch the floodlit castle at its best.

## Grein to Krems: 85 kilometers

From Grein, **retrace** your route along **Road 3** to the **bridge** across the Danube. Pedal over to the **right bank** of the river, then follow the **signed bike route** all the way to **Ybbs.** The bike route does far too much meandering as you work your way through the midsize city of Ybbs, so you'll need patience and sharp eyes to stick with it. Escape the town and pedal on toward **Krummnussbaum.**

Enjoy a striking view of the pilgrimage church of **Maria Taferl** on the ridge above Marbach as you regain **riverside cycling** just before Krummnussbaum. There's a ferry across to Marbach, if you would like to explore the town or its much-visited church. From **Krumm-nussbaum, zig inland** with the bike route to cross a tributary of the Danube just before **Pöchlarn.** If you want to take a look at the attractive little town, stay on the road toward the town **center** as you pedal on.

Revel in more riverside cycling from Pöchlarn, then look for the massive bulk of **Melk Abbey** looming into view ahead. You'll see the twelfth-century **Weitenegg ruin** on a hillside across the river. Cycle past yet another **Danube dam** and swing inland toward **Melk Abbey** not long after. Ride to the lower town, dwarfed by the amazing yellow façade of the abbey complex crowded on the hill above. You can walk up a **steep pathway** to reach the ridgetop buildings from the lower town, or you can **pedal up the stiff hill,** following signs for **Parking—Stift Melk.**

Marvel at the fantastic baroque interior of the abbey church, hand

*Austria greets bike tourers with open arms along the long-distance Danube bike route.*

over the Schillings for a fascinating tour, or simply wander the extensive grounds of the complex before continuing on for Krems. The Benedictine Abbey of Melk was founded in 1089, and the complex and its furnishings will provide you with a memorable afternoon of sightseeing. If time gets away from you, Melk has a youth hostel and a campground. Ask for help with lodgings at the **tourist office** at Rathausplatz 11.

You'll have a route decision to make at Melk. You can stay with the signed bike route along the **right bank** of the Danube, enjoying quiet, pastoral cycling and cruising past the twelfth-century **Schönbühel Castle** along the way. The major disadvantage with the right-bank ride is that the nicest wine towns are on the left bank. However, frequent ferry-crossing points allow access to the cities on the opposite shore.

We cycled the right bank on our first trip down the Danube, so we decided to sample the left bank on our most recent visit. **Cross** the river on the **bridge** below Melk, then pedal a **bike lane** beside the hectic **Road 3.** The ride is unappealing at first, but as vineyards and orchards and small wine villages begin to take over, the atmosphere improves markedly. You'll see lots of **"No Bike" signs** (round sign with a red outer ring and a bicycle inside) along this route. They're used to route you **off Road 3** and through the charming villages along the way. Obey and enjoy!

Pass **Aggsbach** and look for the lofty, lonely **Aggstein ruin** on a ridge across the Danube. **Schwallenbach** is a delightful little town, and **Spitz** is worth a long pause. Check out the parish church, and look for the wine-tasting garlands that adorn the old houses. Pedal on to **Weissenkirchen,** with a fortified church and picturesque streets, then continue to **Dürnstein.**

Although often overrun with ruddy-cheeked tourists, Dürnstein is another Danube treasure, its architectural pearls strung along the enchanting main street (Hauptstrasse). Climb to Dürnstein's wonderful ruined castle (said to be the spot where Richard Lionheart was imprisoned on his journey homeward from the Third Crusade), and savor an enchanting view of the lazy Danube, lying in a bed of green, vine-covered hills.

As you pedal onward from Dürnstein toward **Krems,** following the signed **bike route** along the way, watch for the hilltop **Göttweig Monastery** ruling the ridge across the river. Enter Krems and look for the city **tourist office** at Undstrasse 6. The staff there can direct you to the youth hostel or a centrally located pension. If you're camping, head for the city's well-signed, excellent campground on the Danube shoreline (just to the right off Road 3). Once you've stowed your bicycle and gear, prowl the midsize wine town, savoring the old houses, lively streets, and medieval ambience of Krems and its western neighbor, Stein.

## Krems to Tulln: 45 kilometers

Leave Krems by **backtracking** to the Danube **bridge** and crossing the river to **Mautern.** Follow bike signs for **Radweg Krems Süd** through the busy town of Mautern and out along the river. A bit of zigzagging with the bike route will bring you to the **Danube shoreline** once again. Mile after mile of flat, easy cycling follows as the Danube Valley widens out into a less-impressive version of its former self.

Stay with your riverside route, with only the water, the wildflowers, the grass, and scores of other cyclists for company. You'll be getting close enough to Vienna to pick up racers and recreational cyclists out on day rides from the city as you pedal on with **bike signs** for **Tulln.**

Pass a fascinating example of the "bike culture" along the Danube near **Traismauer,** as you ride by a **cyclists' rest station/restaurant** astride the bike route.

Pedal on to another Danube **dam** where a restricted area results in some zigging and zagging for the bike path. Follow **small roads** through **Zwentendorf, Pischelsdorf,** and **Langenschönbichl.** Then cycle into **Tulln** with the waterside route. To visit Tulln's interesting city center, swing **right** off the waterfront with signs for the *Stadtmitte.* The midsize city's parish church is worth a visit. Adjacent to the church, look for a thirteenth-century funerary chapel with captivating paintings of the Last Judgment.

Tulln has a handful of hotels and scores of shopping opportunities (if you haven't picked up a street map for Vienna yet, do it in Tulln). To find the city's modern campground, return to the waterfront and continue downriver with the bike route. Watch for camping signs leading to the right off the bike path, and reach the large camping area soon after.

## Tulln to Vienna (Wien): 36 kilometers

You'll want to get an early start for your ride into Vienna today. Although the distance isn't long and the terrain is easy, finding lodgings in Vienna can be a challenge. It's best to have plenty of time to work with. From Tulln's **center,** return to the **riverside bike route** and continue down the Danube. The paved shoreline bike path is well signed throughout this section (look for **Radroute Klosterneuburg**). Keep an eye out for painted directional arrows on the asphalt, too— they'll sometimes get you past an unsigned branch in the route.

Cycle past scores of summer homes as you depart Tulln's suburbs. In truth, the development never ceases completely between Tulln and Klosterneuburg. Riding is easy and you'll have loads of company on weekends. Reach a **junction** before the **dam** at **Greifenstein.** (You can cross the Danube on the dam, if you want to pedal the left bank for some reason.) Keep to the **right** with signs for **Klosterneuburg.** Endure some zigging and zagging, then **leave the river** to pedal through **Kritzendorf** and on to **Klosterneuburg.**

Klosterneuburg offers a large and busy campground (signed just off the bike route) for those who would like to avoid cycling into the heart of Vienna. From the campground, it's a five-minute walk to the train station and a quick and affordable commute into Vienna. The campground staff will help you with train schedules and fees. This spot is crammed with cyclists in the summer months, and Klosterneuburg itself is an interesting city, with an abbey and church well worth a visit.

To pedal on toward Vienna, cycle onward past the campground, keeping the **train tracks** on your right and a **small creek** on your left. It's bizarre—after hundreds of kilometers of well-signed bike paths, the signs seem to disappear as you near your goal. (We've decided that bike-route designers all over Europe take intense pleasure in "dumping" trusting cyclists!) Pedal small roads and intermittent bike paths for a time, and work your way into the city snarl. When the bike route **branches** near the **Nordbrücke,** continue with the cycle path along the **Donaukanal.**

(One branch of the bike route crosses the river and follows the Donauinsel, a long, park-ruled island. If you've already done your sightseeing in Vienna from the campground in Klosterneuburg, and you're continuing on for Budapest, this is the way to go. Signs for Donau Radweg Lobau will lead you out of town.)

Stay beside the Donaukanal as you pedal toward the **center.** If you're without a clue as to where you're staying tonight, head for the **tourist information** office at 1010 Kärntnerstrasse (near the Opera House). They'll provide you with a list of accommodation options. One word of caution—Vienna is a very large and very busy city. If you're negotiating its streets with your bicycle in tow, we recommend you take your time and push. Telephone ahead if you're hunting for a vacant hotel room or a bunk in a hostel. Vienna has a handful of youth hostels, several student dormitories, and some inconveniently located campgrounds.

Once you're settled in, hit the streets without your bike and fall in love with a lovely city. Forget you're a cyclist, ignore the cobblestones and trolley tracks, and discover the charms of Vienna. Sip a cup of coffee at a streetside cafe and choose a delicious-looking *Torte* or sweet roll (*Büchteln*) from overloaded display cases that make indecision a delight. Walk to the *Dom* and stare in fascination at its incredible Gothic exterior, or wander for hours in the palace complex of the Hofburg. Grandeur, beauty, culture, and wealth weave a spell throughout Vienna that will tie you to the city with a timeless bond.

# TOUR NO. 12

# A RIVER RIDE TO BUDAPEST
*Vienna, Austria, to Budapest, Hungary*

*Distance:* 386 kilometers (240 miles)
*Estimated time:* 7 riding days
*Best time to go:* May, June, July, or September
*Terrain:* A riverside glide
*Connecting tours:* Tours No. 11 and 13

If you're like many other tourists traveling to Europe these days, you're eager to explore a bit of Eastern Europe, hoping to catch a "feel" for this rapidly changing area where it seems each new month brings history-making events. Hungary is a great place to begin your trek. Although it's probably one of the most westernized of eastern countries, the differences between east and west make traveling here a challenge and a delight. People are friendly, prices are low, and traffic is minimal on the smaller roads. What more could a cyclist ask?

To make this tour even more enchanting, tag it onto the end of our Tour No. 11 (Salzburg to Vienna), or combine it with a trip through Czechoslovakia and central Germany (see our Tour No. 13), and pedal as many kilometers as you can find the time for. One thing's certain: Any time you spend cycling in Hungary will only make you hungrier for more!

The Danube Valley can get downright stifling in the Hungarian summer, so don't plan an August tour unless you want to cook. Prepare for your visit with as much advance reading as you can handle (see "Information" for guidebook suggestions), as twentieth-century Hungarian history is a fascinating and convoluted affair. Any political "savvy" you demonstrate to the Hungarians you encounter will be appreciated, as the people here feel (quite justly) that their country is little understood by the Western world.

As for the Hungarian language—well, if you can master even the simple pleasantries, you've got a very talented tongue. Syllables seem to multiply like rabbits in Hungarian sentences, as do seemingly unpronounceable combinations of consonants. Fortunately, many Hungarians keep a bit of English or German in reserve for tourists.

You won't need to obtain a visa in advance if you're entering the country on your bicycle, and the usual "Eastern" regulations regarding minimum daily currency exchange and official tourist lodgings aren't enforced here. For the most part, you'll find traveling in Hungary to be

hassle free. It is a good idea to keep some Western cash on hand if you'll be leaving the country by public transport, however. The country's hunger for Western currency means you pay for international tickets with Western cash.

**CONNECTIONS.** To reach Vienna and this tour's start, you'll have a host of options. You can pedal in with Tour No. 11 from Salzburg, or you can arrive by train or Danube ferry or airplane. If you're purchasing a roundtrip air ticket to Budapest to cycle this tour, you can hop aboard a Danube hydrofoil for the quick trip to Vienna and the start of your ride.

We heartily recommend combining this Hungarian tour with some cycling in Czechoslovakia. Although we would have preferred to pedal from Budapest to Prague on our most recent trip, time constraints forced us to hop a train (actually, it was the Orient Express), then resume our pedaling from the Czechoslovakian capital. Admittedly, it was a major hassle, but we and our bikes survived. What the Hungarian train system lacks in efficiency it does make up for in economy. You'll find train fares here to be delightfully low, especially if you're traveling to Eastern bloc countries.

**INFORMATION.** As mentioned earlier, the more information you can absorb about Hungary before you go, the more your days in the country will mean to you. Brush up on your twentieth-century history to discover what the modern era's two World Wars meant to this land. Then delve into a travel guide to discover what you want to see while you're visiting. The *Blue Guide Hungary* is a comprehensive, though somewhat dry tourists' reference volume. Turn to *The Real Guide: Hungary* for livelier prose and lots of useful information. One note of advice—always check the guide's publication date before purchasing it. Hungary's government regulations have fallen by the wayside in droves in recent years. You'll want to be sure which rules are still standing and which ones aren't.

Hungary's national tourist organization is IBUSZ. Offices within the country can exchange money, provide you with accommodation assistance, and even sell tickets for public transport. Write in advance to IBUSZ, 1 Parker Plaza, #1104, Fort Lee, New Jersey 07024, and ask for information on travel regulations, on Budapest, the Danube, and cycling. Request the pamphlets *Hungary Tourist Information* and *Hungary Camping,* too.

**MAPS.** This seems strange to be saying in a cycling guide, but Hungary is one country where we found small-scale maps to be a disadvantage rather than a help. Why? Because if the road was small, it was usually also unpaved (we're not talking well-packed gravel here, we're talking 4 inches of dust). Just about every rideable road we traveled was shown on the overall auto map a friendly Hungarian cyclist gave us on our first day out. The scale? It was a whopping 1:650,000!

You can purchase an excellent 1:300,000 map of Hungary that shows sites of interest, campgrounds, and youth hostels. It's published by RV Reise- und Verkehrsverlag and is available in bookstores in Vienna. Simply keep in mind that there are an abundance of unpaved roads in this largely undeveloped country, and not every road this map will show you is one you want to pedal.

If you're considering doing some exploring on your own while in Hungary, contact the Hungarian Cycling Federation, 1146 Budapest, Szabó J. u. 3 for tips. In the week of riding we did here, we encountered more helpful, talkative cyclists than in a month of traveling in any other European country. We heard lots of raves about the cycling possibilities around Lake Balaton, if you're looking for touring ideas.

Please refer to the map suggestions in Tour No. 11 for your ride from Vienna toward the Hungarian border.

**ACCOMMODATIONS.** If you're not camping, you'll probably want to rely on the local or regional Hungarian travel agencies to book your accommodations for you. Rooms in private homes are generally inexpensive and agreeable, although their proprietors don't always welcome one-night stays. Look for signs for *szoba kiadó* or *privat-zimmer* if you want to hunt for yourself. Some cheap hotels and several hostels provide other options.

Hungarian campgrounds are a budget tourist's dream. Pick up a camping pamphlet from a tourist office (or request one in advance by mail), then plan your cycling days accordingly. We found Hungarian campgrounds to be convenient and adequate, although quality can vary considerably from site to site. Best of all, camping in Hungary was a cultural adventure, as we often shared our tent area with travelers from all over Western and Eastern Europe. We'll never forget the busloads of rowdy Polish schoolchildren that enlivened our campground in Tata; and we must admit that accordion music still makes us shudder, thanks to an all-night musician who plagued our campground at Budapest.

**SUPPLIES.** Food in Hungary is a joy—it's cheap, filling, and tasty. Venture beyond goulash (*gulyás*) to sample mysterious offerings on your restaurant menus. You'll encounter plenty of meat and poultry, often smothered in rich sauce. Generally, we found the quality of Hungarian food (both on supermarket shelves and in restaurants) to be a notch below what we were accustomed to in Western Europe. However, as budget tourists, we were delighted with the opportunity that the low Hungarian prices provided us to splurge.

Hungary produces palatable (and very affordable) wine and beer, and be sure to stop in at a Hungarian sweet shop (*cukrászda*) for a cup of strong coffee and a pastry. Of course, all the kilometers you're cycling will allow you to indulge in what seems to be a daily ritual for urban Hungarians—a two-scoop ice cream cone in any one of a vast array of flavors.

Shopping hours in Hungary are generally Monday to Friday 9:00 A.M. to 7:00 P.M. and Saturday from 9:00 A.M. to 2:00 P.M. Shops are closed on Sundays and national holidays (be sure to check your guidebook for a list of dates). You should have no trouble finding bicycle shops in midsize cities here, as cycling is a popular sport. However, if you need parts or equipment, you probably won't see the brands you're accustomed to, at least not at prices you want to pay. Settle for a substitute to limp you through.

## Vienna to Hainburg: 50 kilometers

Please refer to the final paragraphs of Tour No. 11 for information on sights and lodgings in Vienna. From the city **center,** work your way toward the **left bank** of the Danube. (We crossed to the long island called the **Donauinsel** via Vienna's **Nordbrücke,** then pedaled bike paths along its length to leap to the left bank via a pedestrian bridge and **bike signs** for **Lobau** and **Hainburg.**) From Vienna's center, it's probably more direct to cycle through the **Prater,** then cross the Danube on the **A23 bridge** (**Praterbrücke**) before swinging down to the riverside route signed for **Lobau.**

The bike route is fairly well signed, once you're on the left bank. Follow a **shoreline bike path** for a time, then angle **left** through the industrial development at **Lobau.** Press on to gain a **levee bike route** that makes for pleasant and peaceful cycling. Scattered gravel stretches interrupt the mostly paved route. You can swing left to visit **Orth** or **Eckartsau** if you crave a change from the somewhat monotonous scenery.

**Bike signs** for **Hainburg** lead on for mile after mile of quiet riding. More signs will direct you up onto the **lofty Danube bridge** (pause for a great view of the walled city of Hainburg from the span). Leave the bridge and swing down to the **right** and **under the bridge** to continue following the river into **Hainburg.**

If you're hoping to camp, stick with the riverside route to find a delightful (and free) tent campground on the far edge of the city. There are bathroom facilities available (no showers) next to the bar/cafe just down the road. We shared the little riverside site with a group of visiting Hungarian cyclists and a handful of German tourers bound for Budapest. Even though the place was free, we would have happily paid many Schillings for the conversations we shared that night.

If you need a room, leave the river to enter the fortified city (there's a neat old **gateway** on the **west** side of town). You'll find several grocery stores and an interesting blend of shoppers from Austria, Hungary, and Czechoslovakia as you prowl Hainburg's lively streets in quest of supper supplies.

## Hainburg to Moson-Magyaróvár: 64 kilometers

Leave Hainburg with the **bike route** signed for **Pressburg.** You'll come in beside the main road just before **Wolfsthal,** then cycle a bike path through the town. Veer **right** to **abandon the bike route** as you turn onto **Road D50** for **Berg** and **Kittsee.** (The signed bike route continues from Wolfsthal to **Bratislava (Pressburg),** Czechoslovakia. You may want to sneak a peek at Bratislava and set your feet in Czechoslovakia while you're this close. Czechoslovakia doesn't require visas for Americans or Canadians.)

Enjoy easy cycling on **D50** through **Berg** and on to **Kittsee.** The road hits a **T** intersection in Kittsee. Swing **left** toward the **center,** then take the **first right** onto a **small, unsigned road** to gain the route toward **Pama (Pamastrasse).** More quiet, effortless riding follows.

Turn **left** to cycle through **Pama,** and stay with this road to **Deutsch Jahrndorf.** You'll be riding within a stone's throw of the Czech border as you approach the city. In **Deutsch Jahrndorf,** ignore the first right (signed for Bad Nickelsdorf) and pedal to the **far end of town.** Turn **right** just **before the church** to find another silent road leading on to **Bad Nickelsdorf.**

Hit a very busy **main road (Road E60)** in Bad Nickelsdorf, and go **left** to pedal to the **Austrian–Hungarian border.** Be very careful here, as traffic is extremely heavy. We encountered long lines of trucks and automobiles when we crossed the border in the summer of 1991. However, one of the "perks" of being on a bicycle is the opportunity to pedal past lineups of overheating vehicles, claim your passport stamp, and continue on. Welcome to Hungary!

Pause to exchange money at the border (if you wish), then prepare to do battle with the Hungarian road system. With any luck, the troubles we encountered while learning the ins and outs of this country's thoroughfares will save you a few headaches of your own. Hungary's small roads have either no directional signs (i.e., just *where*

*Hungary presents many route-finding challenges to the cycle tourist.*

is this road going?) or very hard-to-read signs. It seemed that every time we ventured off the main road during our early days of cycling here, we lost pavement and/or lost our way.

Grit your teeth and pedal the **main road (Road 1)** to **Moson-Magyaróvár.** (If you're riding a mountain bike and don't mind pedaling on dirt or gravel, there is a paralleling secondary route to the north, along the Lajta River. We tried to ride it, but our narrow tires and heavy loads made it impossible.) Moson-Magyaróvár is a big and busy town, strung out along the main road. There are several grocery stores and lodging possibilities in the city.

You'll find an adequate and well-signed campground at the far end of town (there's shopping nearby). Occasional **"No Bikes" signs** (round sign with red ring around a bicycle) will direct you off the main road and onto paralleling paths as you work your way through town. The bike-path surfaces are usually terrible, but we'll take loose fillings over being flattened by a truck any day!

# Moson-Magyaróvár to Pannonhalma: 66 kilometers

From the main road through the **center** of Moson-Magyaróvár, take the **left** turn signed for **Máriakálnok**. Cross the **Mosoni-Duna River,** and continue with this paved route through flat farmland. Traffic is light and cycling is pleasant to **Máriakálnok,** then continue past town to a **T** junction. Go **right** (unsigned) onto a busier road and pedal on toward the southeast.

You'll pick up signs for **Györ** as you pass through a series of small towns. Ride through **Darnózseli** and on to **Hédervár,** with a well-kept mansion, then stay with signs for **Györ.** The roughly paved road is virtually shadeless, so you'll be simmering if you're riding in the summer months. As you leave **Györújfalu,** watch for a **small paved road** swinging off to the **right** (just before a junction with the no-bikes-allowed main road). Hop on this small road to pedal into Györ **beside the river.**

You'll arrive at the **bridge** across the Mosoni-Duna soon after. Take it to find the heart of the **old city.** Györ is a lively Hungarian city, with a vast town hall, an interesting Carmelite church, a cathedral, a pharmacy museum, and (believe it or not) even a McDonalds! Join the locals for a stroll down Lenin Utca, and duck into one of the countless cafes or ice-cream shops along the way.

When you can tear yourself away from Györ's cheap eats, cross the **train tracks** on the **Lenin Bridge,** and continue south through the city. The road that takes off from the bridge is studded with "No Bikes" signs, so it's better to swing **left two blocks,** then veer **right** to parallel the main road out of town. Get onto **Road 82** toward **Nyúl,** but abandon this busy thoroughfare soon after as you angle **left** onto a quieter route signed for **Nyalka.**

Rough pavement may slow you down a bit, but the cycling is flat and effortless as you pedal southeast to a **junction** signed for **Tap** and **Pannonhalma.** Go **right** for Pannonhalma and enjoy views of the city's massive monastery as you loop around the hill and cycle into the town below. Pannonhalma has a well-signed campground that's within walking distance of the city's major attraction—Pannonhalma Monastery. You'll have a short, steep climb to the campground (and a long, steep hike to the monastery), then hop off your bike, choose a terraced site, and indulge in a glorious hot shower.

If you need indoor accommodations, you should be able to find something in the midsize town that curves around the monastery hill. There are a few grocery stores and plenty of restaurants and cafes to handle the many tourists that make the trek to Pannonhalma. Don't skip a tour of the lofty church complex, home of an abbey founded in 969 (it's now a Benedictine monastery). A guided visit is well worth the *forints* you'll fork over to view the monastery's 300,000-volume library, not to mention the vast hilltop basilica.

## Pannonhalma to Tata: 80 kilometers

We endured two hours of frustration as we tried to find our way northeast from Pannonhalma, and we ended up pushing our bicycles through a seemingly endless cornfield in ankle-deep dust. Simply put, a secondary road that our map showed between Pér and Örkény-puszta never materialized, leaving us stranded in roadless farmland without a tractor. If you want to look for it, feel free. Otherwise, **backtrack** to **Györ,** and leave town on **Road 81** toward **Pér** and **Kisbér.**

Veer **left** off Road 81 on the outskirts of Györ, and gain the secondary road toward **Örkény-puszta** and **Bönyrétalap.** Enjoy easy cycling past acres of farmland as you cruise through Örkény, Bönyrétalap, and on to **Lana.** We shopped and ate lunch in **Bábolna,** then pushed on through flat, boring fields to **Nagyigmánd.** Signs for **Tata** lead on from Nagyigmánd as you **cross** the busy **Road 13** and continue with a peaceful secondary road.

Pick up gently rolling hills through **Kocs** and on to **Tata.** The road hits a **T** in the midsize city. Swing **left** to head toward the twin towers of Tata's church. Continue with the road **past the church** to reach the shore of **Öreg-tó,** the larger of the city's two lakes. There's a pleasant bike/pedestrian path along the lakeshore, and it makes for much nicer cycling than Tata's main street, Ady Endre Utca.

The northern tip of Öreg-tó boasts a derelict castle, an old mill, and a museum. Cycle along the lake's western shore to take a look at the city's handsome old riding school, or find the interesting Ethnographic Museum on Alkotmány Utca. Tata's hotels are clustered around Ady Endre Utca. To find camping, pedal Öreg-tó's eastern shore to a sprawling, less-than-luxurious site on the lake's southern end. Take an evening stroll along the lakeshore and stop in at one of the cafes that troll for tourists here.

## Tata to Esztergom: 50 kilometers

You'll return to the banks of the Danube today, as you ride toward one of Hungary's most captivating cities and the center of Hungarian Catholicism since the year 1000. Leave Tata with **Road 100,** a busy thoroughfare roaring northward toward the Danube shore. Watch for a turn to the **right** signed for **Almásneszmély** about 5 km from the city (**"No Bike" signs** on Road 100 will help alert you to the turn). Swing right to follow this smaller road to a **junction** with **Road 10** along the Danube River.

Go **right** onto this sometimes growling main road (try to avoid cycling this section on a weekend), and enjoy easy riding through a lineup of small towns. Gaze across the water at the green hills of Czechoslovakia as you pedal east toward **Esztergom.** Pedal through **Tát** and swing **left** onto **Road 11** for **Esztergom.** You'll have views of the city's hilltop basilica as you cruise in through busy suburbs.

A visit to the largest basilica in Hungary (completed in 1856) should be at the top of your tourist itinerary for Esztergom. It's a bit of a climb to the hilltop church, but you won't regret the effort. Pay the small fee to tour the basilica's incredibly rich treasury, and make the stifling ascent to the church's cupola. If the narrow stairway doesn't make you lightheaded, the view will. Gaze down on the writhing Danube, its ruined bridge (a casualty of World War II), and the crowded rooftops of the city.

Take time for a visit to the medieval palace on the hilltop, then descend to Esztergom proper to stroll the busy streets and view the Christian Museum (a collection of religious art). Restaurants and hotels should meet your needs here, and there are many rooms available in private homes.

If you're camping, you'll be in for a treat (and a bit of a climb). Esztergom's newest campground is a wonderfully equipped hillside site about 2 km from the center. It boasts a magnificent sunset view of the shimmering Danube and the dome of the basilica. To reach the spot, look for signs for Camping Vas-Kapu as you leave the city center headed east.

## Esztergom to Szentendre: 46 kilometers

Leave Esztergom with the increasingly busy **Road 11** toward Szentendre. You'll be pedaling through the scenic (and very popular) Danube Bend as you push on. A trio of alluring cities rules this famous loop in the Danube River—now that you've seen Esztergom, you'll want to allow yourself plenty of time to pay your respects to Visegrád and Szentendre as well.

Roadside villages and vast fields of sunflowers will line your way as you cycle beside the river. The hills on both sides of the Danube are heavily forested, and you'll be feasting on the scenery as you cycle into Visegrád.

Swing **right** off the main road as you enter town, and continue to Visegrád's ruined medieval palace, once the talk of fifteenth-century Europe. Although some might consider the restoration work on the ruins to be a bit heavy-handed, a leisurely exploration of the site is still a treat. We were "adopted" by an Hungarian cyclist in the preceding village, guided to the palace, and led through a tour of the ruins by a very knowledgeable and gracious host.

Continue with **Road 11** as you endure a marked increase in resorts, development, and traffic on the way to **Szentendre.** You'll swing **left** off the main road to ride to the riverside road below the city core. Whatever you do, don't visit Szentendre on a summer weekend. It would be a shame to spoil this city's charm by being trampled by a camera-clicking tour group.

If you do manage to survive the tourist crowds, you'll certainly agree—Szentendre is a gem, set into a steep hillside above the Danube, its piled, tiled roofs and church belfries tumbling toward the river. Szentendre's shop-lined streets are tumultuous with artists, craftsmen, and hustlers, all plying their wares. Its salesmen will accost you. Its cafes and restaurants will entice you. Its museums will enthrall you. And its vistas will steal your heart. (Climb to the church plaza on **Templomdomb** for the best view in town.)

Seek a room in the city (get help at the **IBUSZ office** at Bogdányi Utca 11) or a site at the nearby campground, stow your bicycle, and set out on foot to enjoy the town. If you have the time and energy, make the very worthwhile detour to see the excellent Village Museum (*Skanzen*) about 2 km out of town. It's signed off of Road 11 on the north side of Szentendre. You can easily blow a day here, walking through the magnificent display of Hungarian homes and rural buildings, and marveling at the tools, the handicrafts, and the housewares.

## Szentendre to Budapest: 30 kilometers

If you're hoping to find indoor accommodations in Budapest, it's a good idea to telephone an IBUSZ office at least a day ahead to try to line something up. Ask for assistance at Szentendre's office if you need advice. Then tighten up your helmet strap an extra notch for the ride into Hungary's growling capital—it's a nail-biter. Leave Szentendre with the **waterfront road.**

As a cyclist, you'll be routed off of Road 11 for much of the way from here to Budapest. Stay with the **cycle path** along the left side of the road for a few kilometers, then gain a **paved asphalt route** paralleling the main road (on the right side). Traffic is intense, so you'll be glad for the space between you and the speeding vehicles.

Watch for a city sign announcing your **entry into Budapest**—a **canalside bike path** leads to the Danube shore from here. Cross the main road carefully and follow the canal to a **riverside bike/pedestrian route** lined with resorts, swimming pools, discothèques, and people. (If traffic is too heavy to cross the main road safely at the canal, continue on the right side of the road until the bike path ends, cross at the traffic light, and ride to the riverside bike route from here.) Pedal deeper into Budapest as you press on. We swung **right** on **Rozgonyip Utca** to reach the immense **Camping Római** between the Danube and Road 11.

Camping Római is probably your most convenient camping option in Budapest. If you visit in the summer, expect crowds, noise, dirt, two restaurants, and a late-night accordion player who may tempt you to commit murder. What the place lacks in atmosphere, it makes up for in convenience. If you don't have a tent, you might check out the bungalows or the adjacent "motel." A short walk leads to a train station on

Road 11, and you can reach the center of Budapest in 30 minutes.

If you're pedaling into the city to search for other accommodations (Budapest has loads of hotels, hostels, and summer-season dorm beds), stay with the **Danube bike path** as long as possible. When this peters out, swing **right** toward **Road 11** (or work your way in on paralleling roads) for the trip toward the **center.** It is *extremely important* to have a good street map of Budapest *before* you cycle in.

From Road 11, hop on the **bridge** (Arpád hid) to **Margit Island** (Margit-sziget) to cross the train tracks and gain quieter cycling on the island. As you leave the island, you'll hit another bridge (Margit hid); swing **right** for **Buda** or **left** to reach **Pest.** There's an **IBUSZ office** to the left at **Nyugati pu** (train station). Turn **left** as you leave the island, cross the Danube, and follow the main boulevard (Szt. István krt.) straight ahead to find the station.

One thing's for sure—you'll want to dump your bike and gear as soon as possible in order to enjoy this city. Find accommodations, buy a transit pass, and explore. Stroll the lively pedestrian avenue of Váci Utca for a taste of cosmopolitan Budapest. Climb to the heights of Castle Hill for a wonderful vista of the city sliced by the Danube. Admire the ornate interior of the hilltop Matthias Church and spend an afternoon in the museums at the Royal Palace. When you're worn out from sightseeing, pull up a chair in a streetside cafe, or "park it" on a doorstep to enjoy an ice cream cone.

If you're ending your cycling here with a plane for home, Budapest's Ferihegy Airport is east of town. For those continuing to another destination by train, ask at an IBUSZ office or at the MAV Hungarian Railways office to find out which station you need (be sure to tell them you have a bicycle, as it may travel on a different train and leave from a different station). Look for a sign for *poggyász feladás* (baggage check), once you're at the train station.

*The soaring pinnacles of Budapest's Matthias Church offer shelter from the blazing summer sun.*

# TOUR NO. 13

# EAST TO WEST

*Prague, Czechoslovakia, to Frankfurt, Germany*

*Distance:* 593 kilometers (367 miles)
*Estimated time:* 10 riding days
*Best time to go:* June, July, or September
*Terrain:* A blend of challenging hills and restful river valleys
*Connecting tours:* Tours No. 10, 11, and 12

If you're seeking an escape from the beaten tourist track, if you're bold enough to brave new territory, and if you don't mind a bit of hard work in exchange for quiet roads and scenic cycling, try this trek from Prague to Frankfurt.

Czechoslovakia is both a challenge and a treat for the cycle tourist. Road surfaces here are excellent, and even the small roads are well signed and easy to follow. Unfortunately, heavy traffic plagues the main thoroughfares during the summer months, and, since no provision has been made for cyclists, you'll want to avoid the country's main roads at all costs. Czechoslovakia (and the neighboring region of Germany to the west) is rugged country, and you'll encounter hilly riding in your pursuit of secondary roads. Lighten your load and toughen your legs—then prepare for a feast of scenery and quietness and culture.

Entering Czechoslovakia is effortless for Americans and Canadians today; thanks to the "Velvet Revolution" of 1989, visa regulations have gone the way of a host of other governmental rules. North American visitors face no minimum currency requirements, either. And the country's accommodation system has loosened up, as well. During our visit to Czechoslovakia in the summer of 1991, we witnessed changes taking place at an almost daily pace. In the neighborhood where we stayed near the center of Prague, a new campground opened every day! Despite the many changes for the good, expect to encounter poverty, unemployment, crime, and a scramble for Western goods and currency while you're in Czechoslovakia. These, too, are the by-products of "progress."

Please refer to the introductory material in Tour No. 9 for background on Germany. After you leave Czechoslovakia, you'll be pedaling westward with the snaking Main River, making your way through an area rich with vineyards, churches, and lovely cities. And, as you're coming from east to west, you'll be able to note the differences that still exist, examining them under the glare of first-hand experience. Best of all, you'll be able to appreciate those differences, thanks to the insights gained from traveling slowly and traveling well.

**CONNECTIONS.** If you arrive in Prague via train from another European country (we rode the Orient Express from Budapest), expect to encounter some hassles as you clear your bicycle through customs. We arrived at one train station, heavily loaded with armloads of panniers, only to be told that our bicycles were awaiting us at another station (only Prague's main station has a customs area for unaccompanied baggage). Needless to say, getting anywhere with a long-term tourer's gear—without a long-term tourer's bike—can be a major headache. (One note of caution should be sounded here. Be extremely careful in Prague's train stations. They give the term "den of thieves" new meaning.)

Prague does have an international airport (west of the city, noted on our first day's ride), if you're considering a direct flight from home. If you *do* fly into Prague, *don't* pedal in. Prague's center is far from cycle friendly. Claim a room or a campsite near the airport and let the city's inexpensive transit system carry you in and out for sightseeing. We pedaled out of the city once—and that was one time too many.

You'll have several route options as you ride this tour. Consider hooking up with one or more of our other Germany rides. For those who have the time, an excellent loop could be designed by combining this ride with Tours No. 10, 11, and 12. You could close the final leg by either cycling from Budapest to Prague or hopping on a train.

**INFORMATION.** Anything you can read about Czechoslovakian history will be a plus as you prepare for your trip. The Czech people have been politically minded for decades—it's a survival skill, not a luxury. Any local you encounter who has a mastery of English is going to want to talk about his country's past, its present, and its future. Prepare yourself to talk intelligently.

Write in advance to Czechoslovakia's state tourist company, Čedok, for information about your visit. The United States address is ČEDOK, 10 East 40th Street, #1902, New York, New York 10016. Ask for a map of Prague and information on accommodation options (mention camping if you're interested).

Bring along the most recent guidebook you can buy to help you through the intricacies of Czech bureaucracy, public transit, shopping practices, etc. Check out *The Rough Guide to Czechoslovakia* and/or *The Real Guide: Czechoslovakia* to get you started. As for the Czech language, a phrasebook might come in handy if you have an athletic tongue and a good attitude. Fall back on German or English in a pinch—both are spoken by a surprising number of Czechs, especially the ones who deal with tourists.

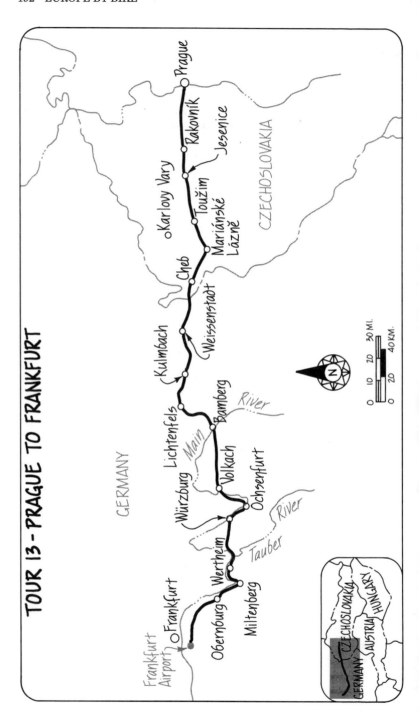

TOUR 13 - PRAGUE TO FRANKFURT

Please refer to the "Information" section in Tour No. 9 to prepare you for your ride in Germany.

**MAPS.** With a little hunting (hit the bookstores in Prague), you can find adequate maps for your ride through Czechoslovakia. We relied on a German map for part of our tour (*Die Generalkarte* at 1:200,000). In the process of displaying a section of the former East Germany, this map shows a hefty wedge of northern Czechoslovakia, as well. However, a 1:100,000 series published in Czechoslovakia is a better option. These maps show campgrounds, hostels, and sights of interest. Look for the *Soubor Turistických Map*—and buy it if you can find it.

Check the "Maps" section in Tour No. 9 for recommendations on German map options.

**ACCOMMODATIONS.** The summer of 1991 marked a tough transition for the Czech accommodation scene. Tourists flooded into the country in unprecedented numbers, and the supply of beds simply couldn't keep up with the demand. Fortunately, the Czech people are among the most enterprising and adaptable in Europe. In Prague and other popular tourist cities, just about anyone who has a spare bedroom is renting it, and the grassy plots that were backyard gardens last year are cozy campgrounds now.

If you're in the hunt for indoor lodgings during your days in Czechoslovakia, you'll probably need to work through a tourist agency of some kind. The state tourist company, Čedok, deals primarily in "upscale" beds, so if you're living on the cheap, check out an independent tourist agency instead. The travelers' grapevine is perhaps the best source for unofficial hostels and inexpensive rooms in private homes. Ask the backpack-toting youths at one of Prague's train stations for recommendations. Please be aware that "scamming" tourists is a common practice in Prague. Don't go anywhere or stay anywhere you feel is unsafe.

As mentioned earlier, campgrounds are springing up faster than the gardens in Czechoslovakia these days, so you should be in great shape if you have a tent. Besides the convenience and economy that Czech campgrounds provide, you'll have the joy of observing the Europeans around you at their leisure. It's a wonderful way to learn about the country and to make new friends.

Please refer to our accommodation information in Tour No. 9 for help with Germany.

**SUPPLIES.** When we think of eating in Czechoslovakia, we think of one thing—ice cream! Maybe it's because we were cycling in July and craving lots of cold things. Maybe it's because it seemed that every other person on the city streets was juggling a cone or two. Or maybe it's because we never could get over the fact that we could buy ice cream for three in Czechoslovakia for less than 50 cents. Whatever it is, it's worth a paragraph—when you're in Czechoslovakia, eat ice cream!

*Czechoslovakian ice cream is a bargain lover's delight.*

In general, we found the Czech food to be consistently excellent and always affordable. Standup *bufets* line the larger city streets, and you can fill up on pizza, open-faced sandwiches, or mini hot dogs and hamburgers in doughy buns whenever you please. Grocery deli counters are filled with delicious meats and cheeses, so picnic lovers won't go hungry, either. And restaurant meals are within reach of even the budget tourist here. Sample freely—even if you can't make out the menu.

The Czech people are justifiably proud of their beers. In fact, much of the beer-making prowess of Bavaria hinges on the inventiveness of Czechoslovakia's Bohemian region. The western city of Plzeň is renowned as the birthplace of beer. If you want to make friends quickly here, lavish praises on the local brew.

Expect to encounter difficulty finding certain products in Czechoslovakian stores. Although things are changing very rapidly, Western goods are still a hot item. Rest assured, the locals will snatch them up before you get near them! We'll never forget the one department store we visited in downtown Prague. Its shelves were sprinkled liberally with Western goodies, and people waited in line more than 30 minutes just to claim a shopping basket so that they could go inside and shop!

You'll find Czech stores open from about 9:00 A.M. to 6:00 P.M., Monday through Friday. Plan on afternoon closures on Saturdays and all-day shutdowns on Sunday. Unfamiliar holidays can sabotage your shopping plans, so check your guidebook for a list of potential closing days. If you run into mechanical trouble in Czechoslovakia, you'll only find bike shops in the larger cities. Try to limp it to the German border if you can.

## Prague to Jesenice: 70 kilometers

Prague is one of Europe's most enchanting cities. Don't be so eager to pedal out that you pass it over. This city deserves close inspection. Begin by buying a good street map at a *tabak* or bookstore. As mentioned earlier, the increasing demand for tourist accommodations has far outstripped the Czech supply—especially in Prague. So start your hunt early in the day.

If you're on a budget, ask around among fellow travelers or seek help at one of the independent services you'll find at the Prague train stations. You should be able to line up a bed at a decent price this way. If you're arriving by air, there are rooms and a campground near the airport. Those camping nearer to the city center will find a neighborhood "campground alley" along Trojská Street, a short distance from Prague's Holešovice Station. Backyard gardens are now lucrative camping operations for the homeowners along this street. Check out the Hajek Autocamp for great facilities and a charming English-speaking host.

Once your accommodation puzzle has been solved, buy a fistful of transit tickets and set out to explore the city. Prague's old town square (Staroměstké náměstí) is a joy, surrounded by handsome buildings and overflowing with tourist bustle. The elaborate old town hall boasts an incredible fifteenth-century clock. Join the crowds that watch the clock go through its paces when the hour strikes. Then explore the tantalizing streets of the old Jewish quarter, just north of the square.

Cross the Vltava River on the evocative Charles Bridge, and climb to the hilltop crowned by Prague Castle for a spectacular view of the city. Visit the castle and duck inside Prague's cathedral, then return to the city streets below to wander to your heart's content. You'll long remember the days you pass in Prague.

Our route from Prague to the German border is a hill-studded journey west, with little deviation for tourist sights. If you'd like to see more of Czechoslovakia than this tour has to offer, we recommend a ride north from Prague along the Labe (Elbe) River. Kralupy, Mělník, Terezín, and Děčín are worth a look, and you'll find vineyards and campgrounds scattered along the river valley. Unfortunately, the

Czech countryside to the west of the Labe has been decimated by coal mining for many years, and environmental hazards are a concern. Primarily because we had a two-year-old child in tow on our last visit, we opted for the pristine and peaceful countryside to the south.

Leave Prague on the horrendous **Road E6/E48** signed for **Karlovy Vary.** You'll endure cobblestones and trolley tracks as you pedal away from Prague's center, and heavy truck and tourist traffic make the way unpleasant. Pass the city's international airport at **Hostivice,** push on to **Jeneč,** and watch for a turn to the **left** signed for **Unhošt.** Hop onto a much quieter thoroughfare to pedal through Unhošt, a busy market town with shopping opportunities, and ride on to **Kýsice.**

You'll return (reluctantly) to **Road 6** for about 4 km. Cycle through **Doksy** and grab a **left** turn signed for **Lány** to gain another pleasant road. Go **left** at a subsequent junction signed for **Lány** and pedal through the small town ruled by a large château. Stay with the signed route for **Rakovník** from here, as the Czech hills begin in earnest. Quiet forested cycling follows.

Endure many **long ups and downs** as you pedal through trees to a shaded **T** in the heart of the forest. Swing **right** for **Rakovník** and continue climbing. A steep descent leads into the city. Rakovník is a charmer, with a busy central plaza, a fortified gate tower, and a Gothic church. Get off your bicycle and seek out an ice cream shop. You probably won't wait more than a minute before a friendly Czech comes up to talk. Rakovník offers a couple of crowded grocery stores and a handful of indoor accommodations. If you're not camping, this is your best bet for quite a while.

To press on for the campground at Jesenice, cruise the length of Rakovník's central shopping avenue, then keep **right** to intersect with a busier road. Go **right** on the main road and pedal a short distance to a **junction** signed for **Jesenice.** Swing **left** here. **Climb gradually** for about **20 km** as you ascend on a quiet route past trees and forest-shrouded lakes. Reach Jesenice at last (there are grocery stores here), and swing to the **left** on the **main road** through town to reach a sprawling campground set next to a lake.

If you're into cultural experiences, you'll adore this spot. With any luck at all, you'll be the only foreigner in the place. A busy bar, some even busier showers (two hot ones for about 400 people), and a tiny campground grocery store offer lots of opportunities to observe the Czechs at leisure. The cost of all this entertainment? Well, there were three of us, and we paid less than $2.

## Jesenice to Mariánské Lázně: 78 kilometers

From the campground at Jesenice, **backtrack** to the signed turn for **Blatno.** Follow this silent ridgetop road with lovely views of the surrounding countryside, then enjoy a gentle downhill glide to Blatno.

Signs for **Karlovy Vary** will lead you back toward the unfriendly **Road E48** once more. Swing **left** onto E48 for a stretch of frightening cycling to **Lubenec,** then pounce on a **left** turn signed for **Chyše.** Now the hard work begins.

A **stiff climb** up a forested hillside leads into an afternoon jam-packed with hills. You'll have quiet roads, smooth pavement, and pleasant scenery to cheer you, but you'll be a tired puppy by the time this day is finished. Pedal on to Chyše, with a well-kept château and a decrepit church, then ride to **Žlutice,** following signs for the town. There's another vast old church at Žlutice. The church's crumbling walls and the city's many empty storefronts give witness to Czechoslovakia's ongoing challenges and woes.

Leave Žlutice with the route for **Toužim.** A **hefty climb** leads into more exhausting **roller-coaster cycling.** Pass one small village after another—each seems to be set apart from its neighbor by a diving and climbing road. Sprawling farm complexes, ramshackle churches, and lots of curious stares will line your route. Stop to ask for water, or directions, or…. You'll be delighted by the hospitality you'll encounter.

Cruise downhill to enter **Toužim,** a sprawling Czech city with lots of shops and industry. (If you're running late or running out of oomph after all the hills, you can probably rustle up a bed in town.) In Toužim, swing **left** on the main road signed for **Plzeň,** then take the **right** turn for **Teplá** on the outer edge of town. We'll always remember Toužim as the place where two friendly locals offered us, our bikes, and our bike trailer a ride in their tiny car, reluctantly accepted our smiling refusal, then reappeared a few kilometers later to present our delighted toddler with a fast-melting ice cream cone.

Enjoy pleasant cycling to Teplá with a slight increase in traffic. In Teplá, a cozy village nestled beside the road, take a turn to the **right** signed for **Mariánské Lázně.** You'll have easy pedaling for a time. Pass a turnoff for a vast windsurfers' campground beside a lake (it's 3 km to the campground from the turnoff), and stay with signs for **Mariánské** to begin your final bout of climbing.

Endure a **steady uphill** push through forested hills. Hit a **junction** with the main road for Mariánské and go **left.** Traffic is much heavier on this thoroughfare, but you can escape it shortly afterward with a **right** turn onto a small road signed for the **Golf Hotel.** An unwelcome ascent away from the main road is soon transformed into a **joyous descent** along a tree-shrouded hillside. Your legs will shout for joy as you cruise into the delightful spa town of Mariánské Lázně.

Once the favored hangout of nineteenth-century royalty, but doomed to neglect and decay during Communist rule, Mariánské Lázně ("Marienbad" in German) has now become the destination of troops of German tour groups. Despite the crowds, the aging spa city is a treat. You'll love strolling the busy avenues, admiring the ornate façades of the brightly painted buildings, lingering in the beautiful central park, and staring at the city's famous colonnaded spa.

Although prices are much higher here than in rural Czechoslovakia, goods are still a bargain. You should be able to celebrate the end of your hill-studded riding day with a plateful of delicious (and affordable) Czech food. Mariánské's campground is 3 km from the city center on the south side of town. There's a Čedok office in the center of town, if you need help with indoor lodgings.

## Mariánské Lázně to Cheb: 33 kilometers

Leave Mariánské with the **road** signed for **Cheb** (Eger in German). Traffic is fairly heavy to **Velká Hledsebe,** where you'll join an even busier **main road** (Road 21) toward **Cheb.** Unfortunately, there just aren't many road options through this border area—hug the wide shoulder and pray for the 17 rolling kilometers to your **junction** with **Road E6.** A quick descent leads to a large lake (campground here) and the E6 junction. Swing **left** for **Cheb.**

Endure harrowing traffic into Cheb's center, keeping **left** at the first main **junction** in the city. Dive **right** into Cheb's lively **pedestrian core** to escape the traffic at last. You'll have fun prowling Cheb's shop-lined streets and spending your final *koruny* here (ours went for ice cream cones!). You should be able to find indoor accommodations without difficulty.

Cheb is a good breaking point for two reasons—there's not much in the way of camping or hotels for the next 50 km on our route into Germany, and Cheb makes a good base for a day excursion to yet another famous Czech spa town, Karlovy Vary. Larger and even more luxurious than Mariánské, Karlovy is well worth a visit. However, cycling here would mean far too many kilometers of suicidal main-road riding. Make your base in Cheb and hop a bus to Karlovy, if you're so inclined.

## Cheb to Weissenstadt: 40 kilometers

Return to the **main road west (Road 6/E48)** as you depart Cheb and head for the **German–Czech border.** We cycled past a solid line of backed-up trucks from the city all the way to the customs office at the border station. Ride through rolling hills, cross the border, and pedal on to **Schirnding.** Cross the **Röslau River** in the little town, marveling at the abrupt change in architecture, automobiles, and general upkeep you'll witness in this German city. Swing **left** for **Arzberg** here, and abandon the traffic of E48 to pedal a secondary road toward that city.

More **wearying hills** lead on to Arzberg, a pleasant midsize porcelain town. **Descend steeply** into the city core, then angle **right** for **Thiersheim** to climb away just as steeply. Follow a quiet ridgetop road with fine views of the surrounding fields and forest. Enter **Thiersheim,** a perky city with an impressive fortlike church, and go **left** for **Bernstein.** You'll **cross** the unappealing **Road 15** soon after. When your road **branches,** keep **right** for **Bernstein** and **Weissenstadt.**

Pedal a pleasant route through rolling hills to Bernstein and on to **Röslau.** Stay with signs for **Weissenstadt** through Röslau (lots of shopping options here), and climb away from the busy city. Push on to Weissenstadt, a pleasant tourist town set beside a popular lake. Weissenstadt will tantalize you with its bakeries and grocery stores and awe you with the sudden abundance of Western goods.

The city has a handful of hotels, if you need a bed. To find Weissenstadt's well-kept, inexpensive municipal campground (swimming pool, washing machine, and lots of visiting Czechs to make you "homesick"), swing right along the city's main street and watch for camping signs leading left. Descend to the lakeside campground, park your bike, and give your aching legs a break.

## Weissenstadt to Lichtenfels: 72 kilometers

Leave Weissenstadt with the main road signed for **Gefrees.** You'll have easy cycling along the lakeshore, then a **long steady climb** into forested hills. Enjoy a gliding descent into **Gefrees,** a busy German city overflowing with attractive buildings. Traffic increases as you leave town on the swiftly climbing road signed for the **Nuremberg freeway.** Stay with the **freeway route** when the road branches 2 km from Gefrees, and continue up and **over the freeway** with a pleasing loss of traffic.

A **steep descent** will take you into **Markt-schorgast.** Keep to the **left** through town, then go **right** for **Pulst** as you leave the city. More climbing follows. **Abandon the Pulst route** to pedal **under the train tracks** and take the first **right** (signed for **Himmelkron**) to gain a silent, unpaved road beside the train tracks. The surface is good and the cycling is superlative as you follow this shaded and solitary route for about 2 km, then emerge onto pavement to continue toward **Himmelkron.**

Cross a busy **main road (Road 303)** and go **straight** to pedal into Himmelkron, an attractive town with a noteworthy church and an unusual collection of elaborate dovecotes. Leave Himmelkron to push on to **Trebgast,** snuggled into the base of a steep, forested hillside. Keep to the **right** for **Kulmbach** and climb steeply through the pretty town, then reach an intersection signed for **Kulmbach** straight and to the left.

You'll have two options here. If you've had it with hills by now, continue straight with the main route and follow the valley of the Weisser Main on its route toward Kulmbach. You'll intersect with the main

*A forested lane leads to the banks of the Main River.*

road into Kulmbach and go left for the final 4½ busy kilometers into
the large city. We opted for a quieter (but much hillier) ride to
Kulmbach, veering **sharply left** from the junction and ascending
**very steeply** to the ridgetop.

Once you're up, you'll have a scenic and silent hilltop ride with wonderful views of the surrounding countryside. A **swift and steep** descent leads into **Kulmbach.** The Bavarian city of Kulmbach, although
marred by much development and industry, possesses an attractive
central core overlooked by the hulking castle of Plassenburg. After all
the hills you've seen in the past few days, you'll probably be more interested in Kulmbach's famous beer than in its hilltop castle. But stop
in at the modern **tourist office** near the old core to gather information on the city and its surroundings.

Leave Kulmbach on the murderous **main road** signed for
**Lichtenfels** and **Mainleus.** Watch for a paved **bike path** on the
**south side** of the road and hop on it. You'll be tracing portions of
the **Main River Bike Route (No. 8)** throughout the remainder of the
day. Unfortunately, it's poorly signed and difficult to follow. Lose the
paved bike path just before **Mainleus,** and **cross the main road**
carefully to pedal through town.

Hop onto the **small paralleling road** to ride through **Schwar-
zach.** The bike route seems to come and go from here. Try to follow it
if you fear for your life. Shudder and ride Road 289 if you hope to get

anywhere quickly. **Cross** to the **south side** of the main road just past **Mainroth,** and gain a **paved route** along the train tracks. Swing **left** for **Maineck** at **Mainklein** (any hints you're following the Main Valley here?).

Endure hilly but much more peaceful cycling as you ride through **Maineck, Prügel,** and on to **Altenkunstadt.** Continue **straight** for **Strossendorf,** another pretty village. Watch for a roadside **lumber mill** (on the right) and take the **next right** onto a **gravel road** marked by a **bike sign.** Pedal this silent route to an unwelcome reunion with the **main road (now Road 173)** at **Hochstadt.** Fortunately, there's a **paved roadside bike route** from Hochstadt to **Trieb.**

**Recross** the main road in Trieb, and **climb** through the village to go up and over the ridgeline. Finish your day with a **quick descent** to the edge of **Lichtenfels. Cross** the main road once again, and gain a **secondary route** into the city center. If you're in the market for a campsite, you'll pick up campground signs from the secondary road. Pedal on to find a pleasant riverside spot with excellent facilities and lots of cyclists.

Lichtenfels's center boasts a handful of hotels, if you need a bed, and the city itself is a delight to explore. It's filled with attractive half-timbered buildings and interesting churches, and the old core is flanked by handsome gate towers.

## Lichtenfels to Bamberg: 42 kilometers

Continue with the secondary road through Lichtenfels's **center,** and shun the turnoff signed for Coburg. Watch for a hard-to-spot turn to the **left** marked by a small sign for **Vierzehnheiligen** and a graphic of two hikers. Hop onto this tiny route and head into a **steady ascent** to reach the hilltop pilgrimage church dedicated to the 14 saints of intercession. The Church of Vierzehnheiligen is an unforgettable example of German baroque, with a heavenly interior that gives new meaning to the word exuberant.

Pause to catch your breath on the church's terrace, and enjoy a tremendous view across the Main Valley to the hilltop **Kloster Banz,** then descend with the auto road from the church to gain the route toward **Staffelstein.** The valley road has a fair amount of traffic, but the terrain is gentle and the towns along the way are picturesque. At **Ebensfeld,** swing **left** for **Schesslitz** to get on a much quieter road toward the southeast. You'll leave the river to **ascend a low ridge,** then pedal on to **Kleukheim.**

Kleukheim is an enchanting village, and the road through town is lined with flower-bedecked houses. Like so many Bavarian villages, Kleukheim is a testimony to the German commitment to attractive, well-kept towns. Continue with your quiet route to **Schesslitz,** and swing **right** with the main road toward **Bamberg.** Traffic increases significantly here, but you'll pick up a paved **bike path** paralleling the main road soon after.

Enjoy pleasant cycling into **Memmelsdorf** (watch for the handsome **Seehof Palace** on the left), and push on into the heart of **Bamberg.** As you enter the city, you'll continue **straight** with the main road (**Memmelsdorfer Strasse**), then swing **left** onto **Ludwigstrasse** to cycle past the train station. There's a **tourist office** nearby on Hauptwachstrasse. From the train station, take a **right** onto **Luitpoldstrasse** to cross the **Main-Donau Canal** and continue into the old core.

Bamberg has two youth hostels, a host of hotels, and a pleasant campground (Campingplatz Insel) about 4 km south of town. (Please read the opening paragraph of our route from Bamberg for directions to the campground and one of Bamberg's hostels.) You may want to take a day off to explore this charming city, as it's filled with worthwhile sights.

Begin at Bamberg's impressive cathedral (*Dom*) and pay your respects to the "Bamberg Rider," a famous thirteenth-century equestrian statue. Then admire the wonderful Domplatz and its terraced rose garden. Bamberg's streets are filled with delights, as well. Colorful buildings, remarkable churches, and a charming riverfront setting provide the town with an unforgettable ambience. And the city's Old Town Hall (*Altes Rathaus*) on its perch in the middle of the Regnitz River will surely tempt your camera trigger finger to fly.

## Bamberg to Volkach: 70 kilometers

Return to the banks of the **Main-Donau Canal** and follow the **bike path** toward the **south** as you ride away from Bamberg's center. If you're pedaling on a weekend, you'll have lots of company on the bike route. Head for the suburb/village of **Bug** (there's a youth hostel here), and continue on the road along the **Regnitz River** to pass a campground turnoff not long after.

Proceed south along the west bank of the Regnitz. There's a paved **bike path** paralleling the road. When the bike path swings away to the **right,** stay with the path, and pedal on to an **intersection** with another road. Go **right** here to ride to **Waizendorf.** You'll cross a secondary road coming from Bamberg here (a more direct route from Bamberg's center if you're not camping) and continue on to **Unteraurach.**

**Cross Road 22** in Unteraurach and stay **straight** with signs for **Stegaurach.** At **Walsdorf,** angle **left** for **Steinsdorf** to begin a **steady climb** through trees. Descend to cycle along the **Rauhe**

**Ebrach,** passing **Schonbrunn, Rauhenebrach,** and **Unter Steinbach** along the way. Attractive villages, bright fields of sunflowers, and quiet pedaling will make the minutes pass pleasantly. Puff through a **steady climb** then enjoy a **quick descent** to **Dingolshausen.** Rolling hills lead on to **Gerolzhofen,** a busy market town with an inviting core.

A much busier road will carry you the 12 km from Gerolzhofen to **Volkach** (there's a bike route as far as Frankenwinheim, if you want to avoid the main road). You'll begin to see vineyards and wine villages as you pedal on toward your reunion with the Main River. **Krautheim** and **Obervolkach** are each a treat. Enter **Volkach** and swing to the **right** through the **town gate** to explore the Hauptstrasse, a flamboyant *Rathaus,* and a host of lovely half-timbered buildings. Volkach has a convenient riverside campground and a handful of indoor accommodations to meet your needs.

## Volkach to Würzburg: 54 kilometers

From Volkach's center, return to the **junction** outside the town gate, and veer **right** to cross the **Main River** toward **Astheim.** Once across the river, take the **left** turn signed for **Dettelbach** to gain a delightfully quiet road beside the river. Pedal along the base of steeply sloped vineyards and marvel at the beauty of the German countryside as you savor a simply gorgeous stretch of cycling. The "party" ends abruptly as you head into a **very steep ascent** to **Neuses** and leave your riverside ride behind.

Continue on across the ridgetop to **Dettelbach,** a charming wine city with streets that beg for exploration. Then continue along a much busier road beside the **west bank** of the Main through **Mainstockheim** and on to **Kitzingen.** You'll pick up a **paved bike route** for your final kilometers to Kitzingen. The lively city boasts several hotels and a deluxe campground.

Leave Kitzingen along the **right bank** of the Main, pedaling the road signed for **Sulzfeld.** Enjoy another stretch of scenic cycling as the road winds past vine-clothed hillsides and fortified wine villages. Each town will tempt you to stop and savor. Abandon the main road at **Segnitz** to pedal down to the banks of the Main. You can cross the river here for a closeup look at **Marktbreit,** another tantalizing Bavarian town.

Return to the **right bank** to pedal on to **Frickenhausen.** Flanked by a pair of stout gate towers, the pleasant town is just a warmup for the day's real charmer—**Ochsenfurt.** You'll have to cross the **river** to enter this gemlike city, but it's worth the detour. Ochsenfurt will delight you with colorful streets lined with half-timbered houses, an ornate *Rathaus,* and a noteworthy church. Linger and enjoy, then return to the **right bank** to pedal on toward **Sommerhausen.** (There is a secondary road along the Main's left bank, but it's narrow and busy.)

Shun the busy right bank road and follow the right bank's **paved riverside bike path** instead. You'll enjoy more enchanting scenery as you swing north through Sommerhausen, **Randersacker,** and on to **Würzburg.** The city's **Marienberg Fortress** will float into your view as you approach the center, hovering above a cloud of vineyards. If you're in the market for a campground, there's a wonderful tents-only site at Würzburg's Kanu Club (kayak club) about 2 km from the center. It's on the left bank of the Main, but you can reach it via a pedestrian bridge (cross and continue downstream) before you hit the city proper.

Pedal on to Würzburg with the river. Although it's a massive city, Würzburg feels quite "comfy" in the pedestrian-friendly neighborhoods beside the Main. You'll find **tourist offices** at the train station and the *Marktplatz.* Get directions to the city's youth hostel or a convenient hotel. Then stow your bicycle and set off on foot to explore this wonderful river city.

Climb away from the Main and into the busy streets of the downtown core for a look at Würzburg's cathedral and a visit to the Residenz. A tour of this bishops' palace is well worth the Deutschmarks it will cost you. And the surrounding park (Hofgarten) is a treat for picnickers and wanderers alike. On the opposite bank of the Main, the Marienberg Fortress invites another climb. The fortress holds a regional museum that's worth a visit, too.

## Würzburg to Miltenberg: 70 kilometers

We decided to cut a bend of the Main River as we left Würzburg on our way to Wertheim, but that meant pedaling up a very big hill to get across the ridge. If you have the time and inclination, stay beside the river and meander toward Wertheim instead. You'll cycle more than double the kilometers, but you may have a more pleasant ride.

If you do decide to "lop the loop," leave Würzburg by crossing to the **left bank** of the Main, then get on the **small road** signed for **Frankenwarte. Climb precipitously** as you leave the river valley. The hill just seems to go on and on. You'll finally gain a secondary road at **Höchberg.** (If you don't mind steady traffic in exchange for a more gradual climb, take Road 8 for Frankfurt out of Würzburg, and climb to Höchberg with this route.) From Höchberg, follow signs for **Eisingen,** then pedal on to **Waldbrunn.**

Beyond Waldbrunn, you'll be forced to go **left** on the busy **Road 8/ U30** for a short stretch, then escape with another **left** for **Helmstadt** and the **freeway entrances.** Pedal through Helmstadt and **Holzkirchausen,** then continue **straight** for **Markt-Heidenfeld.**

Angle **left** when the road branches to cycle on to **Kembach** on a wonderfully silent road.

A **long downhill glide** leads through **Dietenhan** and **Urphar,** where you'll finally rejoin the **Main.** Pedal a **bike path** along the main road as you push onward through a forested river valley to arrive at the fascinating riverside town of **Wertheim.** Swing off the road to pedal into the city, situated at the crossroads of the Main and Tauber Valley bike routes. Wertheim is crammed with bike tourers in the summer months, and you'll probably enjoy simply sitting in a doorway and watching the tourers pedal past.

*Wertheim is a crossroads of German bike routes.*

If you're not set on cycling to Frankfurt for any reason (i.e., a flight home, a leap to Heidelberg and the start of Tour No. 10, or a hookup with the Rhine bike route toward castle country and the north), consider heading south from here instead. The Tauber Valley bike route (*Taubertal Radweg*) is a winner, and you'll enjoy the quiet pedaling it offers a whole lot more than you'll enjoy the harrowing cycling the Frankfurt area holds in store.

Whatever direction you're heading from Wertheim, don't leave before you pay homage to this delightful little city. Stroll through the lively *Marktplatz,* and walk to the nearby Gothic church (*Stadtkirche*). It's filled with carved tombs for the Counts of Wertheim and overlooked by Wertheim's lofty castle. If you need a room, Wertheim has plenty of hotel keepers willing to accommodate sweaty cyclists.

Before you push on toward Frankfurt, you may want to seek advice from one of the tourers arriving from that direction. When we pedaled this route in 1991, the secondary road on the right bank of the Main boasted both the signed bike route and gobs of traffic, while the main road on the left bank appeared to have a bike route under construction. We pedaled the **left bank** and endured heavy traffic there, but the river valley is narrow and scenic and the cycling is effortless.

There are several campgrounds on the way to **Miltenberg,** but you'll find a very convenient site on the **right bank** of the Main, just across from Miltenberg's captivating center. If you're in need of indoor lodgings, hunt around in Miltenberg's old core, taking time for a stroll along the attractive Hauptstrasse or a cold drink in the picture-perfect *Marktplatz.*

## Miltenberg to Frankfurt (Airport): 64 kilometers

Leave Miltenberg along the **right bank** of the Main and pedal the road signed for **Gross-heubach.** It's worth following the **signed bike route** through here, as many of the early kilometers are along a nice asphalt path beside the river. Eventually, the bike route will deposit you on a fairly busy secondary road toward **Erlenbach.**

Swing down off the main route to cycle a **smaller road** through **Erlenbach.** Angle **left** just before crossing the **train tracks** when your small road heads back toward the busier route. Gain more quiet, forested cycling as you pedal on, then veer **left** to cross the **Main** before **Elsenfeld** (the turn is signed for **Obernburg**). Ride through Obernburg's compact center, flanked by watchful gate towers, then depart the city with the road toward **Gross-Wallstadt.**

Suffer through 3 km of busy road, then watch for a **bike-route sign** leading **left** for **Grossbostheim** (it's just before your road crosses over Road 469). Savor a paved and peaceful route through endless fields as you follow a straight-arrow road to an **intersection** with the secondary road for **Grossbostheim.** Go **left** here and cycle the paralleling

**bike path** to the city. It seems redundant—but Grossbostheim is a charmer, too, full of more half-timbered buildings and as clean and perky as a German town can be.

Unfortunately, the cycling deteriorates from here. It seems that Frankfurt spews forth cars in ever-expanding rings, and you'll find little in the way of quiet pedaling between Grossbostheim and the Rhine. Our advice is this—don't ride anywhere near Frankfurt. If you want to see this enormous city, or if you're simply heading in so that you can head out on a flight for home, hop aboard a train in Grossbostheim or Aschaffenburg. Train travel with bicycles is a breeze in Germany. You can buzz into Frankfurt's central train station, do your sightseeing, pack up your bike—then buzz out on a 12-minute airport-bound line. Spend a few Deutschmarks and save yourself a lot of frightening kilometers. Please.

If you're intent on pedaling to the airport, or if you're bound for Mainz and the Rhine Valley (as we were), swing **right** in Grossbostheim for **Aschaffenburg,** then go **left** just after for **Schaafheim.** Pedal this secondary road to Schaafheim, then angle **right** to ride toward **Babenhausen.** You'll hit a **main road** before Babenhausen and go **right.** Then veer **left** just after to pedal into the city.

Ride through Babenhausen and press on with signs for **Rodgau.** The towns are long and unfriendly as you pass through **Nieder-Roden, Ober-Roden,** and on toward **Rödermark.** Watch for a **bike sign** leading **right** for **Dietzenbach** before you hit Road 486 (suicide), and attempt to follow this poorly signed cycle route through **Dietzenbach, Götzenhain, Dreieich,** and **Buchschlag.** Deciphering the bike route is a royal pain, but if it keeps you off the main roads for a while, it's probably worth the trouble.

You'll reach a sign for the **Frankfurt airport** leading **right** onto a terrifying red road. If that's the way you're headed, good luck! We shuddered through some spine-tingling kilometers on this road, then dove off as quickly as we could, bound for Mainz and the Rhine River.

# TOUR NO. 14

# PEDALING ON THE PELOPONNESE

*Patras to Athens, Greece*

*Distance:* 899 kilometers (559 miles)
*Estimated time:* 14 riding days
*Best time to go:* April, May, June, September, or October
*Terrain:* Murderous hills and magnificent scenery
*Connecting tours:* Tour No. 15

Greece. Just the word evokes visions of sparkling blue sea and brilliant beaches, haunting ruins and pulsating sun. But Greece for the cyclist is so much more—endless hillsides of shimmering olive trees trembling in the afternoon breeze, the quiet smiles of black-garbed women sitting atop dusty donkeys, a welcome pause to watch as a flowing melody of bell-collared goats crosses a lonely road.

But Greece, despite its incredible richness in scenery, climate, and culture, is not a land that bestows its treasures without charge. And the Peloponnese Peninsula is one of the most generous and yet most miserly of all Greek hosts. So lighten your load and train your body for a hill-studded ride that will challenge, exhaust, and test you. Then let the harsh and aching beauty of this ancient land wash away your weariness with the warm massage of gentle Mediterranean waves and with the titillating scent of oleander on the evening breeze.

**CONNECTIONS.** The Greeks have had a maritime civilization for thousands of years, and one of the best ways to reach the country is by sea. You can get to Patras and the start of this tour via ferries from Yugoslavia or from Ancona or Brindisi, Italy. If you'll be entering and leaving Greece from the international airport near Athens, you can load your bicycle on a train or pedal the Piraeus-to-Patras portion of Tour No. 15 to reach this tour's beginning.

**INFORMATION.** Write in advance to the Greek National Tourist Office, 645 Fifth Avenue, Olympic Tower, New York, New York 10022, and be sure to ask for the excellent Athens map they provide. Once in Greece, consult offices of the Greek National Tourist Organization (GNTO) for free English-language literature. Rand McNally's *Blue Guide Greece;* Michelin's *Green Guide Greece; The Real Guide: Greece;* and *Let's Go: Greece and Turkey* are guidebook options for your visit. If

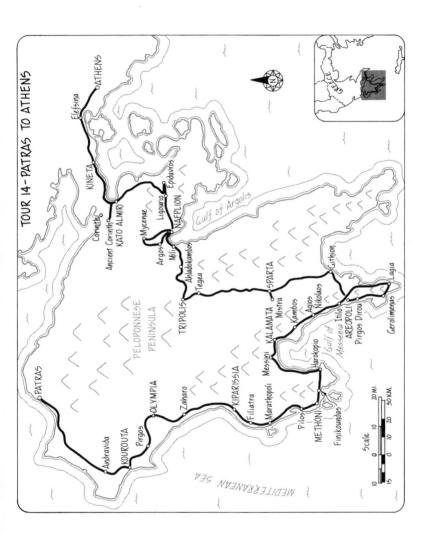

you're particularly interested in archaeological sites, the *Blue Guide* provides comprehensive coverage. Of course, if you feel like one Swiss cyclist we met, who admitted he was "tired of looking at a bunch of toppled stones," there's always the luxurious Mediterranean to welcome you at the end of your cycling day.

**MAPS.** For route finding, Map No. 5, *Peloponneso-Peloponnese,* published by Efstathiadis Group, is available in bookstores in Greece. It has a scale of 1:300,000 and gives place names in both Greek and Latinized forms. (The Latinized forms may differ slightly from map to map, so be prepared to do some creative interpreting.) An alternative map, *Peloponnese,* by Clyde Surveys Ltd., has a scale of 1:400,000, but Greek spellings are not provided.

**ACCOMMODATIONS.** Greece is a camper's paradise. Imagine a hillside, a spreading panorama of sea and olives before you, a tent tucked beneath the silver and green branches of a twisted olive tree. This dream is reality on the Peloponnese. Organized campgrounds in Greece are plentiful, inexpensive, and well equipped. The hot-water supply is often based on solar power, so showering in the evening will usually produce more steam than a morning "waker upper."

Although freelance camping is not officially allowed in any part of the country, ask permission from the friendly Greek landowners and be amazed by their unhesitating hospitality. We were able to camp in olive groves and on beaches, and were constantly delighted by the beauty that greeted us through the open doorway of our tent.

Lodgings in hotels are generally affordable, especially in the off-season, when prices usually drop. Greek hosts are relaxed about bicycles, and they'll often provide a secure shed or a lobby corner for overnight lockups.

**SUPPLIES.** Shopping in Greece is an exercise in ingenuity and endurance. Products are often scattered among dozens of shops, each specializing in vegetables, fruit, cheese, beverages, or bread. Simply let go of your Western "one-stop-shopping" mentality, and you'll be delighted by the results of your excursions. Instead of meeting one shopkeeper, you'll meet five; instead of emerging with a plastic-coated hunk of tasteless cheese, you'll carry a paper-wrapped lump of tangy *feta;* instead of acquiring a hard, cold loaf of bread, you'll cradle a hot bundle that begs for immediate consumption.

"The climate is always right" is the rule Greek shopkeepers live by when establishing their store hours. Shops open about 8:00 A.M. and close in the evening at 7:00 or 7:30 P.M., with a midday respite from the heat that lasts from 1:30 to 5:00 P.M. Saturday morning is the last sure bet for weekend shopping, and the majority of stores are closed Saturday afternoon and Sunday.

If you need bike parts in Greece, only the large cities offer much of a selection. There are several good bicycle shops in Athens, clustered near Omonia Square on Eolou Street.

## Patras to Kourouta: 85 kilometers

The tour begins in Patras, the largest city on the Peloponnese Peninsula and a major port for ferry traffic with Yugoslavia and Italy. Check at the **GNTO office** near the ferry terminal to pick up armfuls of free literature on the country. Patras has a conveniently located youth hostel, as well as several campgrounds 5 to 10 km east of the city. Pedal east from the ferry terminal on the harbor road, and you'll see camping signs within a few kilometers. There are several hotels in Patras, too.

To begin the tour, leave Patras on the **main road west,** following signs for **Pirgos.** (Most main road signs give names in both Greek and Latinized forms.) The flat, four-lane road skirts the sea. Traffic lessens and the road narrows as you draw away from the city. For a brief escape from the cars, turn off toward **Rogitika** onto a **small road** beside the sea. The road deteriorates, becoming dirt after about 5 km. Swing inland to regain the **main road** just before you lose the pavement.

The nicely surfaced main road has a wide shoulder most of the way to **Kourouta.** The New National Road and the Old National Road intertwine along this section, sometimes going their separate ways, sometimes merging into one. Both are signed for Pirgos. The New Road is smooth and fast, but the Old Road is more interesting, winding through the small towns along the route.

Try this combination. Follow the **Old Road** to **Kato Ahaia,** the **New Road** to **Andravida,** then the **Old Road** once more through **Gastouni** and on to where it loses itself in the **New Road.** At the **main turnoff** for **Kourouta** (ignore the first Kourouta sign pointing down a gravel road to the sea), follow a paved road to the **right** to reach a pleasant campground just before the small town. Take time for an afternoon swim on the excellent beach near the campground.

## Kourouta to Olympia: 40 kilometers

Return to the **main road** and follow signs for **Pirgos.** Pause to practice your multistop shopping in Pirgos's frenetic downtown. You'll emerge with a good appetite and the makings of a great picnic lunch. Walk your bicycle through the city hubbub, then remount to follow signs for **Olympia,** branching **left** after the **center** of town.

Hills increase and the road narrows during the 21 winding kilometers to Olympia. We realized we were on a popular sightseeing route when a toddler waved and called to us from the roadside, "Hello tourist, hello tourist." In Olympia, choose among three campgrounds, several hotels, and a youth hostel. Camping Diana is the closest campground to the archaeological site. Tucked into a hillside above the city, it's well equipped, clean, and offers solar-heated showers.

*The remnants of an ancient pillar grace the ruins at Olympia.*

Olympia rolls out the tourist carpet in a big way. Collect English-language reading material, maps, and postcards in the shop-infested downtown, then escape to the archaeological site on the edge of town to wander the extensive ruins, stirred by visions of those first Olympic athletes. If you can tear yourself away from the haunting beauty of the stones, visit the museum nearby.

## Olympia to Kiparissia: 59 kilometers

Leave Olympia on the **Krestena** road and climb a **short, steep hill** before descending to the **Alfios River.** Turn **left** toward **Krestena** after crossing the river, and follow the valley to **Makrisia,** a fascinating little city on a hill. Pedal through town, peeking in doorways to watch old women and black-robed priests on their morning shopping rounds. Then continue on the rolling road toward Krestena.

At the **unmarked junction** just **before Krestena,** turn **right** and pedal over a small **hill,** then go **left** on the **main coast road** signed for **Kiparissia.** Pass through pine forest and olive-covered hillsides with the sea beyond. Small ascents and descents break up the mostly level riding. Watch for the old fort on the hill above Kiparissia, a midsize town with lots of shops and a sprinkling of hotels.

## Kiparissia to Methoni: 62 kilometers

Continue along the **coast road,** following signs for **Pilos. Filiatra** is a confusing jumble of streets and intersections, but stay with the labyrinthine route signed for **Pilos** and you'll make it through. Veer **right** onto a paved turnoff for **Ag. Kiriaki** 4 km beyond Filiatra. At the **T** intersection that follows, turn **left** to ride on a quiet asphalt road along the coast, passing discos and vacation homes along the way.

If you're looking for a secluded beach for camping, there are several opportunities in the area. We camped on a lovely beach behind a small cafe, enjoyed an evening of conversation with its friendly Greek-American owner, and woke at dawn to watch a shepherd lead his flock along the water's edge.

The **secondary road** continues along the flat coast to **Marathopoli.** Here, you can turn left to regain the main road at Gargaliani (8 km), thus guaranteeing a look at **Nestor's Palace** (and a steep climb, as well). Or you can continue on the quiet **secondary road,** trading the ascent to Nestor's Palace for about 5 km of unpaved road (area residents assured us the road would be paved in a few years, so hope for the best).

For the latter route, turn **right** at the **junction in Marathopoli,** then go **left one block before the sea.** This is a confusing section, and it's subject to changes because of ongoing roadwork. Muddle through the unpaved kilometers (don't try it after a heavy rain!), regain the **paved road,** and turn **left** to reach the **main thoroughfare** toward **Pilos.** Go **right** on the **main road** and pedal up a steep incline just before the **Kalamata junction.** Turn **right** at the junction and continue climbing for **Pilos,** then descend steeply to the sea.

From the compact harbor town of Pilos, follow signs for **Methoni** up a grueling **2-km ascent.** Proceed past the turnoff for Mesohori and continue following signs for **Methoni,** sailing down a silver ribbon of road through whispering olives. Signs in Methoni lead to the impressive seaside fortress. There are lodging options in the small city, and there's a campground that stays open until mid-October.

# Methoni to Kalamata: 80 kilometers

Leave Methoni and follow signs for **Harokopio.** Climb a **long, steep hill** to **Evangelismos** and let the beauty of the Greek landscape recompense you for your labor. A **steep descent** leads to the sea at **Finikoundas,** a town set on a curving white beach. Follow the sea for a short while, climb a short, steep hill, then descend again. Pass a pretty seaside campground and begin a **long, punishing climb** from the sea. The road turns to gravel for about 200 meters but returns to asphalt soon after.

Pedal through **Akritohori** and continue climbing toward Lamia. At the **junction** before **Lamia,** ignore the road branching off to the left and continue **straight** into town. In customary Greek fashion, the road surface goes from good to awful in Lamia, then improves again after the city. You'll be rewarded for the day's toilsome climbs and bumpy passages by the smiling Greeks working beside their patient donkeys, by the laughing men who fly by in their dented pickups and honk enthusiastic greetings, and by the panorama of hill after hill of olives, somber green against the dancing blue of the sky.

Enjoy a **long descent** toward **Harokopio** and cruise up a short hill just before town. At the **junction** in the city, veer **left** for **Kalamata.** If you have the time and energy, you can make the 8-km round trip down the hill to **Koroni.** The seaside city has a large, dilapidated Venetian fortress and an attractive harbor. Unfortunately, it also has a 4-km climb back to Harokopio and the main road.

Follow the gently undulating coast along the brilliant blue Gulf of Messenia, drinking in views of the cliff-faced mountains across the water. Climb a slight hill before **Rizomilos,** then gain the main **Pilos–Kalamata road.** Traffic increases here, but it's not unpleasant and drivers are polite and friendly (friendly in Greece means lots of honks). There are several campgrounds along the coast in this area.

Cycle through **Messini** and join the **main road** approaching **Kalamata** from Megalopoli. Pass through **Asprohoma** and take the turnoff to the **right** marked for the **New Beach Road** (it's just past a large **factory**) to bypass the Kalamata congestion. Descend along this secondary road and turn **left** at the **junction** for **Kalamata,** then go **right** at a sign for **Areopoli.** The way is unmarked from here. Skirt along the edge of Kalamata's harbor, passing a large docking area and turning **right** to follow the road to the sea.

There are several campgrounds to choose from along the beach just past Kalamata, or you can swing up into the city if you need a room.

# Kalamata to Areopoli: 79 kilometers

Follow the **coast road** along the Gulf of Messenia and turn **right** at the **T** intersection for **Areopoli.** The road begins to climb at **Alniro.**

The grade is moderate to **Kambos,** a small town watched over by a ruined castle and by dozens of men in streetside cafes. Descend briefly to the rugged **Koskaras Defile** and stop on the bridge to enjoy the impressive view. Climb again, winding among dry golden hills and snaking across gorges, curving around steep, mounded hillsides covered with olives—climbing, climbing, climbing.

Reach the summit at last and look down on the sea and 8 km of **switchbacks to Kardamili,** a handsome resort town with campgrounds, shops, and a well-stocked grocery store. The descent is steep and loaded with sharp curves, so don't let the exhilaration of speed keep your fingers too far from your brakes.

Stay beside the sea between Kardamili and **Agios Nikolaos.** If it's late in the day, you might want to stop at one of the campgrounds or hotels along the way. A gruesome series of **switchbacks** that seems to last forever awaits you after Agios Nikolaos. Struggle up the **punishing hill,** and try not to watch the progress of the cars that pass you if you'd rather not see how far you have left to climb.

Reach **Platsa** after about 8 km, with the worst of the hill behind, and enjoy a ridgetop ride through tiny towns of tumbled stone—towns with unique dome-topped churches, men who cheer your courage, and women who laugh and wave from doorways. From **Itilo,** there's a striking view of the ruined fortress of **Kelefa,** its old walls tracing a massive rectangle on the hillside.

Plunge down a **steep descent** to the sea and follow the road along the beach to **Limeni,** a small town with a gemlike harbor and a toppled church. A **4-km ascent** up another steep grade leads to **Areopoli,** hotel rooms, and a blissful release from your bike. There is no campground in Areopoli, but the olive groves outside town provide a wealth of quiet tent spots from which to choose (don't forget to ask permission to camp on private land).

## Areopoli to Areopoli (via the Mani Peninsula): 78 kilometers

If you have the time and your legs still have the strength, don't skip a day trip around the unforgettable Mani Peninsula, using Areopoli as your base. Hauling your gear along this route would be a punishing affair, but you can manage the 78-km loop as a strenuous one-day trek if you get an early start—and if you don't stop to shoot every single roll of film you own on the scenery.

What an incredible day of riding you'll have on the Mani Peninsula! The hills are every bit as tough as the inhabitants—a people never conquered by the Turks, even when all their comrades fell around them. The terrain will exhaust you, but the scenery will repay you

*Climbing toward the Mani tower town of Lagia*

generously for all your labor. Make the elliptical loop in a clockwise direction, cashing in on the morning sun on the mountainous eastern side of the peninsula and tackling the challenging hills early, before heat and fatigue make them too cruel.

In our 78-km day of cycling in this lonely section of Greece, we were passed by fewer than thirty cars. However, we did have to deal with one very pokey flock of sheep and several "haawwnking" donkeys. Be sure to carry a pump, emergency repair tools, and lots of liquids, as towns are few and far between.

Pedal south through **Areopoli** and turn **left** at the **junction** for **Kotronas** 2 km beyond the city. The road climbs to **Himara,** then descends to **Loukadika,** a stone city guarding a ridge that overlooks the sea. **Descend steeply** to a turnoff for **Kotronas** and turn **right** for **Kokala.** Everywhere you look you'll see lonely square towers perched on the rugged heights and clustered in the somber towns, their stout walls giving testimony to the war-filled history of the area.

A series of short ups and downs leads to **Kokala** on the sea, then a **punishing climb** up a golden, tower-studded ridge leads to the lofty town of **Lagia.** From Lagia, continue around the hillside and up another short hill to gain a fine vista of the sea. Descend steeply to **Alika,** and turn **right** at the **junction** for **Gerolimenas,** a more modern Mani town with a nice harbor and a grocery store. Climb a short hill and then enjoy the relaxing 22 km back to Areopoli along the peninsula's western shore.

If time allows, the 5-km descent to the caves near Pirgos Dirou makes a pleasant addition to the day. Turn left at the **junction** in **Pirgos Dirou** to reach the **well-signed caves.** A 45-minute boat ride through cool passageways glittering with frosted white formations provides a welcome break for hill-weary legs. Unfortunately, the steady climb back up the road for Areopoli is the unavoidable aftermath of the sidetrip.

## Areopoli to Sparta: 70 kilometers

Leave **Areopoli** on the road for **Githion,** climbing a gentle hill, then following a creek bed down a **long, gradual descent.** The road follows valleys cut between mounded hills, providing easy riding and pleasant scenery. Just before Githion, follow the edge of the sea past bright citrus groves and several large campgrounds. Climb a small hill and swing down to the attractive harbor town of Githion. (You can make ferry connections to Piraeus and Crete from here, or, if you're in the mood for solitude, you might consider skipping Sparta and taking the more easterly coastal route toward the north instead.)

Follow the **waterside route** through town to an intersection where the road branches in a **Y.** Take the **left** branch (unmarked when we were there) and wind through a small business district before reaching the **edge of town** and a sign (in Greek) for **Sparta.** The narrow, twisting road climbs into the hills, **ascending steeply** away from Githion. Enter a gentle valley, then pedal up another long, steep hill.

Climb until just past the turnoff for Monemvassia, with spectacular views of terraced, olive-covered hillsides. Beyond the junction, descend steeply and follow a rolling route toward **Sparta.** The final 20 km of the ride offer impressive views of the rugged mountains to the west, but heavy traffic and lots of horn-happy drivers make the riding hectic.

Sparta is a modern-looking town that gives little evidence that it was once the home of the illustrious warriors who ruled this harsh and rugged corner of Greece. Explore the mounded hillock on the edge of town, and the past will come alive in its quiet sunken theater and the etchings on its timeworn stones.

Sparta has several affordable hotels, dozens of cafes and shops, and entertaining city streets. There is a luxurious campground (complete with a swimming pool) 2 km outside town on the road toward Mistra. Be sure to follow the well-marked route to **Mistra** (7 km), a hauntingly beautiful Byzantine city on an olive-speckled hillside. The climb to Mistra is gradual, but the final 1½ km between the modern town and the archaeological site are steep. Set aside a morning to visit the spot. You won't be disappointed.

## Sparta to Tripolis: 60 kilometers

Leave Sparta following signs for **Tripolis.** You'll discover what made the ancient Spartans so tough as you **climb steadily** for the next **20 km** through mounded hills, barren except for scattered olive trees and scores of beehives. A steep but disappointingly short downhill leads into another **10 km of climbing,** then on into a splendid high valley rimmed by golden mountains. Reach a ridgetop 45 km beyond Sparta and savor the view of Tripolis on its green and yellow plain of apple orchards, vegetables, and olives.

Descend quickly to the flatland below, but sneak a look at the trim, tile-roofed town of **Manthirea** along the way. We bypassed Tripolis and shortened our route by taking the turnoff to the right for Tegea. If you need to find a bed, continue toward Tripolis on the main road and follow signs for the city. Leave Tripolis on the route for Argos the next morning.

To take the **shortcut** route and avoid Tripolis' urban sprawl, turn **right** for **Tegea.** Follow the quiet road past the small **Tegea museum,** turn **left** at the **T,** then go **right** toward **Lithovounia.** Follow the road straight into **Lithovounia,** then angle **left** as you pass the small town. Cross some typically treacherous Greek **train tracks** and turn **right** on the road for **Argos.** You'll have acres of wild campsites to choose from, and you can spend the night, as we did, sheltered by a lone olive tree and happily trading the lights of the big city for the brilliant Mediterranean sky.

## Tripolis to Nafplion: 60 kilometers

Pedal the **Argos road** through the long **Tripolis Plain.** Climb along a steep hillside, passing above Ahladokambos in the valley below. Cross a high ridge after **5 km of climbing** and make a **steep, switchback-studded descent** to the sea. Be careful on this scenic but dangerous downhill. Gain the coastal road to **Nafplion** by turning

**right** at **Mili,** which is located a few kilometers beyond **Lema.**

Approach Nafplion and enjoy fine views of the harbor town, shadowed by its massive fortress and fronted by a tiny fortified island in the bay. There are a campground and a hostel in Nafplion and you'll find plenty of hotels in the lively, touristy downtown. Go for an early-morning walk along the harbor and watch sun-tanned fishermen working on their boats, or dive into the city streets and absorb the unique flavor of a midsized Greek town.

## Nafplion to Nafplion (via Tiryns, Mycenae, and Argos): 47 kilometers

If your appreciation for toppled stones is still intact, consider a day trip to Tiryns, Mycenae, and Argos from your base in Nafplion. Leave **Nafplion** on the road toward **Argos** and turn off for the ruined fortress of **Tiryns 3 km** later. It's just off the road, to the right. The site is well marked by road signs.

Return to the **main road** and go **right,** then take the next **turnoff** marked for **Ag. Trias.** Follow signs for **Mikines** along the level secondary road, passing orchards and small towns. Climb a short hill just before Mikines, turn **right** into the touristy city, and follow signs for **Mycenae** (**Mycenea** on the signs). Climb sharply to reach the archaeological site 2 km from town.

Some of the most impressive archaeological discoveries in modern history have been made in Mycenae. Marvel at the engineering wonder of Agamemnon's tomb, linger over the beauty of the Lion's Gate, and sense the striking loneliness of this 3,000-year-old city of tombs and tumbled stones, tucked into a wild hillside above Argos and the Gulf of Argolis. If you decide you want to linger longer, Mycenae has a youth hostel and two campgrounds.

To return to Nafplion, you can simply retrace your route back to the city if you prefer quiet riding, or you can take the **main road** from **Mikines** toward **Argos** if you'd like a look at that fortress-guarded city. The main road has a smoother surface than the secondary road, but heavier traffic makes riding less pleasant. In Argos, follow signs for Nafplion to pedal the 13 level kilometers back to your base.

## Nafplion to Kato Almiri: 79 kilometers

Leave Nafplion, following signs for **Epidavros.** Climb gradually for 25 km, passing through pleasant countryside and many small towns. In **Ligourio,** go **right** at the junction for **Epidavros,** then turn **left 3 km later** to reach the site. The amphitheater at Epidavros is like no other. Set among tree-dotted hills, the stone seats await their long-dead occupants, and the air within the structure trembles like a finely tuned instrument, amplifying the most delicate sounds with incredible clarity.

Some maps show a road from Epidavros directly to the sea, but the way was barricaded when we were there and road workers told us the route is no longer open. Retrace the ride **back to Ligourio,** then turn **right** in the city at the **junction** for **Nea Epidavros** and **Athens.** Throughout your ride from this point on, you'll see signs for Athens spelled in a variety of ways (Athene, Athine, Athina). All versions are recognizable.

Coast downhill, staying with signs for **Athens.** Descend almost to the sea, then pedal up a long, steady incline to cross a ridge. Descend steeply above a lovely bay, then climb once more up a gradual hill. There are fine views of the sea throughout the ride, and evergreen forests provide a welcome change from endless olives. From the final summit of the day, you'll get an enchanting look at the curving blue coastline stretching toward the Corinth Canal and mainland Greece.

Descend rapidly to the seaside town of **Kato Almiri.** There are several campgrounds on the beach. We shared our supper at Camp Poseidon with a friendly dog, two puppies, and a cheese-eating cat, then walked to the beach for a midnight swim under the stars.

## Kato Almiri to Kineta: 54 kilometers

From Kato Almiri, follow the **coast road** through **Loutro Elenis.** Turn **left** and climb gradually toward **Xilokeriza** and **Examilia.** Enter **Examilia** and turn **left** at the small town's **main intersection** (it's unmarked from this direction). As the road traverses the tip of the peninsula, look for the fortress of **Acrocorinth** ahead, its walls like jagged teeth on the mountainside. Pedal the 3 km to the **main Corinth road** and turn **left,** following signs for **Ancient Corinth.**

While the archaeological sites of Greece are gripping in their stark simplicity and wild beauty, the tourist towns that squat beside them are often quite depressing in their tacky commercialism. Save your mood for the site, and cruise through Ancient Corinth as rapidly as possible to seek the sun-bleached ruins just beyond the town.

Lock your bicycle under the watchful gaze of the ticket-booth attendant and spend a quiet hour wandering the extensive grounds. The Temple of Apollo with its fantastic sky-piercing columns is a definite highlight of the visit, and the on-site museum has several nice exhibits.

**Backtrack** to **Loutro Elenis,** then continue on the coastal road to reach the mouth of the **Corinth Canal.** Cross the canal on the **drawbridge** and get on the **nontoll road** for **Athens.** Follow the flat coastline east along the sea as the narrow, quiet road winds between the busy freeway and the seashore. At first it's rather dull, with ugly refineries, but these soon give way to millionaire mansions patrolled by barking German shepherds.

There are a few large **campgrounds** just **before Kineta,** or you can ask a friendly looking local for permission to camp on the beach. An evening under the glowing stars and a late-night swim in the sparkling phosphorescent lights of the Mediterranean will do much to wash away the traffic-induced tenseness of the day.

# Kineta to Athens (Campground): 46 kilometers

Beyond **Kineta,** the road climbs to wind along a cliffy section of coast, then descends before **Megara.** Follow signs for **Athens—Old Road** or **Athens—NonToll Road** to avoid the freeway route. **Bypass Megara** and climb a short hill before descending to the sea again. **Elefsina,** with a freighter-filled bay and truck-heavy streets, is an unpleasant interlude after the peace of the Peloponnese. As Athens draws nearer, noise, traffic, and big-city congestion follow.

Cruise through **Elefsina** and join the **main road** just beyond the city. There is a wide shoulder and lots of traffic. Skirt along the **edge of the bay,** then turn inland to climb a **long, gradual hill** with fleets of coughing cars and trucks. Reach the top and **Dafni,** with a Byzantine monastery church and a large, tree-shaded campground. The site is about 11 km from Athens's center, a thrilling 1/2 hour by bus. Be forewarned, though, that after a few nerve-rattling bus rides into Athens, you'll be convinced that all Greek bus drivers are former Indy 500 champs.

Another option for those who don't want to camp is to continue into Athens by bicycle. Proceed with care. The relaxed Greek drivers of the Peloponnese are nowhere to be found in the tire-squealing din of this enormous city. If you have to cycle in, do it on a weekend or during the midafternoon lull in traffic.

Head for the **Greek National Tourist Office** located in Syntagma Square. If you made it this far, you must have a city map, but you'll be able to get information on the sights and help with accommodations here. Athens boasts a score of inexpensive lodgings. Choose carefully, as quality and price can vary dramatically.

If you're ending your cycling trip in Athens with a flight for home, you can swing right for Piraeus after Elefsina to do an end run around the tangle of the enormous city and reach the **airport** to the south. There are several hotels in Piraeus, and there are campgrounds on the coast beyond the airport. Piraeus also offers ferry connections to Greece's sparkling islands, and you can hook up with Tour No. 15 from this busy port.

# TOUR NO. 15

# VISIONS OF THE ANCIENTS
### *Iraklion to Patras, Greece*

*Distance:* 668 kilometers (414 miles)
*Estimated time:* 10 riding days
*Best time to go:* April, May, June, September, or October
*Terrain:* Mix of moderate flatlands and punishing hills
*Connecting tours:* Tours No. 14 and 16

Crete is just big enough, just far enough from the Greek mainland, and just diverse enough in terrain, culture, and history to hang onto a tough independence that sets it apart from the rest of Greece.

You'll sense a difference in the people here if you've spent much time on the mainland or in the Peloponnese. Perhaps it's due to their familiarity with the thousands of tourist "invaders from the sea" that arrive each spring. Perhaps it's due to their pride in a heritage that reaches back to the Minoan Period (2600 to 1100 B.C.) and the roots of European civilization. Or perhaps it's simply because they're from Crete. Whatever the reason, the warm spontaneity of the Peloponnese Greeks is not as evident on Crete. You won't be awash in floods of honks when you're on the roads, and you won't find as many ready smiles, especially in the heavy tourist areas. You might even get a few refusals when you ask permission to camp.

But delve beneath the surface hardness of the Cretans with persistence, politeness, and sincere expressions of appreciation for the riches the island offers, and you'll uncover the wonderful Greek generosity and warmth that makes a visit here so special.

For a fantastic month of riding in some of Greece's loveliest and most challenging terrain, combine this tour of Crete and Delphi with the Peloponnese ride in Tour No. 14.

**CONNECTIONS.** You can get to Iraklion, Crete, and the start of this tour by taking a ferry from Piraeus, Athens's tumultuous port. If you fly into Athens, the airport is about 10 km from Piraeus's harbor. If you're cycling this tour as a continuation of Tour No. 14, pedal from Athens to Piraeus to catch the ferry. It's a 12-hour ride from Piraeus to Iraklion, and ferries run twice a day. Check at the tourist office in Athens or the ferry office in Piraeus for timetables and prices.

**INFORMATION.** Review the introductory material for Greece in

222

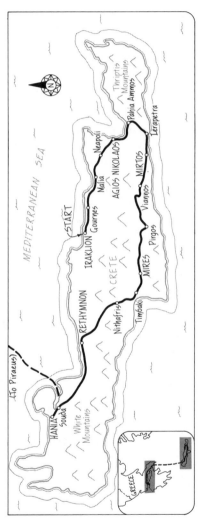

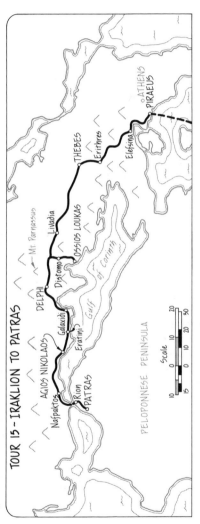

Pedaling on the Peloponnese (Tour No. 14) to prepare for your ride.

**MAPS.** There's an excellent 1:200,000 map of Crete available in bookstores on the island. Published by Freytag and Berndt, it shows hostels, campgrounds, hotels, archaeological sites, and churches, and provides small street maps for the island's major cities.

**ACCOMMODATIONS.** Refer to the accommodations information provided in the introduction to Tour No. 14.

**SUPPLIES.** Look for details on shopping hours and food purchases in the introduction to Tour No. 14.

## Iraklion to Agios Nikolaos: 68 kilometers

Arrive by ferry in Iraklion, Crete's main port and largest city. Despite its size and industry, Iraklion is an attractive spot. A Venetian fortress, arsenals, and other interesting remnants of Venetian rule make a walk through the city enjoyable. Don't skip a visit to the Archaeological Museum. It's a standout, even among its excellent Greek peers, and you'll begin to develop a concept of Crete's illustrious past from the hours you spend there.

From the ferry dock, follow signs for the **Archaeological Museum** to reach **Eleftherias Square** on the east side of the city. The **GNTO office** is across the street, and you can pick up literature on the city and the island there. Iraklion offers several affordable hotels, a less-than-charming youth hostel, and a large campground 5 km to the west, if you're planning an overnight stay. If you do stay in Iraklion, you can make the short day trip to **Knossos,** 6 km south of town, to visit the reconstructed palace of King Minos. It dates back to 1950 B.C.

To ride for Agios Nikolaos, leave **Eleftherias Square** on **Ikarou Street,** following signs for **Sitia.** Descend to ride through the city suburbs. Ignore the first right turn signed for **Agios Nikolaos,** and take the **second signed turn** to gain the **old road** beside the sea. The coastline is dotted with hotels and dirty beaches as you pedal east toward **Gournes,** where the old and new roads merge. Continue on to **Malia,** pedaling past hotels and roadside tourist towns.

Malia is a hopping tourist spot with a main street lined by cafes and postcard racks. There's a youth hostel in the city, or you can cycle about 12 km east to find Camping Sissi. Besides its popular beaches, Malia centers its tourist trade around the **Palace of Malia,** 3 km east of town. This is one of the three great Minoan palaces on Crete, along with those at Knossos and Phaestos. To reach the palace, cycle through Malia and swing **left** at a **sign for the archaeological site** beyond the town. Stroll among the prostrate stones and stretch your imagination with your legs.

Return to the **main road** and go **left.** The road **branches** soon after, with the new road swinging right to pass through the Gorge of

Selinari and the **old road** going **left** to take a curving, climbing route through the hills above. The new road collects most of the traffic and avoids the climb by diving into a long tunnel. You'll have a safer, more enjoyable ride if you angle **left** to weave through the hills. Ascend in **steep switchbacks** to **Vrahasi,** and enjoy a look at an unspoiled Cretan town, then descend to ride for **Neapoli.**

Follow signs for Neapoli and coast down into the city. Veer **left** at the **main square** in town, then go **right** soon after to gain the **old road** toward **Agios Nikolaos.** Continue on toward **Nikithianos,** watching for the stone windmills that overlook the olive groves. Keep **right** for **Agios Nikolaos** when the road **branches,** and pass thousands of olive trees as you ride over gentle terrain to **Houmeriakos.**

Pass **under the new road** and continue on to **Xirokambos.** Join the **new road** after Xirokambos, and go **left** soon after for the **center** of **Agios Nikolaos,** a pretty town set on a shining blue harbor. Shop-lined streets slope down to the boat-speckled bay, and outdoor cafes fill the waterfront. The city is one of Crete's most popular tourist spots. Listen to the clamor of languages being spoken by the tourists that swarm its streets, and you'll wonder how people from so many lands found such an out-of-the-way spot.

Agios Nikolaos's **tourist office** is on Koundourou Street, not far from the harbor. They'll be able to direct you to the city's youth hostel or to one of its scores of hotels.

## Agios Nikolaos to Mirtos: 50 kilometers

From Agios Nikolaos's **center,** climb away from the harbor and follow signs for **Ierapetra** to gain the **main road** southeast along the sea. Enjoy scenic riding as you cycle through undulating terrain, passing cliff-encircled bays of brilliant turquoise. Follow the up-and-down route to **Gournia,** the site of Crete's best-preserved Minoan town. You'll have a good view of the excavated city from the road.

Swing **right** for **Ierapetra** just past **Pahia Ammos,** and **turn inland** to cross to Crete's southern coast at the island's narrowest point. To the east, the sheer faces of the Thriptis Mountains spring from the valley floor, and you'll spot tiny white churches and scattered settlements as you **climb gradually** for about 6 km. Sail down the final stretch of road to Ierapetra while the valley winds whir in the flying blades of modern windmills in the fields along the way.

Ride **through Ierapetra,** a resort town with lots of lodging options, and turn west for **Mirtos.** You'll have flat seaside riding with some short hills as you pass dozens of greenhouses on the 15-km ride to Mirtos. This small town attracts scores of solitude-seeking travelers to its quiet beaches. There's no campground at Mirtos, but there are lots of rooms available in the town.

# Mirtos to Mires: 100 kilometers

As you ride away from Mirtos, you'll be leaving "tourist Crete" behind and exchanging hotels and postcard racks for several hours of tough mountain riding, a few kilometers of rough dirt roads, and an abundance of magnificent scenery that will make your days a joy. The farther you pedal from the tourist towns, the warmer the greetings, the more enthusiastic the waves, and the readier the smiles from people you pass along the way.

Leave Mirtos on the road signed for **Viannos** and **Iraklion.** Climb gradually for 2 km, then leave the valley to **ascend steeply** into olive-sprinkled hills. The road surface is good, traffic is light, and the inclines are murderous. The views out over the surrounding countryside will soothe your soul, even as your legs beg for mercy. Scattered level stretches and an isolated downhill or two break up the **14-km climb.**

Reach **Pefkos** and enjoy a short descent, then climb steeply to a ridge where a lone memorial guards the heights. The view from the point is almost worth the climb! You'll have mostly level riding beyond the ridge, then a quick **3-km descent** to **Viannos,** a small hillside town with a church and a handful of cafes. Climb a final **ridge** from Viannos, then **descend steeply** for 4 km toward **Martha.**

Veer **left** toward **Skinias** just past a **turnoff** for Martha, and coast down gradually past Skinias and on toward **Demati** and the Anapodaris River. Cross the bridge above the **Anapodaris River.** Swing to the **right** up a very steep hill into **Demati** and follow what may still be an unpaved road around the hill past **Favriana** and on toward **Kato Kastelliana.**

Scattered signs mark the route toward **Pirgos.** Stay to the right at **Ano Kastelliana** to bypass the town and reach a **signed junction.** Continue **straight** for **Pirgos.** Cruise into **Mesohori** and veer **right** for **Pirgos.** Then cycle the 6 km to the midsize town. Several cafes and small food stores line the main street.

From Pirgos, swing **right** for **Iraklion** and pedal into the level expanse of the broad, heavily cultivated **Mesara Plain.** You'll have stunning views of Crete's Mount Ida massif as you cycle along the valley floor. The snow-capped peaks seem out of place in the southern reaches of Greece, and their wild beauty contrasts sharply with the cultivated lands below.

Cycle easy terrain toward **Protoria** and go **right** toward **Iraklion,** then veer **left** just afterward for **Asimi.** Ride a gently rolling route along the northern edge of the plain, and pass through Asimi and **Stoli** on the way to **Ag. Deka** and the Roman ruins of **Gortys.** Gortys was the capital of Roman Crete and was once the largest city on the island. Stop to look at the sixth-century church of **Agios Titus** (to the right of the road), said to be the site of the first bishopric of Crete. The tumbled stones of the Roman *Agora* lie beside the church, and beyond the Agora is the Roman *Odeum,* where a law code from 500 B.C. is inscribed in stone.

From Gortys, continue through level terrain with gradually increasing traffic to **Mires,** where the day's early hills will probably send you in search of a room. There are no campgrounds in the vicinity. Timbaki, 12 km farther on, also has hotels.

## Mires to Rethymnon (Rethimno): 80 kilometers

Follow signs for **Timbaki** away from Mires. Reach the turnoff for **Phaestos** about **6 km** beyond Mires. The Minoan palace at Phaestos is comparable to those at Malia and Knossos. If you want to take a look, it's a 2-km climb from the main road to reach the hilltop site. Then continue on the main road to **Timbaki,** a midsize town with a busy main street.

Pedal **straight** through town and continue toward the sea. Bypass the turnoff for Kokkinos Pirgos and **climb steeply** to a **ridgetop junction.** Turn **right** to follow a quiet, 61-km route toward **Rethymnon.** Pass through countless tiny mountain towns as you labor up and over the backbone of Crete. You'll have spectacular views of mountains, sea, and twisted olive trees to make up for your muscles' screams. Climb steadily to **Apodoulou,** following signs for Rethymnon. The road ascends more gradually after Apodoulou, winding past hillsides where lone shepherds watch their flocks.

Ride through **Nithafris** and **Kouroutes,** cross a ridge to **Apostoli,** then coast down to the narrow canyon beyond. Follow the canyon to **Filakio,** then enjoy a short stretch of level riding before climbing once again. Cross a ridge and descend steeply to **Prasies,** then continue on to reach a final downhill to the sea. At **Perivolia,** turn **left** on the **old coast road** to pedal the final 3 km into **Rethymnon.** If you want to camp, go right at Perivolia to reach a campground soon after.

Rethymnon's **tourist office** is near the waterfront. Stop for information on the town or to get help with your search for lodgings. There's a youth hostel in Rethymnon, as well as several hotels. Rethymnon is a wonderful city for strolling. It's big enough to be interesting, yet small enough to cover in a single afternoon. Walk along the old harbor to the Venetian fortress that rules a bluff above the sea. Turn into the city's narrow streets, overhung with balconies and lined with shops and cafes, and walk back toward your room, watching for minarets along the way.

# Rethymnon to Hania: 61 kilometers

From Rethymnon, follow signs for **Hania** as you pedal out of town. The road branches at **Atsipopoulo,** with the **new road** going **straight** and the **old road** angling to the **left.** The new road is level, smooth, and direct, but the old road is a better choice on heavy traffic days. We pedaled the new road.

Except for a short hill outside of Rethymnon, the riding is level for the first 20 km along the coast, and you'll have fine views of Crete's White Mountains as you pedal. There are scattered campgrounds along the way, and sandy beaches beckon beside the road. Swing inland to **climb gradually** for about 12 km, passing through fragrant pine forests and catching glimpses of the snow-capped mountains to the south. Old and new roads cross several times during the climb, so you'll have lots of opportunities to trade.

Angle toward the sea, descending to **Kalami** and continuing along the edge of **Souda Bay,** where dozens of ships rest at anchor. At **Tsikalaria,** about 5 km after you return to the sea, abandon the main road and swing **right** for **Souda.** Avoid a steep hill by pedaling through Souda, then follow the busy 6-km route into **Hania** from there.

Head for the Hania **tourist information office** at the city's Venetian harbor to get information on lodgings and ferry connections to Piraeus. You'll have to cycle back to Souda to catch the overnight ferry for the mainland. There's a youth hostel in Hania, as well as lots of hotels and pensions. Two campgrounds lie to the west of town. This is a delightful place to relax while you prepare for your return to mainland Greece.

Be sure to visit the Agora, a huge covered food market in the center of town. It's a visual delight of color, texture, and movement, and the sensual avalanche of smells, sounds, and tastes you'll find there will make the supermarkets back home seem incredibly dull. Walk through the old Venetian district behind the harbor, shop for sandals or a fisherman's hat in one of the shops, or climb the fortified hill west of the old city for a great view of the tiled roofs of the town.

The **ferry** from **Hania (Souda)** to **Piraeus** runs daily. Reserve a bunk or a room for the overnight trip, or simply claim a dark corner on the deck (protect your valuables) and snooze the hours away to your early morning arrival.

# Piraeus to Thebes: 75 kilometers

Arrive in the ship-filled, pollution-hazed harbor of Piraeus, and begin your ride to Delphi, Patras, and (perhaps) a ferry trip to Italy. If you're cutting this tour short with a flight for home, the international

*The covered market in Hania is a produce lover's paradise.*

airport at Athens isn't far away. To ride for Delphi, cycle along the edge of the **harbor** in a **counterclockwise** direction, and turn **right** on **Ag. Dimitriou.** Follow the busy street for about 2 km, then veer **left** at a sign for **Perama.**

Stay on this road to a **Y** intersection and then angle **right** for **Athens** (Athina) and **Patras** (Patra). Veer **left** for **Patras** soon after. This road was in the midst of a major construction project when we cycled it, so some of these turns may change. Basically, you'll be riding **toward Elefsina** from Piraeus.

Traffic to Elefsina is heavy and annoying, and you'll have a **steady climb** as you cycle away from Piraeus. A gradual descent leads to **Skaramangas.** Join the **main road** for **Elefsina** there. Abandon the main route about **8 km** later, turning **left** at the **sign** for **Non-Toll Road—Elefsina.** Pedal into Elefsina, following signs for **Corinth** (Korinthos), then go **right** onto the road for **Thebes** (Thive). Climb gradually past **Mandra,** then ascend a **punishing hill** to **Agios Sotira.**

Coast down into a cultivated valley, then climb another steep ridge. Descend steeply to **Inoi,** then pedal gradually upward through a gentle valley that gives way to tougher hills. A seemingly endless climb (about 14 km) ends at a ridge above **Erithres.** Sail down a 10 percent grade into the city.

Throughout this exhausting day of riding, you'll be encouraged by the friendliness of the rural Greeks you encounter. One truck driver stopped at the bottom of a long hill to offer us and our bicycles a ride, then passed us again just as we struggled to the crest. His enthusiastic honks of congratulations cheered us almost as much as the sight of the downhill on the other side. The hills are merciless, but traffic is light, the road surface is good, and the Greek countryside is lovely.

Descend gradually after **Erithres,** then gain level riding as you pedal the final 13 km to **Thebes.** Follow signs for **Livadia** and **Delphi** as you wind your way through Thebes. If you're not camping, Thebes is the last good opportunity to find a room until Livadia, 46 km farther on.

Thebes has a place of honor in Greek history. At one time the city was the capital of all Greece. According to tradition, Thebes was the home of the tragic King Oedipus. You can visit the city's archaeological museum to learn more about the area.

## Thebes to Ossios Loukas: 81 kilometers

Leave Thebes on the road for **Livadia** and **Delphi,** and enjoy easy riding across the flat Teneric Plain. Watch for the elusive peak of **Mount Parnassus** lurking in the clouds ahead. Livadia is a large, busy market town with lots of shops. Follow signs for **Delphi** as you cycle through the city, then climb gradually from the valley floor. There's a **300-meter tunnel** near **Tsoukalades.** It's straight and not too bad to ride through if traffic is light, but you can avoid it by turning off for Tsoukalades and taking the **old road** over the hill.

Continue a steady ascent with lovely mountain scenery for several more kilometers, then descend briefly to the turnoff for **Distomo** and **Ossios Loukas.** You'll have a couple of options here. We asked permission to stash our bags beside an auto shop at the junction, made the 24-km round trip to Ossios Loukas Monastery without our gear, then continued on for Delphi. Or you can cycle on to Distomo (3 km), get a room in town, then ride the final 9 km to the monastery. There are no lodgings available at Ossios Loukas itself.

Swing **left** for **Distomo** at the **junction,** and pedal into the compact town. Signs for **Ossios Loukas** will direct you to **Stiri.** Pedal on to a junction for Kiriaki and angle **right** for **Ossios Loukas.** Climb steadily through almond orchards, then enjoy a swift descent to the lonely monastery on its hill.

You won't regret the energy you spend to reach Ossios Loukas, a quiet group of buildings strikingly situated on a hillside above a wide, tree-dotted valley. The well-kept grounds, the surrounding almond trees, and the glittering mosaics in the monastery church combine to leave the visitor with a sense of the richness and time-lessness of Greece.

## Ossios Loukas to Delphi: 36 kilometers

**Retrace** the route to **Distomo** and continue to the **main road.** Go **left** to resume the climb to **Delphi.** A final **12 km of steep uphill** on a winding, mountain-shadowed road leads to **Arachova.** The small city of Arachova, perched at the crest of the long climb to Delphi, is buried in shops and postcards, trinkets and tourists. It will always be linked in our minds to the persistent, blanket-toting shopkeeper who followed us down the road out of town calling, "No money—just look!" Despite the commercial overkill, Arachova is a beautiful spot with a fantastic view of the shimmering Gulf of Corinth.

As a cyclist, you'll prize Arachova even more, for it marks the end of your grueling ascent from Piraeus. Fly through a joyous 10 km of crazy **switchbacks** to arrive at the site of **Delphi,** where a wooded cleft in the side of Mount Parnassus holds the most sacred ruins of Greece. Just around the bend, the modern city holds scores of hotels, restaurants, and cafes, but in the quiet beauty of the wooded glen, when dawn turns the columns golden or sunset paints them pink, you can marvel at the sacred stones in solitude.

There are two campgrounds near Delphi. The closest is 1½ km out-side town. There's a youth hostel in the city, and you can visit the **tourist office** on the main street for help with finding a hotel room.

## Delphi to Agios Nikolaos: 62 kilometers

Leave Delphi and coast down a winding road to the **olive groves** below, enjoying vistas of the Gulf of Corinth as you go. Turn **left** at a **small sign** for **Itea,** and pedal a quiet road through olive groves be-fore joining the **main road** to cycle on toward Itea. On the **outskirts of Itea,** go **right** for **Nafpaktos** and **Galaxidi.** You'll have 17 km of gently rolling terrain as you hug the coastline to **Galaxidi,** an attrac-tive seaside town with a pretty harbor. Continue on toward **Eratini** on the up-and-down road along the sea.

Swing down off the main road to cycle into **Eratini,** a built-up sea-side town with lots of hotels and a long sandy beach. You can find a room in Eratini if you need one, or continue for 10 km along the coast to camp at Agios Nikolaos. Take the **beachside road** through Eratini

*Dawn light at Delphi*

and continue out of town to rejoin the **main road.** Cross a ridge before descending to **Agios Nikolaos.** Watch for a campground sign to the right as you approach the town.

Agios Nikolaos offers ferry connections to Egio on the Peloponnese Peninsula, and you can pedal on to Patras from there. We decided to stay on the north side of the Gulf instead, delaying our ferry ride until Antirrion.

## Agios Nikolaos to Patras: 55 kilometers

From Agios Nikolaos, continue on toward **Nafpaktos.** The hills are gentle and the road surface is good. Light traffic and views of the sea and the ever-present olives make for pleasant riding until just **before Nafpaktos,** where you'll join **another road** and pick up heavier traffic. Explore the midsize town of Nafpaktos with its handsome Venetian castle and the small medieval harbor. Continue on through the city and cycle the **9 km** to the **Antirrion turnoff.**

Veer **left** for **Antirrion** and the **ferry,** and pedal to the **ferry dock,** where there are frequent departures for **Rion,** just across the water. Arrive in Rion, and follow signs for the **new road** and **Patras** to pedal toward the city. There's an old road to Patras, as well, but it's narrow and has heavy traffic.

Cycle into Patras and head for the waterfront. The **ferry terminal** is on the north edge of the docking area, and there's an office of the **GNTO** nearby. Check on ferry connections to Ancona and Brindisi at either spot. There are dozens of hotels and pensions in Patras. If you want to camp, follow the harbor road northeast past the ferry terminal. You'll see campground signs within a few kilometers.

# TOUR NO. 16

# TOURING TUSCANY
### Ancona to Genoa, Italy

*Distance:* 668 kilometers (414 miles)
*Estimated time:* 9 riding days
*Best time to go:* May, June, September, or early October
*Terrain:* Lots of challenging hills with a few easy days
*Connecting tours:* Tours No. 15 and 17

You'll pedal through the green heart of Italy on this tour through Umbria and Tuscany, and you'll get a chance to visit four of Italy's loveliest cities along the way. Assisi, Siena, Florence, and Pisa will dazzle you with art and architecture, and the vine- and olive-covered Tuscan hills and the cliff-lined Mediterranean Coast will thrill you with natural beauty.

Italian drivers have a world-wide reputation for speed, recklessness, and incessant honking. Although a brief ride we made between ferry ports in southern Italy supported that reputation, the northern drivers continually surprised us with their friendliness and courtesy. And Italy's reputed proliferation of tourist-preying thieves didn't materialize either. Instead, we found easygoing, smiling people in the country; helpful, honest shopkeepers in the cities; and a magnificent blend of landscape and art that made our time in Italy a "masterpiece" of good experiences.

You'll love the Italian tradition of *Passeggiata,* the evening "parade." The strollers come out before supper, when the coolness of the evening descends, and the city streets are filled until well after dark with talking, laughing crowds of neatly dressed Italians. Join the window-shoppers to get a feel for Italian culture at its most gregarious.

Avoid the high-intensity (and high-temperature) months of July and August when you're scheduling your trip. Your days in Italy will be more pleasant, your quest for accommodations more successful, and your visits to churches and museums less crowded if you do.

**CONNECTIONS.** Ancona was once a popular stop for ferries from Zadar, Split, and Dubrovnik in Yugoslavia, and still is for ferries from Patras, Greece, so you'll have lots of options for hookups with cycle tours in those countries (be sure to check on current political situations and/or ferry schedules). Ancona is also served by rail lines from cities throughout Italy and northern Europe.

**INFORMATION.** Write to the Italian Government Travel Office, 630 Fifth Avenue, #1565, Rockefeller Center, New York, New York 10111, and request specific information on cycling, camping, and sightseeing. They'll provide a list of campsites and an overall map. Ask for street maps of the larger cities you plan to visit, too.

Michelin's *Green Guide Italy* is a good reference source for your trip—well worth its weight, even on the Tuscan hills. Other guidebook options include Baedeker's *Italy,* two *Blue Guides, The Real Guide: Italy,* and *Let's Go: Italy.*

**MAPS.** Pick up detailed maps for route finding once you arrive. The Auto Club of Italy, with offices in many of the larger cities, sells regional maps at 1:275,000 scale. There's also an excellent 15-map series at 1:200,000 scale published by the Touring Club Italiano. It's available in bookstores. Tourist offices are plentiful in Italy, and staff people usually speak English. You should be able to get free literature, city maps, and accommodation information without difficulty.

**ACCOMMODATIONS.** Campgrounds in Italy are pleasant, convenient, and easier on the budget than sky-high hotel rates. Most big cities have at least one site near the city center, and you can get campground listings from tourist offices. Freelance camping is acceptable, too, but always ask permission first.

If you're staying in hotels, expect to pay plenty. The least expensive rooms can be found in a variety of private establishments (called *albergo, pensione, soggiorno,* or *locanda*). According to law, prices must be posted on the door of every room, so double-check the price when you check the springs. You'll usually have to pay extra for a shower, and you'll invariably have to give up your passport for paperwork.

**SUPPLIES.** Italy is a hungry cyclist's dream. Few foods fill a growling stomach like pasta and pizza. And the huge meals that are an Italian tradition will seem just right after you've pedaled an 80-km day. Compared with other southern European countries, Italy isn't cheap, however. Restaurant meals can set you back quite a bit, so if you're on a tight budget, you may be doing lots of picnicking. But that's no hardship here.

Wonderful cheeses like Bel Paese and Gorgonzola, tasty lunch-meats, excellent produce, and lots of fresh-baked rolls (*panini*)—what more could a picnicker ask? And, if you grow tired of sandwiches, most supermarkets offer deli-counter pizza at affordable prices as well. One word of warning—in Italy a "pepperoni pizza" is a "green-pepper" (the vegetable) pizza and bears little resemblance to our meat-laden North American version.

Italians are addicted to sweets, and you'll have an overwhelming assortment of cookies, pastries, and chocolates from which to choose. Again, prices can be surprisingly high, but a few bites will convince you that your lire were well spent.

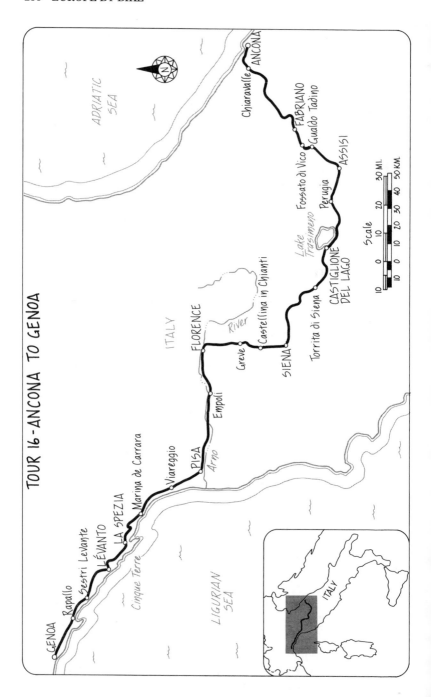

TOUR 16 - ANCONA TO GENOA

Shopping hours in Italy vary between the city and the country. You can almost always find something open in big cities like Florence or Genoa, although you will find Sunday closures everywhere. In small towns, shops shut down between 1:00 and 3:00 P.M. while the Italians escape the heat and enjoy their main meal of the day. Most of Italy's museums and cathedrals adhere to the afternoon lockup, too, with Mondays the most common for all-day closures. (Please remember that Italy is a very religious country. Short shorts or revealing blouses—even for a cyclist—are not appropriate attire in churches.)

Needless to say, cycling is big in Italy. Well-stocked bicycle shops abound in larger cities, and you'll be dazzled by the scope and variety of products. Of course, touring gear is buried by the avalanche of racing equipment, so you may have to hunt for specialized needs.

## Ancona to Fabriano: 75 kilometers

Ancona is crowded, busy, and loud—a startling (but true-to-life) introduction to big-city Italy. But despite the traffic and industry, Ancona is an attractive town, climbing away from the sea on a steep hillside and ruled by a hilltop cathedral (*duomo*).

Leave the **ferry dock** and follow signs for **Rimini** and **Pesaro** as you pedal along the coast. If you need to buy maps in town, swing **left** onto **Corso Stamira,** and walk into the downtown core to find the Auto Club of Italy (ACI) at Corso Stamira 78. You can buy detailed maps for your ride at the office. Ancona's main **tourist office** is at the train station, although a branch office sometimes operates at the Stazione Marittima.

Return to the **Rimini/Pesaro road** and leave Ancona, riding beside the sea and the train tracks. Keep **straight** when the main road angles left for Rimini and Pesaro. Follow signs toward **Falconara.** Join **Road 16** for **Rimini** soon after, cross the **Esino River,** and angle **left** onto **Road 76** for **Chiaravalle** and **Iesi.** Cycle through gentle terrain, paralleling the main road as you pass farms and scattered industrial districts.

Cross **under the A14 freeway** and ride through **Chiaravalle,** following signs for **Iesi.** Chiaravalle is a pleasant small town, a welcome contrast to the hubbub of Ancona. Traffic increases on the secondary road between Chiaravalle and Iesi, so you might want to opt for the wide shoulder of the main road and roomier pedaling. Swing **left** to reach the main road **after Chiaravalle,** following signs for **Rome** (Roma) and **Ancona,** then turning **right** for **Rome** when you reach the **wide thoroughfare.**

**Road 76** parallels the main route for **20 km** beyond Iesi before the two roads **merge.** If you're pedaling this tour in the fall, you'll be treated to a lovely palette of autumn color as you ride—dark brown fields of freshly turned soil next to broad yellow swathes of corn stubble, and tightly trellised vines painting the hillsides with brilliant streaks of red and gold.

Begin a climb into **hillier terrain** as the two roads merge. There are a series of uncomfortably long but well-lit **tunnels** ahead as Road 76 dives into the hills. Avoid the tunnels and gain a winding route through a beautiful river gorge by turning **left** onto a **small paved road** at the **large gravel plant** just before the **first tunnel.** Play hopscotch with Road 76 and its tunnels to **Gattuccio,** then climb a **small hill** while the main route burrows through the mountain. Rejoin **Road 76** just beyond.

Follow signs for **Fabriano** along Road 76. Truck traffic increases and the road narrows for the final kilometers into the midsize city. Fabriano has a handsome central square, a seventeenth-century cathedral, and many medieval buildings. You'll be able to find a *pensione* in the city if you need a bed.

## Fabriano to Assisi: 60 kilometers

Leave Fabriano on **Road 76** for **Rome** and begin a climb into the hills. The **rugged terrain** will challenge and reward you for the remainder of the day. Follow the narrow, winding route beside the river to **Cancelli** and pedal through a **tunnel.** Turn **right** for **Camodiegoli** just afterward, to avoid a second, longer tunnel. Cross an **overpass** and go **left** at the **T** to climb steeply up and over a long hill. You'll have lovely vistas of green hillsides sprinkled with oak and maple as you pedal up the seemingly carless secondary road.

Descend steeply to rejoin **Road 76,** then veer **left** for **Fossato di Vico** less than **1 km** later. Cross the **train tracks** on a somewhat suspect **bridge** (we walked), and ride through Fossato di Vico before following signs for **Rome** onto **Road 3.** Continue on Road 3 toward **Gualdo Tadino,** and veer **right** for **Perugia** and **Assisi** onto **Road 318** on the edge of town. Ride **3 km,** then go **left** for **Assisi** as you begin a **long climb** away from the valley floor, passing through **Grello** and cycling on to **Osteria di Morano.**

Coast down a short hill, then climb a **steep hill** beyond Osteria, enjoying one beautiful vista after another. You'll have a stretch of level riding before **San Presto,** then **descend steeply** to the river below. Cross the **river** and swing around the hillside for your first glimpse of Assisi, an enchanting city perched on a mounded hill, its towers standing guard above its walls.

Assisi's campground is on a steep hill above the city core. To reach the **campground** (or the youth hostel next door), turn left as you enter the city and puff up the **via Santuario delle Carceri.** There are signs for the campground (2 km from the city center). Rooms in Assisi are scarce during high season, but things are quieter in spring and fall. Seek out the tourist office on the Piazza del Commune if you need help.

The medieval streets and picturesque alleys of Assisi are a treat to wander through. And Assisi's churches—particularly the magnificent Saint Francis's Basilica—will take you several hours to explore. Marvel at the wealth of paintings in the basilica dedicated to the city's most famous son, St. Francis, and then pedal out into the surrounding countryside to sense the beauty that inspired him to worship.

## Assisi to Castiglione del Lago: 80 kilometers

From **Saint Francis's Basilica,** take the **via Frate Elia** down the hill and turn **right** to follow signs for **Perugia** to the **valley floor** beyond. Cycle west on **Road 147** through flat agricultural land, joining the **main road** toward Perugia **15 km** from Assisi's center. Cross the **Tevere River** and take the **first exit** off the main road for Perugia. Go **left** at the **T.**

The road **branches** soon after, with signs for Rome (Roma), Florence (Firenze), and Perugia. Continue **straight** for **Perugia,** pedaling cautiously in the thick traffic. Climb a **long, steep hill** into the city **center.** Perugia squats atop its mounded Umbrian hill like a grim dragon turned to stone. The city has an abundance of regal buildings, ornate façades, and massive palaces. Stop to admire the view out over the surrounding countryside from the small park across from St. Peter's Church.

Continue upward through the Porta San Pietro toward the Piazza 4 Novembre, Perugia's central square. The Great Fountain (Fontana Maggiore) in the impressive square is a masterpiece of Italian sculpture. Walk around and around it, deciphering the stories in the carved panels. Perugia's **tourist office** is in the Priors' Palace on the plaza.

To leave the city, follow the **via dei Priori** west from the Priors' Palace to the **Oratory of San Bernardino,** a beautiful fifteenth-century church. Then take the **via A. Pascoli** down the hill, veering left at the **T.** Continue downhill and follow signs for **Roma** and **Firenze.** Go under the **train tracks** and keep to the **left** for **Rome,** then go **right** for **Florence** a short distance later.

Follow signs for **S. Sisto** to gain **Road 220** southwest from Perugia. Coast downhill, climb a short, steep hill, then descend into **S. Sisto** on a lightly trafficked secondary road. Stay on **Road 220** for about **13 km** more. Then angle **right** for **Mugnano,** following signs for **Magione** and pedaling through acres of olive trees.

Ascend a gentle hill, then coast to an **intersection** with **Road 599.** Veer **left** for **Chiusi.** Pedal **8 km** along the flat, marshy lakeshore and angle **right** for **Castiglione del Lago.** Enjoy easy, quiet riding before joining the **main road** into Castiglione for the final 7¹/₂ km of the day. There are several campgrounds along the lake in this area, or you can look for a room in Castiglione, a pretty lakeside town with a fourteenth-century castle. The city **tourist office** is at the Piazza Mazzini.

## Castiglione del Lago to Siena: 80 kilometers

Leave Castiglione by pedaling west on **Road 454** for **Pozzuolo** and **Montepulciano.** Negotiate a series of small hills covered with vineyards and yellow-faced sunflowers, and enter a long valley dominated by the distant form of Montepulciano on its hilltop. Follow signs for

*Siena's* duomo *is Italian architecture at its most exuberant.*

**Montepulciano** and **Siena** past Pozzuolo and Acquavua to arrive at **Nottola.** From Nottola, you can make the 7-km trip to Montepulciano if you'd like a closer look at the lofty town. Otherwise, turn **right** for **Siena** in Nottola, and follow signs for Siena and **Sinalunga** through **Torrita di Siena.** Pedal through rolling hill country of vineyards and small towns. Ride through **Sinalunga** and join **Road 326,** veering **left** toward **Siena** and a final 38 km of busy main-road riding.

You'll have level going at the start, then a final stretch of **roller-coaster hills** as you approach Siena. Armaiolo is a particularly attractive town, with a lovely bell tower embellishing its medieval silhouette. Reach a junction just before Siena and savor the view of the city on its hill, with its many fine buildings standing out against the sky. Go **straight** at the **junction,** following signs marked **Siena Stazione.** (The route signed for Siena Centro does a huge loop around the town, adding several confusing kilometers to your ride.)

If you want to camp during your stay, there's a well-marked campground on via Scacciapensieri near the train station, and there's a youth hostel northwest of the old city as well. Climb the hill to the city center and head for the magnificent Piazza del Campo, using the tall tower of the Palazzo Pubblico as your guide. The **tourist office** is at Piazza del Campo 56, and you can get a city map and a list of hotels there.

Siena stands out among Italian cities. The fan-shaped Piazza del Campo is one of the most impressive plazas in Europe. The mesmerizing *duomo,* with its shocking striped exterior of multicolored marble and its exquisite interior of inlaid stone, will demand at least a couple of hours of your time. And the streets of the city, full of talking, laughing, strolling residents, will delight you with their variety and life.

Be sure to savor the culinary treasures Siena has to offer, too. Slices of moist white bread piled with chunks of fragrant Gorgonzola cheese, and a tasty after-dinner treat of nutty *panforte,* rich with candied fruit and honey, will make your stomach rumble with contentment.

## Siena to Florence: 70 kilometers

Leave Siena on the **via di Camollia** and follow signs for **Florence** (Firenze) as you ride. After a few kilometers, reach a **junction** signed for Florence to both left and right. Veer **right** and follow signs for **Castellina in Chianti** onto **Road 222.** Stay on Road 222 for Florence throughout the day.

Climb through **challenging hills,** with vistas of steeply sloped vineyards and vibrant green fields. Short descents and brief level stretches break up the mostly uphill riding to Castellina, an attractive town of old houses ruled by a tower-topped fortress. Descend from Castellina, then climb a **long hill** past acres of vines. Pedal on to **Greve,** a midsize town with lots of stores, then ride through short rolling hills to Strada.

Follow signs for Florence down a long hill to **Grassina,** cross under the **A1 freeway,** and enter the outskirts of the city. You'll arrive in Florence on the south bank of the **Arno River,** then swing west along the shore to pedal toward the **city center.** The view of Florence's old core, dominated by the mighty *duomo* and the bell tower of the Palazzo Vecchio, is a fitting finale to a day of lovely Tuscan hills.

There are several bridges across the Arno into the heart of the city. Florence has several **tourist offices.** Take the **Ponte Santa Trinita** across the river, and continue north to reach the office at the train station. Or try the office at via Manzoni 16. You can get a city map and lodging information here. There are two campgrounds in Florence. Italiani e Stranieri, on the olive-covered hillside east of the Piazzale Michelangelo, is closest to the city center and offers a wonderful view of the city across the Arno. There's also a campground next to the youth hostel, a few kilometers northeast of the city center.

Moderately priced rooms abound on the streets around the main train station and the *duomo,* but you'll have to convince some of the proprietors to let you haul your bicycle inside. Many of the rooms are up several flights of stairs.

Florence, city of Michelangelo and artistic capital of Tuscany, is a lovely town that is best appreciated during the off-season, when tourist crowds begin to thin. You'll have a long list of "must-see" attractions here, with the magnificent cathedral, the Uffizi Gallery, and the Palazzo Vecchio near the top of the heap. Try to get out on the streets early to avoid the crowds. Dive into the museums and churches to savor Florence's art. Climb to the Piazzale Michelangelo or struggle up the campanile's 414 steps to get a panoramic view of the city. And stroll the jam-packed shopping streets after dark to experience Florence's throbbing urban life.

By the way, if you're convinced a tour of Italy wouldn't be complete without a visit to Rome, Florence makes an excellent base for a train ride to the south. We left our bicycles and gear tucked away in a courtyard at our *pensione,* then made the four-hour trip to Rome for a few days of frenzied sightseeing.

## Florence to Pisa: 82 kilometers

Cross to the **south side** of the **Arno River** and cycle west onto **Road 67.** Follow **blue road signs** for **Pisa** as you draw away from Florence (but abandon the blue freeway signs to stay with Road 67). The mostly flat, easy ride to Pisa follows the Arno River on Road 67 throughout the day. During your early kilometers on the winding secondary road, you'll pedal through lush green valleys of vines, olives, and oak, and small towns along the way provide interesting breaks in the scenery.

Pass through two short **tunnels** near **Capraia,** about 24 km from

*Pisa's Leaning Tower is no slouch with sightseers.*

Florence. Just past **Empoli,** you can veer **right** for **Fucecchio** to cross the **Arno** if you'd like to abandon Road 67 for a **smaller thoroughfare.** Traffic is just as heavy on the north side of the river, however, and a long succession of towns overlooks the road. The final 30 km into Pisa are dull at best.

Enter Pisa either by crossing the **Arno River** into the old city (from Road 67) or by approaching from the east (on the secondary road). Head for the *duomo* on the northwest edge of the city center. You'll never forget your first look at Pisa's famous Leaning Tower beside the massive Pisa Cathedral. The bizarre tilt of this skinny white cylinder, set off against the perpendicular lines of the hulking church beside it, is a spectacular sight. And the overall picture created by lush green grass, the white wedding-cake cathedral, the dome-shaped baptistry, and the drunken tower produces a remarkable composition.

Venture inside the *duomo* and the baptistry for a look at Italian architecture at its finest. Unfortunately, visitors are no longer able to ascend the Leaning Tower, due to safety concerns. The city **tourist office** is just across the lawn from the Leaning Tower. There are several competitively priced *pensioni* near the cathedral, and there's a large campground just outside the western city gate on Viale delle Cascine. It's within walking distance of the *duomo*.

One note of warning—the coastal section of this tour (from Pisa to Genoa) is, for the most part, busy and heavily developed. If you're not cycling on to France, not particularly fond of seaside resorts, or not intent on seeing Italy's remarkable Cinque Terre, consider ending your ride in Pisa.

## Pisa to La Spezia: 85 kilometers

Leave Pisa by cycling west from the Piazza del Duomo onto **Viale delle Cascine.** Ride past the campground and continue on to an intersection with **Road 1.** Follow Road 1 for **14** busy **kilometers** toward **Genoa** (Genova) and **Viareggio.** Veer **left** for **Torre del Lago Puccini** to gain a smaller road, still with lots of traffic. Pedal on through level terrain to **Viareggio.**

In Viareggio, follow signs for the **center,** circling across the **train tracks** and working your way down to the beach and your first look at Italy's Mediterranean Coast. The solid succession of restaurants, hotels, shops, and campgrounds probably won't impress you. Follow the flat seaside road through a string of small resort cities to **Marina de Carrara.** Cycling this stretch during high season could be quite unpleasant, despite the wide road.

Things lighten up a bit after Marina de Carrara. Cross the **Magra River,** then turn **left** for **Montemarcello, Ameglia,** and your introduction to the Italian Riviera. Ameglia is an attractive town of tall, fortlike houses. Labor up a **long, steep hill** to **Montemarcello,** passing through fragrant pine forests and terraced olive groves. There's a fine view from the top of the ridge.

Pedal through rolling terrain to a **junction** for **Lerici** and **Sarzana.** Turn **left** and **descend steeply** to **Lerici** and the sea. Lerici is a busy resort town with a castle-guarded harbor. Follow signs for **La Spezia** from here, climbing with **Road 331** along the sea. There are several campgrounds along this section, if you want to camp before La Spezia. Otherwise, follow the seaside Road 331 into the city and ride along the busy harbor. Look for a room in the city center.

# La Spezia to Lévanto: 42 kilometers

Continue through La Spezia on the **harbor road,** veering **left** at the edge of town for **Portovénera** and **Riomaggiore.** Then go **right** to ascend a **steep hill** signed for **Riomaggiore.** Enjoy stunning views of La Spezia and the sea before you dive into a well-lit **tunnel** of about $^1/_2$ km. The vistas beyond the tunnel are more spectacular still, as you ride along a hillside high above the Mediterranean.

Gaze ahead to Italy's matchless **Cinque Terre,** the Five Lands. Five tiny fishing villages cling to this cliffy, curving section of coast, linked by the sea, by train tracks, and by a rocky cliffside footpath. Although a connecting road between the towns is scheduled for construction, the project will probably take several years.

Arrive at a **junction** signed for **Riomaggiore** and **Manarola.** If you feel like exploring (and working very hard), make the steep descent to Riomaggiore and take a look around the compact town. You can continue on to Manarola from Riomaggiore by pushing your bicycle along the path called the **Via del Amore,** but it's really not a hike for a bike. A better option is to stow your bicycle and gear in Riomaggiore and walk the trail, then return to the city by train.

You'll have spectacular views of the whole section by simply keeping to the high road and pedaling through. If you choose to see it this way, continue **straight** at the Manarola/Riomaggiore **junction,** ride through another **tunnel,** then go **right** for **Volastra** up an **extremely steep hill.** The incline will probably have you off and shoving before you reach the top.

Come to a **junction** signed for **Vernazza** and **Lévanto.** Go **right** for **Lévanto** onto a **dirt road** (may be paved by now) and wind through a high pine forest with wonderful views of the sea. The surface isn't too bad and you'll regain pavement after about 6 km. At a **T** signed for **Lévanto** and **La Spezia,** veer **left** for **Lévanto** and descend a **steep hill** to **another junction.** Turn **right** here to continue a **long descent** to the sea.

If you want to camp, there's a nice site in a hillside olive grove about **2 km above Lévanto**, and there are two more campgrounds closer to the city center. Watch for the campground signs as you coast down the hill. Lévanto offers hotels and *pensioni,* as well.

# Lévanto to Genoa: 94 kilometers

From Lévanto, follow **blue road signs** for **Genoa** up a **long, steep hill.** As you climb, you'll have fantastic views of the cliffs and beaches below and of the jagged coastline stretching toward Genoa. Turn inland for the final leg of the 19-km ascent to the **Bracco Pass.** Reach the crest of the hill and continue on to **Road 1.** Go **left** for **Genoa** on Road 1.

Cycle a short level stretch, then fly down a **precipitous descent** to **Sestri Levante** and the heart of the Italian Riviera. Hotels, restaurants, villas, and nonstop traffic will accompany you for the remaining 56 km to Genoa. From Sestri Levante, the riding is pleasant to **Chiávari,** with only **one tunnel** to make your skin crawl. **Climb steeply** from Chiávari, then descend to **Zoagli,** sharing the road with Mercedes, Porsches, and a few Rolls Royces along the way.

Ascend again from Zoagli and swing **left** onto a **side road** around the ridge to avoid another **tunnel.** Speed downhill into **Rapallo** and follow **blue Genoa Road 1 signs** through town and up another **steep hill** to (guess what) another **tunnel.** Enjoy a final **steep descent** to **Recco** and the sea.

The 7 km between Recco and **Bogliasco** are rolling and winding—tough riding after a hard day. The terrain moderates after Bogliasco, and Genoa reaches out to draw you in with heavy traffic and solid development. At **Nervi,** the narrow coast road grows into a more comfortable four lanes. Follow signs for **Genova Centro** into the throbbing heart of the city.

Genoa is Italy's largest seaport. It's sprawling, loud, and dangerous, so ride with caution. If you're ending your tour here, you'll be heading for either the train station or the airport west of town. Since Tour No. 17 starts in Genoa and departs to the west, you can check the start of that tour for directions to the airport. To reach Stazione Brignole, continue following signs for Genova Centro to Piazza Verdi, the Brignole train station, and a city **tourist office.**

# TOUR NO. 17

# RIVIERA ROCK AND CLASSICAL PROVENCE

*Genoa, Italy, to Carcassonne, France*

*Distance:* 857 kilometers (533 miles)
*Estimated time:* 14 riding days
*Best time to go:* April, May, June, September, or October
*Terrain:* Fairly easy throughout
*Connecting tours:* Tour No. 16

This tour follows the Mediterranean coastlines of Italy and France for much of its length, so if you're searching for solitude and quiet roads, this is *not* the tour for you. Europe's Mediterranean Coast is busy and crowded. It has its merits, but quiet cycling isn't one of them. You will have a brief respite from the heavily developed seaside areas when you swing inland for a look at the pastoral loveliness of Provence (avoiding the urban chaos of Marseilles along the way) but, overall, this is a ride for those who are willing to accept the "Med" as is—beautiful, trendy, and woefully overused.

**CONNECTIONS.** You can reach Genoa and the start of this tour by plane or train, or you can cycle in via Tour No. 16 (Ancona to Genoa). Genoa's airport is west of the city, and the Brignole train station is in the center of town. As befits Italy's largest port, Genoa is also served by ferries—you can arrive by boat from either Corsica or Sardinia.

**INFORMATION.** For preparatory information on Italy, read the introduction to Tour No. 16. Please look at Tour No. 4 for material on France.

**ACCOMMODATIONS.** One warning note. If you're cycling this tour late in the year, be aware that many hotels, pensions, and campgrounds along the Riviera are closed up tight in November and/or December, while management takes a holiday. You'll have to scramble to find rooms in some of the smaller Riviera towns.

**MAPS.** You'll need maps for two different countries on this tour. Read the "Maps" section in Tour No. 16 for help with Italy, and check the map information in Tour No. 4 for information on France.

**SUPPLIES.** For information on shopping hours and food purchases in Italy and France, refer to Tours No. 16 and 4, respectively.

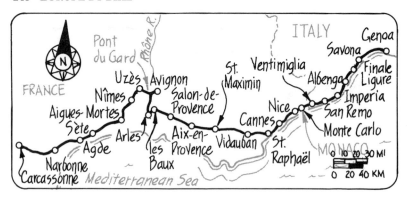

## Genoa to Finale Ligure: 71 kilometers

From the Brignole **train station,** head south on **Viale Brigata Bisagno.** Follow signs for **Pegli** and **Savona.** Take **Corso A. Saffi** to the **right** just before the harbor, and climb a small hill, cycling above the water. The **freeway** will be on your left. Descend and join **via Sopraelevata Gramsci** to continue beside the freeway, and stay with **blue signs for Savona.**

Continue following the blue road signs for **Pegli** and **Savona** as you pedal away from the city on **Road 1.** Pass the airport turnoff and cycle on to Pegli as the noise and pollution of Genoa begin to fade. Ascend a small hill at **Arenzano** and climb another just past **Cogoleto.** Traffic is not too bothersome along this section, and there are pleasant interludes of sea, cliffs, and olives between the built-up seaside towns.

**Varazze** has a long stretch of sand beside it. Pedal on toward **Savona** and pass through **two short tunnels** before the busy city. Stay along the sea as you ride through Savona, following signs for **Imperia.** Cycle on to **Noli,** an attractive fishing town, and come to a scenic stretch of curving road cut into the cliffs. Speed through several short tunnels along the level, winding route.

Enter **Finale Ligure** (actually a string of small villages) and choose from several campgrounds, hotels, and *pensioni.* The small downtown area beside the palm-lined beach at **Marina** makes a pleasant setting for an evening stroll.

## Finale Ligure to San Remo: 74 kilometers

Begin your last full day of riding in Italy by pedaling away from Finale Ligure, continuing southwest on **Road 1** toward **Imperia.** You'll have lots of level riding and fewer built-up areas to block your views of the placid Mediterranean along the way. Swing **left off Road 1** to explore **Albenga,** a handsome town with a thirteenth-century cathedral and a fifth-century baptistry. Cross the **river** in Albenga and turn **left** to follow signs for **Imperia** on a smaller road beside the sea. **Rejoin Road 1** soon after.

You'll have a small hill at Cape Santa Croce and a fine view as well. Descend to **Alássio,** a resort town sprawled beside the sea, then climb to Cape Mele and another impressive vista. Pedal on **past Cervo,** a unique village perched on a hill above the road, and endure a **long, steady climb** to Cape Berta just before **Imperia.** Follow signs for **San Remo** and **Ventimiglia** through Imperia. The city's old quarter, on a small promontory to the left of the road, will tempt you to stop and explore.

There are several campgrounds just beyond Imperia, if you decide to end your riding day. The road is level between Imperia and San Remo (26 km), running close to the sea and passing through small villages along the way. Ride past whispering olive groves, vineyards, and vibrant fields of flowers as you approach **San Remo,** capital of Italy's "Riviera of Flowers." Carnations, chrysanthemums, roses, and mimosa are grown along this temperate coastline and sold all over Europe.

The quiet beauty of old villages and flowers gives way to traffic and hotels as you enter San Remo. Follow signs for **Ventimiglia** to pedal through the town and reach the year-round campground on the western edge. You'll be within walking distance of the city center (about 3 km) from the large, well-equipped (and expensive) site, or you can hop a bus into the city from a stop near the campground.

Explore San Remo's colorful, palm-lined promenade, and rub shoulders with furs and three-piece suits while you window-shop for pearls or count Mercedes. Then climb into the twisted streets of the old city, and join the locals bartering at a vast outdoor market where the opulence and wealth of the Riviera seem very far away.

## San Remo to Nice: 56 kilometers

Follow **blue road signs** for **Ventimiglia** as you leave San Remo on **Road 1. Ospedaletti** is an attractive resort town nearly buried in palms. Continue on to Ventimiglia, a hilltop city of tall, rectangular houses, and prepare to say "bonjour" to France. Cross the **river** on the far side of Ventimiglia and follow signs for **France—SS1.** Turn **right** to ascend a **short hill,** then pedal through a long uphill **tunnel.** You can avoid the tunnel by swinging left after the river, then circling up and around the point to rejoin Road 1.

Reach a **junction** signed for the **French border** (left or straight). We went **left** to avoid a climb but endured a few **tunnels** along the way. **Menton,** just across the Italian–French border, is a large Riviera resort with a pretty waterfront. Keep to the **left** to stay along the sea as you pedal through the town.

Follow signs for **Nice** to climb a steep hill away from Menton, and rejoin the **main road (now Road N7)** to ride toward **Monaco.** Look for signs for **Monte Carlo's center,** and descend to the wealthy capital of Monaco. Watch for the unique license plates of the small principality on the cars that pass you as you ride. Signs in Monte Carlo lead past high rises, hotels, and shops to the **Casino,** a classy-looking building set on a flower-filled avenue.

Swing **left** to get a closer look at the Casino and continue down to the waterfront to marvel at the money floating in the yacht-filled harbor. Continue pedaling along the sea on **Road N98** for **Nice.** Just beyond Cap-d'Ail, we hit a road closure that resulted in a detour up a long, steep hill and back to **Road N7.** If you can stay on Road N98 for the ride into Nice, you'll avoid the hill and enjoy a much more pleasant ride.

Nice's **tourist office** is just off the waterfront at 5, Avenue Gustave V (near the Place Masséna and the Municipal Casino). There's another office at the main train station. There are two youth hostels in Nice, but neither one is centrally located. Get a room instead, and stay close to the street life that gives the city its appeal. Head for the old city (*Vieille Ville*) to search for budget accommodations. The old city is a fascinating enclave within the modern city, and there are lots of inexpensive hotels to choose from along its tangled streets.

Nice is a wonderful city for walking. After you've exhausted the alleyways of the *Vieille Ville,* head for the Promenade des Anglais along the sea and join the waves of walkers there. Modern Nice has attractions of its own, with shops, movie theaters, and restaurants, but it has little of the charm of the somewhat seedy old town.

# Nice to St. Raphaël: 77 kilometers

Leave Nice by cycling west along the **Promenade des Anglais,** following signs for **Cannes.** Pass the Nice airport and continue on the busy **Road N98** for about **2 km** before veering **left** for **Villeneuve-Loubet-Plage.** Follow the road along the sea to **Antibes,** a midsize Riviera city with a pleasant old core. You can add some scenic riding to your day by cycling the small road around the Cap d'Antibes and rejoining Road N98 beyond.

Otherwise, follow signs for **Cannes** onto **Road N7** as you pass through Antibes, and **abandon N7** about **8 km** later, angling **left** for **Palm Beach.** Cycle around a small promontory and enter Cannes along a lovely waterfront road. Pass a tree-filled city park where men bowl in the afternoon sun, and continue on through the city, following the seaside **Road N98** to **la Napoule-Plage.**

Climb a long hill just beyond **Théoule-sur-Mer,** then descend to ride along the **Corniche de l'Esterel,** a strikingly scenic route that winds beside the sea from Cannes to **St. Raphaël.** You'll have views of the inland peaks of the Massif de l'Esterel, as well as looks at the Mediterranean, the red cliffs, and the scattered mansions tucked among them as you ride.

There are several campgrounds between **Agay** and **St. Raphaël,** including some deluxe, Riviera-priced sites near the city. St. Raphaël is a pretty resort town with a harbor full of expensive boats and a tidy downtown core. Take a final look at the opulence of Riviera life in St. Raphaël. Pastoral, peaceful Provence is ahead.

# St. Raphaël to St. Maximin: 90 kilometers

Ride through St. Raphaël on **Road N98,** and follow signs for **Aix.** Turn inland with N98, then cycle through **Fréjus,** an ancient Roman town with the remains of the oldest amphitheater in France. Veer **left** for **Aix** and **Road N7** just before the train tracks, then turn **right** at the **T** to pass under the **tracks** and N7. Go **left** onto **N7** for **Aix.**

Cycle along the comfortably wide shoulder of the uncomfortably busy N7 for the 24 km to **Vidauban.** Take a brief break from the traffic on the way by pedaling through **le Muy** when the main road makes a loop around the handsome town. Pass through **Vidauban** and turn **right** for le Thoronet, leaving the traffic on N7 behind. Ride a winding route on **Road D84** beside the **Argens River,** passing fields of vines and deep forests on the quiet road.

Leave the river to climb to **le Thoronet,** and cycle **through town,** continuing uphill to a **turn** toward **Carcès.** Go **right** to **regain D84,** then descend to cross the **Argens River** and join **Road D562** toward **Carcès.** Cycle the 7 rolling kilometers into Carcès and follow signs for **Brignoles,** continuing on **D562.** Pedal **gradually uphill** for the 12 km to **le Val.** You'll fall in love with rural France as you cycle quiet roads past olive groves and vines, exchanging *bonjours* with smiling field workers along the way.

Just past the center of **le Val,** turn **right** on **Road D28** for **Bras,** and climb gently beside the Ribeirotte River. **Ascend steeply** through a scraggly forest of aspen and oak. Reach the ridgetop, keep **right,** and descend into the small town of **Bras.** Follow signs for **St. Maximin** in Bras, and stay on **D28** for the final 10 km to that city. The road is level most of the way.

St. Maximin is a midsize town with a good selection of shops and a handful of inexpensive rooms. Visit the Gothic church or explore the narrow streets of the city core, and nibble on a crispy baguette from a local *boulangerie.*

## St. Maximin to Aix-en-Provence: 38 kilometers

Follow signs for **Aix** out of St. Maximin and pedal **steeply uphill** on **N7** for about 4 km. From the crest, you'll have mostly downhill and level riding the rest of the way to Aix-en-Provence. Traffic is heavy on N7, but you'll make good time through the easy terrain. Views of the rocky white mountains to the north increase the pleasantness of the ride. (If you don't mind cycling a little extra distance in exchange for quieter roads, swing right off N7 to ride through Pourcieux, then continue to Pourrières and Puyloubier. You can pick up Road D17 into Aix from here.)

If you stay on N7, you'll follow the course of the **Arc River** into a scenic canyon, then continue into **Aix.** Look for signs for the **center** (*centre*) as you climb a gradual hill on **Cours Gambett**a to enter the city. Continue straight, walking your bicycle through a bustling pedestrian area on rue d'Italie. Proceed to Place Forbin, where **Cours Mirabeau** angles left toward the beautiful Fontaine de la Rotonde.

Cours Mirabeau is Aix-en-Provence's lovely main boulevard. Lined with cafes and dotted with fountains, it leads to the main **tourist office** on Place Général de Gaulle (on the left across from the fountain). Get a city map, literature on the city, and accommodation information at the tourist office. There's a youth hostel in Aix, and there are lots of hotels in the streets around Cours Mirabeau. If you want to camp, you'll find an assortment of campgrounds 3–5 km from the center.

Spend your afternoon strolling beneath the plane trees, browsing in the city's many bookstores, or sitting at a streetside cafe, and watching people watching people.

## Aix-en-Provence to les Baux: 67 kilometers

From the Aix tourist office, take **Avenue Bonaparte** to **Boulevard de la République,** and continue on past a large **supermarket,** then veer **left** at the next intersection onto **Road D10.** Cycle under the **train tracks** and over the **freeway,** then go straight on **Road D17** for **Eguilles.** Climb steadily to Eguilles on the quiet secondary road. Veer **left** onto **Road N543** at **Eguilles,** then continue straight onto **D17** for **Salon-de-Provence** and **Pélissanne.**

Descend gently to Pélissanne, an attractive small town, and swing **left** onto **N572** toward Salon. At the far edge of Pélissanne, go **right** to **regain D17** for **Salon.** Pedal the 5 km to Salon's **center,** entering on a long boulevard lined with plane trees. Come to a **T** by the fountain and town hall. Go left to get a look at the city castle, built between the tenth and the fifteenth centuries.

Return past the fountain (walk—it's the wrong way on a one-way) and turn **right** by the **large church.** Continue on this street to a junction with **Road N538.** Veer **right** toward **Avignon,** then go **left** a short distance later to gain **D17** for **Eyguières.** You'll have short ups and downs for the 9 km to Eyguières, another pretty Provençal town approached by a long, tree-lined boulevard. In Eyguières, swing **left** onto **Road N569,** then go **right** onto **D17.** Intersections aren't well marked.

Pedal away from the city on D17 toward **les Baux,** climbing gently, then continuing on level terrain. The lush fields of vines give way to dry, rocky olive groves as you continue west toward **Arles.** Descend a short hill to the **D5 junction,** and go **right** toward **Mouriés** and **les Baux.** There's a campground at **Maussane,** and it makes a good base for cycling to les Baux and St. Rémy (uphill) without your bags.

If you need a room, you can pedal the 9½ km from Maussane to **St. Rémy** on **D5,** then backtrack to visit les Baux on the following day. St. Rémy has several Roman remains, including a triumphal arch and a mausoleum, but you'll have a stiff climb to reach the town.

Whatever you do, don't skip a visit to les Baux. It's an amazingly situated village, perched on a stern outcropping of stone and guarded by the walls of a medieval castle. To reach ancient les Baux, turn onto **D5** for St. Rémy at **Maussane.** Ride gradually uphill for 2½ **km,** then turn **left** for **les Baux.** Pedal **steadily uphill** through shimmering olive groves with the stone city on the ridge luring you on. Pass through the modern tourist village to arrive at the long-dead city on the ridgetop (entry fee), then pace backward through the centuries to gain a spectacular view from the summit of the hill.

# Les Baux to Arles: 20 kilometers

Continue around the **hill** from les Baux, following signs for **D17** and **Arles** as you descend past olive groves. Go **right** on **D17** to pedal the final 13 km into Arles. Ride through **Fontvieille** and continue on to **Montmajour Abbey** with the twelfth-century Church of Notre Dame. The abbey's massive walls command a hill beside the road.

Turn **left** onto **Road N570** and follow signs for Arles's *centre* into town. There are several inexpensive hotels in the charming city, and you'll have a host of sights to induce you to an afternoon of wandering. Begin at the **tourist office** on the **Boulevard des Lices.** To reach the office, head for the Roman Arena as you pedal into town, and continue south past the Roman Theater to the pretty Jardin d'Eté. The tourist office is just beyond the garden.

If you're planning to do some heavy-duty sightseeing in Arles, invest in a *billet global,* an overall ticket for the arena, the theater, and several other attractions. It will save you a fistful of francs and introduce you to one of the most personable cities in Provence. Don't miss Arles Cathedral with its elaborate carved portal depicting the Last Judgment, then take a melancholy walk along the Alyscamps, a quiet lane whispering with golden-leaved trees and lined with empty Christian tombs. Vincent Van Gogh painted this spot when he lived in Arles.

## Arles to Avignon: 45 kilometers

Although the ride from Arles to Avignon isn't a long one, you can expect a battle if the wind is blowing down the Rhône. Unfortunately, it usually is. From Arles's **tourist information** office, continue away from the city core with the **Boulevard des Lices,** then swing **left** onto the **Boulevard Emile Combes** (with the main road). Pedal on to a busy **roundabout** at the **Place Lamartine** and stay with signs for **Fontvieille** and **les Baux.** Cross under the **train tracks,** then veer **left** at the traffic **light** approximately 100 yards farther on. You'll go **right** immediately afterward onto the **Avenue de Hongrie.**

Keep to the **left** at the subsequent **Y** (it's unsigned) to gain **Road D35** toward **Tarascon.** Signs for Tarascon lead north with D35, and you'll lose most of your traffic as you draw away from Arles. Enjoy effortless cycling to **Lansac,** and continue with **D35** toward **Tarascon.** Look for the riverside château in the distance as you approach the city. You'll hit a **junction** marked by a hard-to-spot sign for **Cellulose du Rhône** (a factory) and go **left** to cross the **train tracks.** Keep **right** at the subsequent **roundabout** to cycle into Tarascon, entering the city through unappealing industrial suburbs.

Look for signs for *centre ville* as you enter town. Tarascon offers a youth hostel and a campground, if you're considering an overnight stop. In the heart of town, you'll hit the main road crossing the Rhône toward Beaucaire (you can go left here to view that city and its château, leaping the Rhône with the bike lane on the bridge). To stay on the left bank of the Rhône and continue toward Avignon, **cross** the **main road,** and go **left** along it very briefly. Then dive **right** just **before the Rhône bridge** with signs for **Vallabrègues.** Pedal past Tarascon's hulking fortified **château,** and continue out of town on a quiet road beside the river.

Keep to the **left** for **Vallabrègues** to gain **Road D183,** then stay with signs for **Avignon** to join **Road D183A** as you depart Vallabrègues. With a campground and a tiny bull ring, the little village might tempt you to linger, but cruise onward along the flat, orchard-dotted valley, making your way north toward Avignon. You'll run smack into **Road D402** as it leaps the Rhône toward **Aramon.** Go **left** here, **cross the river,** then dive **right** onto **Road D2** for **Avignon.**

Several kilometers of flat, busy cycling follow, then stay with signs for **Villeneuve-lès-Avignon** to cycle past the first and gain the

**second** of Avignon's two auto bridges across the Rhône. (The turn onto the bridge is signed for **Avignon.**) Pedal onto the bridge, and watch for a turn for the **Ile de la Barthelasse.** If you're hoping to camp or to claim an inexpensive bed in Avignon, **Camping Bagatelle** is your best bet. Swing **right** off the bridge to loop around to the campground. (There's an *auberge* inside with hostel-type lodgings.)

To continue into Avignon's **center,** pedal onward with the Rhône bridge to reach the left bank and the city walls. Avignon's **tourist office** at 41, cours Jean Jaurès is on the opposite side of town, not far from the train station. Probably the simplest way to reach the office is to stay **outside the walls** and cycle the circling road until you come abreast of the station. Then dive **left** through the city gate to get on **cours Jean Jaurès.** The efficient and helpful staff at the tourist office can supply you with a city map, a list of accommodations, and information on the sights.

Visit Avignon's Papal Palace (Palais des Papes), where the roaming and Rome-less popes settled in for 100 years. The palace is a handsome structure, and it totally overwhelms the little church beside it. Then climb to Le Rocher des Doms, a wonderful park with a superb view of the Rhône and the twelfth-century Pont St. Bénézet. Avignon's old core has many fine buildings, lots of tempting shop windows, and the self-satisfied look of a popular tourist town.

# Avignon to Nîmes (via the Pont du Gard): 65 kilometers

We'll preface this ride from Avignon to Nîmes with a bit of advice for cyclists who feel they've seen about all of the Mediterranean coast (and its traffic) that they care to. Our route, as written, takes you south from here, with a stop at the tantalizing city of Nîmes enroute to the Camargue and the busy "Med." However, on our most recent visit to the area, we bypassed the coast in favor of a much quieter ride to Narbonne. The hills of Hérault are lovely and lonely—not heavy on tourist sights but very nice. Consider a more northerly route to Narbonne if you've had enough of condos and resorts.

As you continue your ride toward Nîmes, the first 10 km of your cycling day will be a "rerun." **Backtrack** from Avignon by crossing the **Rhône bridge,** then go **right** for **Villeneuve-lès-Avignon** and **right again** just afterward for **Aramon.** You'll swing around and **under the Rhône bridge** to find your way to the busy **Road D2** along the river's right bank. Pedal the flat thoroughfare away from town and south along the river valley. Escape D2 happily as you swing **right** onto **Road D126** to enter **Aramon.**

Keep to the **right** as you pedal through this attractive fortified village, and hop on the road signed for **Théziers.** Lovely, pastoral cycling follows as you enter the Provence of poetry and legend. Look for shimmering olive trees, slender green cypresses, rocky vineyards, and barren ridges set against a sky of dancing blue. You'll pass the gemlike Romanesque church of **St. Amand** just before **Théziers.**

In Théziers, swing **right** for **Remoulins,** and pedal **Road D19,** then **Road D19B** as you continue with the signed *Route des Vins.* You'll see as many cherry orchards as you do vineyards as you cruise on toward Remoulins. Cross under the **A9 freeway** and intersect with the disagreeable **Road N100** just before Remoulins. Go **left** here to cycle toward the city, and continue **straight** at the **roundabout** with signs for the **Pont du Gard/Rive Droite.**

Pedal Remoulins's main street past several *patisseries* (be sure to gather your picnic for the Pont du Gard on the way through town), then keep **left** at the far end of the city with more signs for the **Pont du Gard/Rive Droite.** You'll cross the **Gardon River** and go **right** on **Road D981** toward France's most famous aqueduct. Pass a campground, a **tourist office,** a parking lot, and loads of postcard racks as you near your goal. Somehow, the Pont du Gard soars above it all, triumphing through the beauty of its design, the ingenuity of its construction, and the longevity of its rule.

The massive Roman aqueduct makes a spectacular picnic spot, and you can wheel your bicycle out onto the ancient stones of the span to claim your seat. You'll find a great photo angle if you descend to the Gardon River with the path that leaves from the far end of the aqueduct. And be sure to explore the top tier of the span (if you're not afraid of heights!) to see the channel that allowed the Romans to carry water from the Eure River all the way to Nîmes.

Road D981 crosses the Gardon in the shadow of the Pont du Gard. Continue with D981 to join the **main road** from Remoulins (becomes **D981**) and go **left.** Traffic is fairly steady on this thoroughfare, although it's wide and straight. If you want to see the charming midsize city of **Uzès,** stick with it. Otherwise, dive **left** for **Collias** after about 3 km, and pedal the much more enjoyable **Road D112.** Go **left** again a few kilometers later for **Collias,** then follow **Road D3** to the little town (campground here).

In Collias, swing **right** onto D112 toward **Sanilhac,** and continue through vineyards, orchards, and fields of asparagus with your quiet route. Pedal toward **Pont St. Nicolas** from Sanilhac, and enjoy a gentle downhill glide to the Gardon. You'll hit **Road D979** coming from Uzès (those who made the detour to visit Uzès will join our route here), and go **left** to enter the tiny village of **Pont St. Nicolas,** named for its thirteenth-century bridge.

Cross the **Gardon River** and pause to enjoy the scene, then prepare yourself for a **long ascent** as you climb away from the river with D979, snaking upward through a rocky canyon. Things level out after about 7 km, then pedal onward through a **military area** and past a French military base. Pick up views of Nîmes's high-rise buildings as you plunge down an olive-sprinkled hillside into town.

Reach the edge of Nîmes and continue with your **main route** (becomes the Avenue Vincent Faita). You'll hit a sign for the **center** leading onto the **Boulevard Saintenac**—follow it. Endure hectic city cycling onto the **Boulevard Gambetta,** then watch for a sign for the **Maison Carée.** Go **left** here onto the **rue Auguste** to find Nîmes's **tourist information** office. You can claim a city map and a list of accommodations here.

Unfortunately, Nîmes's municipal campground has an inconvenient location far to the south of the city center. If you hope to do any sightseeing, hunt for a cheap hotel instead. Or claim a bed at the city's youth hostel (they may allow camping for hostel cardholders).

The first-century Roman Arena in Nîmes is an impressive monument to the city's prominence in the Roman world. And its busy streets, glittering shop windows, and brightly lighted movie theaters give testimony to its modern-day prominence. Be sure to visit the city's Roman Arena and the cathedral, and take a walk up the hill to the Tour Magne for an impressive view of the sprawling metropolis. The extensive gardens around the tower make a great spot for a picnic.

*An amazed tourer stands within a vast arch of France's unforgettable Pont du Gard.*

*Mottled plane trees line a quiet road near Uzès in southern France.*

## Nîmes to Aigues-Mortes: 45 kilometers

Your early kilometers of pedaling will be far from idyllic today as you fight your way out of Nîmes and its urban sprawl. Ride carefully! From the city's Roman Arena and **Place de Arenes,** angle **right** onto the **rue de la République** and stay with this busy route to the **Boulevard Jean Jaurès.** Go **left** here and cycle this hectic road to a **roundabout** on an even more hectic ring road. Go **right** onto the

**ring road** and pedal to the next **roundabout,** where you'll go **left** with signs for **Générac.**

Continue away from Nîmes on the surprisingly busy **Road D13,** passing the city's municipal campground along the way. Intersect with **Road D135** and go **right** at the roundabout with signs for **Générac.** Grab a **left** shortly after to continue with **D13** toward **Générac.** Pedal through orchards and vineyards, and keep to the **right** through Générac to gain **Road D139** for **Beauvoisin** and **Vauvert.**

Traffic finally eases as you cycle to Beauvoisin and continue with signs for **Vergèze** and **Vauvert.** You'll be pedaling through an area of Provence known as the Camargue as you zigzag south toward Aigues-Mortes. The Camargue is a marshy plain created by the Rhône River, and it holds rice fields, vineyards, and a 33,000-acre reserve for migratory birds. If you're lucky, you might spot a flock of pink flamingos on your ride. As for the much-touted wild horses of the Camargue, they seem to have all signed on as "hired hooves" for the myriad "dude ranches" in the area.

**Cross Road D135** and swing **right** onto **D56** for **Vergèze** shortly afterward. You'll abandon D56 as you continue **straight** with **Road D139** and ride toward **Perrier.** Look for the factory buildings of the famous bubbly water straight ahead as you veer **left** onto a **tiny road** crossing a **canal** (there's a small road sign for **St. Pastour**). Keep to the **right** at the subsequent **Y** (it's unsigned), and cycle this silent road past greenhouses and nurseries to reach an unsigned intersecting road (Road D104). Continue **straight** across and hit **Road D979** soon after.

Go **left** on D979 and pedal to the wild **Road N313.** Cross carefully and continue **straight** on the small road through the fields (don't go left into Aimargues). You'll encounter a short section of roadway with no-entry signs (for no apparent reason). Continue through with caution to hit **Road N572.**

You'll pick up signs for **Marsillargues** here as you continue **straight** on your small-road route, cycling past vineyards and fields of asparagus. Cross the **Vidourle River** and enter **Marsillargues,** then angle **left** through town to find the road signed for **Aigues-Mortes.** Pedal this route to **Road D979** and continue **straight** across into **St. Laurent-d'Aigouze,** then go **right** onto **Road D46** toward **Aigues-Mortes.**

Keep to the **left** through St. Laurent to stay on D46, then cycle onward past windswept rice fields and grazing white horses to reach the lonely **Tour Carbonnière,** northern outpost of the walled city of Aigues-Mortes. Pedal on with D46 to an intersection with **Road D58,** and stay with signs for **Aigues-Mortes** to reach this touristy little town surrounded by wonderfully preserved medieval walls.

St. Louis sailed from this port on a crusade to the Holy Land in 1248. Climb to the top of the wall for a view of the city and the sea. You can walk the entire circuit if you have the time. Venture down into the streets of the city if you dare, but be prepared to resist the neon pink flamingos, fragrant lavender sachets, plastic Camargue horses, and a host of other "tourist attractions" being offered by the shops that line the way.

Look for the city **tourist office** on the place St. Louis. You can line up your own personal "wild" horseback ride here or simply ask about accommodations. The city has a handful of hotels and a deluxe campground. (If you'd like to see more of the Camargue, try a day ride southeast toward Saintes-Maries-de-la-Mer. It's lovely on a sunny day.)

## Aigues-Mortes to Frontignan: 47 kilometers

Leave Aigues-Mortes south on **Road D979** for **le-Grau-du-Roi.** Cross the **bridge** in the old port city, and stay beside the sea to gain **Road D255** for **la Grande-Motte,** a bizarre resort settlement filled with modernistic buildings, immaculate parks, and tidy tennis courts.

Go **left** for **Carnon-Plage** in la Grande-Motte, then turn **right** onto **Road D59** to ride between the sea and the main coast road. Traffic is heavy in this area, as the massive city of Montpellier isn't far away. Ride through **Carnon-Plage** and keep to the **left** for **Palavas** on **Road D62E.** Watch for flamingos in the lake to the right of the road. Reach a junction with **Road D986** and go **right** for **Montpellier** and **Villeneuve.**

Pedal **3 km** and veer **left** for **Villeneuve** onto **Road D185.** Ride through Villeneuve and follow signs for **Mireval.** Angle **right** to join **Road N112** after Mireval and pedal on toward **Frontignan.** There's a small year-round campground (on the left side of N112) 3 km before Frontignan. If you're looking for a room, try Frontignan or continue on to Sète.

## Frontignan to Narbonne: 85 kilometers

Stay on the busy **N112** through Frontignan, and pedal the 7 km to **Sète,** a large port in the French region of Roussillon. Sète is a main port for trade with North Africa. Follow signs for the *centre* and **Béziers** as you ride through Sète. Cross a **canal** and go **left** for **Béziers,** staying beside the sea. Reach an **intersection** at the far end of town, and veer **left** for **Béziers** and **Agde.**

Pedal a flat, boring 20 km of seaside road to **Agde.** Go **straight** at the **intersection** just before town to abandon N112 (N112 becomes a ring road) and continue into the city. With its forbidding black cathedral and narrow streets, Agde makes a great lunch stop—if you haven't already fallen prey to the sandy Mediterranean beaches on the route in. Follow signs for **Béziers** through Agde, crossing the **Hérault River** and continuing on **Road D912** with a marked increase in traffic.

Pass a **turnoff** for Portiragnes, descend a **short hill,** and veer **left** off the main road at the bottom. Then go **right** onto **Road D37** and ride to **Villeneuve.** Leave Villeneuve south on **D37** toward **Sérignan,** and swing **right** to cross the **Orb River** into Sérignan 5 km later. Follow signs for **Vendres** through the city, and ride on **D37** through Vendres and on to **Lespignan.** Vendres, Lespignan, and Fleury are all delightful small towns.

Go **left** onto **Road D14** for **Fleury** in Lespignan, and cross **under the A9 freeway** and over the **Aude River.** In Fleury, follow signs for **Salles d'Aude** and ride on **Road D31** to **Coursan.** Join **Road N113** for the final 7 km to **Narbonne.** If it's late in the day, Coursan has an inexpensive (albeit primitive) municipal campground. It's near the city soccer field.

Enter Narbonne on N113 and head for the Cathedral of St. Just. The cathedral is on the left, just before the Canal de la Robine. Narbonne's **tourist office** is on Place Salengro, north of the cathedral. You'll find an outstanding selection of English-language literature on the city, and you can get information on Narbonne's campground (1½ km from the center), hotels, and pensions from the office staff.

Narbonne's cathedral is an architectural freak, but it's a magnificent one. The church was begun on a grand scale in 1272, but it was never completed. As a result, the lofty Gothic choir has been left without a nave. Explore the lovely interior, exchange winks with the staring gargoyles in the cloister, then continue on to the Archbishop's Palace right next door. You'll be delighted by the sights this southern wine town has to offer. Use the tourist-office map to direct your wandering.

# Narbonne to Carcassonne: 77 kilometers

The ride to the walled city of Carcassonne provides scenic pastoral surroundings and lots of quiet cycling. However, the wind coming out of the west can be a fierce enemy on the Narbonne–Carcassonne ride. If the gales are howling when you're ready to head out, consider delaying a day or hopping aboard a commuter train for the trip. We tried to fight the tempest one day—and ended up being blown right back to Narbonne's campground!

Hop on the growling **Road N113** running south through the center of Narbonne, then swing west with this main road to pedal out of the city, following signs for **Carcassonne.** You'll have to endure this thoroughly unpleasant thoroughfare for about 4 km, hugging the shoulder and choking on truck exhaust, then grab a **left** turn onto **Road D613** for **Bizanet** and the **Abbaye de Fontfroide.** Aaah….

Much more pleasant cycling follows as you pedal a quiet road past a ruined hilltop château, mournfully guarding its vineyards. Stay with **D613** when the road branches to the right for **Bizanet.** Cross under the Carcassonne-bound **freeway,** and pedal onward to a **left** turn signed for the **Abbaye de Fontfroide.** If you have the time for a 4-km (roundtrip) detour, consider making a visit to this secluded eleventh-century abbey.

Cruise on with D613 toward **St. Laurent,** negotiating gentle hills on a delightfully peaceful road. You'll be pedaling past the vineyards that produce Corbières wine as you glide through St. Laurent, then climb to a junction with **Road D3** toward **Lagrasse.** Go **right** here and ride through **Tournissan,** a small town set on a long avenue of spotty-trunked plane trees.

**Climb steadily** for a time, then enjoy a **swift descent** into the rocky **Alsou Gorge.** The road hugs the little river as it curves and bends toward **Lagrasse.** Be sure to pause in this delightful village, its medieval streets tucked into the vine-swathed hills of the river valley. A ruined abbey, an ancient bridge, and a picturesque market square make the little town a treat. There's a campground here, if you decide to linger.

From Lagrasse, continue with the twisting river gorge as it fights its way through rock-encrusted hills. You'll have a gentle climb before **Pradelles-en-Val,** then pass **Monze,** a tiny village snuggled into a blanket of vines. Rolling hills commence as you follow the roller-coaster route of D3 past **Fontiès d'Aude**, across the **freeway,** and on to **Road N113** toward **Carcassonne.**

Rejoin **N113** for the final hectic kilometers into **Carcassonne** (you can escape to the right on Road D303 through Berriac for a time, if the traffic is unendurable). You'll see the turreted walls of the old town (la Cité) on a hill above the road as you approach your goal.

You can turn off N113 to climb the hill to la Cité, but if you're looking for a cheap room, continue on to the modern town on the banks of the Aude River and do your looking there instead. Seek help from Carcassonne's **tourist information** office at the place Gambetta. There are a few hotels within the walls of la Cité, but you'll pay plenty for the atmosphere. There is a superbly situated youth hostel on top, however.

If you want to camp, watch for a sign for Carcassonne's campground just before N113 crosses the Aude to enter the modern city. The campground is an easy walk from both la Cité and twentieth-century Carcassonne. Plan to spend several hours exploring the cobblestone streets of la Cité, and be sure to visit the beautiful Cathedral of St. Nazaire with its impressive collection of stained glass. A walk along the golden-hued walls of la Cité at dawn, with a view of the snow-capped peaks of the Pyrenees beckoning from Spain, will make your visit a memorable one.

If you're ending your cycling at Carcassonne, head for the train station and load your bicycle aboard a baggage train toward Paris and its airport (or points beyond). Please remember that you'll need to send your bicycle two or three days in advance to ensure it arrives on time.

Those with the time and inclination for more riding could continue with the Canal du Midi toward Toulouse, swing north toward Castres and Albi, or choose another route instead. On our first visit to Carcassonne, we continued into Spain, pedaling on to the enchanting city of Barcelona, then following the Spanish coast all the way to Gibraltar. You'll be able to pick up the start of Tour No. 18 in Seville if you choose this route. (Please be forewarned that the Spanish coastal roads are plagued with very heavy traffic, though.)

# TOUR NO. 18

# SOUTHERN HOSPITALITY
### Seville to Madrid, Spain (via Lisbon, Portugal)

Distance: 1,288 kilometers (800 miles)
Estimated time: 16 riding days
Best time to go: April, May, June, September, October, or November
Terrain: A blend of easy pedaling and horrendous hills
Connecting tours: Tour No. 17

Spain is a vast, diverse, and rugged land, and the Spaniards are friendly, easygoing hosts. Spain's culture, history, and spectacular natural beauty combine to make this country an excellent place to explore by bicycle. Be cautious on the busier roads—more because of the speeding northern European tourists than the local drivers. And use common sense about your money and belongings in big tourist cities like Seville, Toledo, and Madrid. Be careful, enthusiastic, and appreciative, and you'll discover a treasure-filled land of art, architecture, and religious heritage that will make your visit special.

Try to work on your language skills while you ride. The Spaniards won't ridicule your fumbling. Instead, they'll greet even your weakest efforts with warmth and appreciation. If you have time, read a book on Spain before you go, and gain some understanding of this country that once ruled much of the New World. James Michener's *Iberia* is an excellent place to begin.

Portugal, the second country you'll visit on this tour, is exhilaratingly beautiful and painfully poor. You'll see a good cross-section of the country on this ride, and you'll surely wonder how the pristine loveliness of the Portuguese countryside can exist beside the big-city madness of Lisbon. Portugal's fantastic monasteries, colorful villages, and enchanting countryside more than make up for its rough road surfaces and bitter hills. And the Portuguese people, with their warmth, enthusiasm, and ready smiles, will win a special place in your heart.

**CONNECTIONS.** You can reach Seville and the start of this tour by pedaling the Spanish coast from Carcassonne and the end of Tour No. 17, riding through Barcelona, Valencia, and Málaga along the way (this is the route we took). But the Spanish coast is woefully overdeveloped and overcrowded, and coastal roads can be terrifying at best. Or you can travel to Seville by plane or train from

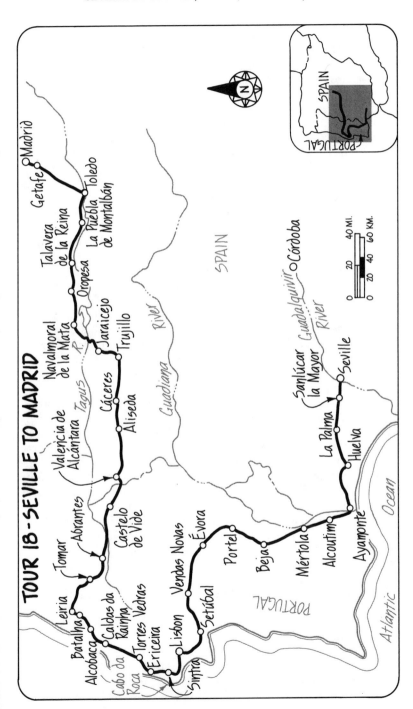

Madrid, thus making the tour a complete loop.

**INFORMATION.** Write ahead to both the National Tourist Office of Spain, 665 Fifth Avenue, New York, New York 10022 and the Portuguese Government Tourist Office, 590 Fifth Avenue, New York, New York 10036 for information on specific cities, city maps, campground listings, etc.

For Spain, it's nice to have a good overall guidebook such as the *Blue Guide Spain, The Real Guide: Spain,* or Michelin's *Green Guide Spain.* A nice combination volume that covers both Spain and Portugal is *Let's Go: Spain and Portugal.* Once in Spain, look for *turismo* offices. In Barcelona, Madrid, and Seville, you can stock up on beautifully illustrated English-language pamphlets for the whole country.

Guidebook options for Portugal, in addition to the previously mentioned *Let's Go,* include Michelin's *Green Guide Portugal,* the *Blue Guide Portugal,* and *The Real Guide: Portugal.* Local tourist offices within the country (*turismo*) are heavily stocked with English-language literature, probably because Portugal is a favorite vacation spot for British tourists. These offices will provide area maps and information on camping and hotels.

**MAPS.** For route finding on this tour, you can use Michelin's 1:400,000 series for Spain (Nos. 446 and 447) and its 1:500,000 map (No. 37) for Portugal. The Automobile Club of Portugal (ACP) also offers a 1:550,000 map of the country, with a 1:250,000 cutout of the Lisbon area. It lists *pousadas* (hotels) and shows campgrounds and sights of interest.

**ACCOMMODATIONS.** Campgrounds in Spain are usually available near large cities and major tourist attractions. They're generally clean and moderately priced. Tourist offices supply the *Mapa de Campings,* a pamphlet that lists campgrounds all over Spain by area and by rating. The Spanish rating system has little to do with the price of a campground; however, it can have a bearing on the quality of the facilities. Freelance camping is acceptable as long as you stay away from populated areas. Always ask for permission.

Rooms in Spain are quite affordable and Spanish hosts are usually good natured about finding a spot for a road-weary bicycle. Look for *fondas, pensiones, hostal-residencias,* and hotels. Check out rooms in advance and look for the prices listed on the doors. Breakfast may or may not be included, and showers usually cost extra.

If you want to splurge, the Spanish government maintains a network of *paradors* in castles, palaces, and historic buildings that make for special one-night stops. Ask for a list from the Spanish National Tourist Office. You may need reservations.

Camping is cheap in Portugal, but you won't find many sites away from the coast or main tourist towns. Freelance camping is permitted, but you *must* obtain the landowner's permission.

You should be able to afford a little more luxury when choosing accommodations in Portugal. Rooms are inexpensive, with a *pensão* being one of the cheapest ways to go. The government-run *pousadas* (hotels) have nicer facilities—and a higher price tag. There are more than thirty of them in the country, and you'll need to make reservations in advance.

**SUPPLIES.** Eating well in Spain is an inexpensive treat. Specialties in restaurants include the delicious rice and seafood dish called *paëlla* and a huge assortment of seafood such as squid (*calamares*) and cod (*vizcaina*). Picnic materials also abound in Spain, with a host of regional cheeses, lots of tasty lunchmeat, and incredibly inexpensive tins of tuna and sardines.

Spanish beer (*cerveza*) is excellent and a bottle of red wine (*vino tinto*) accompanies almost every Spanish meal. Don't leave Spain without sampling a breakfast snack of *churros*—a deep-fried treat that will line your stomach walls with lead—along with a cup of delicious Spanish coffee.

Stores are generally open Monday through Friday from 9:00 A.M. to 7:00 P.M., with an afternoon shutdown between 1:30 and 5:00 P.M. You can shop on Saturday morning for the weekend, but most Spanish shopkeepers lock up Saturday afternoon and all day Sunday.

The Spaniards are serious about cycling, so there are scores of good bicycle shops in the country. Of course, "cycling" means racing here, so you won't find too much specialized touring gear. You will find helpful, interested bike shop owners, however.

Portugal is one of the few bargains left in Western Europe, so treat yourself to some delicious restaurant meals during your stay. Try the seafood specialties that dominate Portuguese cuisine. Dishes with cod (*bacalhau*) are especially good. Portuguese pastries are tasty, too, and there are local specialties for every region you'll ride through. Try the small, round sheep and goat cheese for lunch. Piled on heavy Portuguese potato bread (*broa*), they make a filling picnic.

Portugal is world famous for its port wine, but this is definitely not a drink designed to keep you light on your pedals or your feet, so try something with a little less kick if you still have some cycling to do.

Shops in Portugal are usually closed from 12:30 or 1:00 P.M. to 3:00 P.M., but they stay open until 6:00 or 7:00 in the evening. Most shops are closed Saturday afternoons and Sundays. Museums and other tourist attractions are generally closed on Mondays in both Spain and Portugal.

Plan to carry spare cables, spokes, tubes, and patches for your ride in Portugal, as bicycle shops are scarce and quality touring gear is scarcer still. And make it a habit to check your nuts and bolts at the end of every rattling riding day. (You might want to check your fillings, too!)

# Seville to Huelva: 96 kilometers

Seville has one of the highest concentrations of American students and tourists in Spain, and it's easy to see why. The city is a delight, filled with architectural treasures and cultural revelations. Although it's Spain's fourth-largest city, Seville is relatively "comfortable," even for a cyclist.

Begin your sightseeing at Seville's **tourist office** at Avenida de la Constitución 21B. You can pick up information on lodgings and attractions here. Seville has a youth hostel and a few inconveniently located campgrounds. You should be able to find an affordable room without difficulty, as long as you're not looking during Seville's *Feria de Abril* (April Fair) or *Semana Santa* (Holy Week).

Don't miss a visit to Seville's cathedral, a fantastic structure of soaring stone that will mesmerize you for hours. Climb to the top of the cathedral's *Giralda,* a Moorish minaret transformed into a Christian church tower. The view from the top is magnificent.

Seville has too many treasures to list here, and its wealth increased with the visit of the 1992 World Expo, so be sure to pick up some English-language literature and plan to invest a couple of days in the city. Since this tour turns west toward Portugal from Seville, you might want to consider a one-day detour by train or bus to see Córdoba, the Muslim-influenced city to the east. It's a two-hour ride by train; buses are slightly slower and more expensive. A visit to Córdoba's unique cathedral/mosque makes the trip worthwhile.

From Seville's **cathedral,** follow signs for **Huelva** to gain the **Paseo de Cristóbal Colón** along the banks of the **Guadalquivir River.** Cycle north along the river and turn **left** just before the **train station** to cross the **Guadalquivir,** following signs for **Huelva.** The road turns into freeway after it crosses a second bridge. Take the exit marked for **Road N431** and **Castilleja,** and climb a **steady hill** away from Seville.

Ride through Castilleja and **Espartinas,** cycling roller-coaster terrain. Descend swiftly after **Sanlúcar la Mayor.** You'll see olives, vines, citrus orchards, cork, and eucalyptus as you pedal the lightly trafficked **N431** toward **La Palma.** Swing **left** off the main road to pass through La Palma, and look for the stork nests on top of the city church. **Rejoin N431** outside of town.

Climb a short hill at **Niebla,** a small walled city, and continue through level countryside to **San Juan del Puerto.** Follow signs for **Huelva** and pedal into the midsize port city. In 1492, Christopher Columbus sailed for the New World from the Huelva estuary, and he returned in 1493, to change the face of Spain forever.

You can find cheap accommodations in the streets around Huelva's **train station.** There's a campground several kilometers beyond the city. It's noted in the next section.

*Seville's cathedral is the hub of a lovely city.*

## Huelva to Alcoutim (Junction): 90 kilometers

From Huelva, follow signs for **Punta Umbria** and **Ayamonte**. Cross a long **bridge** on **Road H414** over the estuary, and take the route signed for **Ayamonte** and **Portugal** to join **N431** heading west. There's a campground on the road to Punta Umbria, about 10 km from Huelva. Go **left** on **N431** and pedal through **rolling terrain** for the 36 km to **Ayamonte** and the **Spanish/Portuguese border**.

In Ayamonte, an attractive seaside town, follow signs for **Portugal** to reach the **ferry** across the **Guadiana River**. Crossings are frequent, short, and inexpensive. Arrive at the small border town of **Vila Real** and dive into Portugal. There's a **tourist office** next to the customs building at the border. Stop to pick up literature for your ride. By the way, you'll need to set your watch back an hour with the border crossing, as Portugal is an hour off Spanish time.

We were filled to the brim with the tourist trappings of the biker-unfriendly Costa del Sol, so we decided to pass up a ride west along Portugal's famed Algarve Coast, riding north instead to search for more serene inland riding. As a result, we enjoyed two days of incredibly tough hills, uncomfortably rough roads, and some of the loveliest scenery and most uncluttered countryside we found in all of Europe.

If you don't have camping equipment, you may want to look for a room in Vila Real and ride for Mértola (72 km) the following day. Lodging options are few and far between once you leave the coast. If you're camping, carry an evening meal and plenty of liquids.

From Vila Real, follow signs for **Lisbon** (Lisboa) and **Castro Marim** out of town. Turn **right** for **Castro Marim** and **Lisbon** on **Road N122** and cycle past Castro Marim's brightly painted houses and hilltop fort before winding into the Portuguese countryside on a roughly paved road. You'll have **grueling uphills** and bone-rattling downhills as you ride through a gorgeous blend of farmland and cork forests.

We watched women doing their laundry in streams beside whitewashed villages and waved to men plowing vast fields behind straining teams of oxen and felt as though we were pedaling back in time. Battle the hills past small towns like **Azinhal** and **Odeleite,** and let your legs dictate the day's distance. We pulled off the road a few kilometers before the Alcoutim junction, pitched our tent while the stars glimmered overhead, and fell asleep feeling hill weary, road rattled, and deeply in love with Portugal.

## Alcoutim (Junction) to Beja: 82 kilometers

The **terrain is brutal** for the 35 km to Mértola. It's an almost constant series of ups and downs, and the rough road surface makes even the downhills a challenge. The vibrant green countryside and the smiles of black-garbed women in the fields will ease your suffering while you ride. Mértola is a stunning fortresslike city crowning a rounded hill, and pink, blossom-laden trees color the slopes below it.

Life will come to a stop in the small town as you pedal through, but the staring locals will offer friendly smiles in return for yours. Stay on **Road 122** for **Beja** as you leave Mértola. Climb a **long hill** to the **Alentejo Plateau.** The hills flatten out as you enter a gently rolling landscape of green fields dotted with cork and olive, carob and eucalyptus.

Pedal into **Beja,** an attractive city with a busy agricultural trade. The thirteenth-century castle on the northern edge of town is worth exploring, as is the nearby former Convent of the Conception. And the old streets around the castle, lined with tile-fronted buildings and overhung with wrought-iron balconies, are a treat to wander through.

Beja's **tourist office** is at Rua Capitao Joao Francisco de Sousa 25. There are several *pensões* in the city, and there's a municipal campground southwest of town.

## Beja to Évora: 78 kilometers

From Beja's **castle** (look for signs for *Castel*), angle to the **left,** following signs for **Lisbon** and **Évora.** Coast downhill to the Alentejo Plain. Stay with signs for Évora, cycling north on **Road N18.** Enjoy easy riding through flat wheatlands for the 23 km to **Vidigueira,** an attractive whitewashed town. Stay on N18 toward **Évora** and climb into **rolling hills** covered with cork trees. Portugal is the world's leading producer of cork, and you'll see why as you pedal past endless rows of trees.

Pass **Portel,** a small, castle-shadowed town, and continue north through rolling hills. Then cruise through a **long descent** to **Monte de Trigo.** Traffic is light and the road surface is good along the way. The terrain softens after Monte de Trigo, and you'll cycle through a wide, wheat- and cork-covered plain.

Barring recent improvements, expect a molar-loosening **4 km of rough cobblestone** road just before the intersection with **Road 256.** Rattle through to the **junction,** then gain gloriously smooth pavement, swinging **left** (still on N18) to sail the final 16 km into **Évora.** Enter Évora and follow signs for the **city center.** The **tourist office** is in the central square, Praça do Giraldo. You can get a map of town and accommodation information there.

Évora offers a youth hostel, a campground, and several inexpensive *pensões.* The city dates back to Roman times, and one of its chief treasures is the second-century Temple of Diana, a beautiful collection of standing marble columns that looks like it should be in Greece. The twelfth-century cathedral (*Sé*) is also a treat, with carved choir stalls and an interesting treasury. And don't miss the Ossuary Chapel of the Church of San Francisco. This "chapel of bones" is a sight that will send a shiver through to yours.

After your day of sightseeing, join the Portuguese for their evening "parade," and explore the balcony-shadowed alleyways, the lovely tiled houses, and the flower-brightened corners that make Évora a special town.

## Évora to Setúbal: 103 kilometers

You'll need an early start and lots of energy to make the distance in this lengthy stretch of riding. Unfortunately, the final section of the day offers little in the way of appealing accommodation options. If you're doubtful about completing a 103-km day, start looking for a bed or a tent site well before the industrial wasteland of Setúbal.

Leave Évora on **Road 114** toward **Lisbon** (Lisboa). The road sur-face is excellent and the terrain is gently rolling to **Montemor-o-Novo,** a fortress-guarded town on a hill. Traffic increases at **Vendas Novas,** and the hills flatten out to become dry pasturelands dotted with cork. Continue west toward **Pegões-Cruz** and **Setúbal.**

In **Pegões-Cruz,** swing **left** onto **Road 10** for **Lisbon** and **Setúbal,** and pedal a short stretch of narrow, rough road. You'll rue the passing of pastoral Portugal as you draw near Lisbon. Traffic in-creases, cars travel faster, and cities grow more industrial throughout the day. In **Marateca,** swing **right** with **N10** for Setúbal, and pedal 21 km into the sprawling port city.

The **A2 freeway** to Lisbon starts in Setúbal. Stay **left** and follow the **Setúbal signs** to cycle **N10** into the city. Trace a labyrinthine route through the heart of town, watching for **white signs for Lisbon.** You'll stay on **N10** as it climbs away from Setúbal when you leave.

There are lots of accommodation options in Setúbal, including a municipal campground. The **tourist office** is in the old town on Largo do Corpo Santo, across from the Church of Santa Maria. While you're in Setúbal, be sure to pick up a street map of Lisbon in preparation for your upcoming visit.

## Setúbal to Lisbon: 40 kilometers

Leave Setúbal on **N10** for **Lisbon** and climb a **long, steep hill** with moderate traffic. Descend through rolling coastal hills and pedal on to **Coina.** Traffic increases from here, and you'll ride past a long succes-sion of factories and congestion as you follow **white road signs** for **Lisbon** on **Road 10.**

Reach **Corroios** and follow signs for **Cacilhas** (Lisbon signs go to the freeway). Pedal on to reach the **ferry** that will carry you across the **Tagus** (Tajo) **River** to Lisbon's harbor. You'll see the massive freeway bridge on your left and the overwhelming sprawl of Lisbon across the water as you pedal into Cacilhas. Ferries run throughout the day.

You'll be deposited in the heart of Lisbon at either the Praça Duque de Terceira or the Praça do Comércio in the busy harbor district. From the **Praça do Comércio** (to the right along the harbor from the Praça Duque de Terceira), head straight into the city on **Rua Agusta.** Con-tinue through the Praça Dom Pedro IV (*Rossio*) with its statue of King Pedro IV, and reach the **Praça dos Restauradores.** Lisbon's munici-pal **tourist office** is on the the square in the Palácio da Foz.

You'll be able to get lots of English-language literature at the tourist office, and the staff can help you with accommodations, too. There are hundreds of cheap *pensões* in Lisbon, and there are a youth hostel and a campground. Try the streets on either side of the wide **Avenida da Liberdade** as a starting place in your hunt for a bed. And please be sure to keep a close eye on your bicycle and gear in this immense and sometimes dangerous city.

You'll have lots to see in Lisbon, and there are plenty of opportunities to stretch your legs if you like to walk. Climb through the narrow streets of the Alfama, the oldest part of the city, and enjoy the tile-fronted houses, the streetside fish markets, and the flower-filled balconies that make the district famous. Visit the hilltop Castle of St. George above the Alfama, and claim a vista of the Tagus River and the city sprawled beside its harbor. Or stroll along the grand Avenida da Liberdade, a mile-long avenue lined with theaters, cinemas, hotels, and travel agencies, and eat a picnic lunch in Edward VII Park, where you'll have a fine view of the mighty maritime city sloping down to the water.

# Lisbon to Torres Vedras: 85 kilometers

From Lisbon's **Praça do Comércio,** cycle **west** along the harbor on **Avenida Das Naus,** pass through Praça Duque de Terceira, and continue on to **Avenida 24 de Julho.** Follow signs toward **Cascais** and **Estoril.** Pass Lisbon's beautiful **Hieronymite Monastery** and the **Belém Tower** as you leave the city. If you didn't visit the monastery during your stay in Lisbon, be sure to stop for a look inside. The cloister is one of the finest in Europe.

Continue along the coast on **Road 6,** passing through small resort towns and gently undulating hills. In **Estoril**, swing **right** for **Sintra** and **climb steeply** inland. Stay with signs for Sintra, joining **Road 9,** then climb more gently toward the city. Sintra was the summer home of Portugal's kings for 600 years, and the city boasts a royal palace (open for tours) and an attractive old core.

If you have time, you can also visit the lofty **Moors' Castle** commanding a hilltop 3 km outside the city, or explore the **Pena Palace,** another hilltop attraction. Sintra's **tourist office** is at Praça da Republica 19. There's a campground on the coast, not far from town. From Sintra, you can also make a day ride to Cabo da Roca, the westernmost point in continental Europe. Buses run from Sinta to the cape.

Follow signs for **Ericeira,** pedaling away from Sintra and entering an area of green rolling hills, fresh ocean breezes, and intensively cultivated farmland. You'll have a gradual climb as you leave Sintra, then level riding on nicely surfaced road. Stay with signs for Ericeira on **Road 247.** Pass through **Carvoeira,** and follow the coast road along the bluffs.

Endure a series of short but **steep ascents and descents.** From Ericeira, follow signs for **Torres Vedras,** staying on **Road 247** through **Ribamar** and **Barril,** then turning inland to gain mostly level riding for the rest of the day. We saw many signs of Portugal's poverty in this farming region—women planting seed by hand, men breaking mounds of soil with hoes, and wrinkle-faced grandmothers pushing heavy wheelbarrows along the road.

Torres Vedras is a pleasant midsize town, overlooked by a Moorish castle and made colorful by the characteristic tile-fronted buildings that enliven Portuguese towns. There are a couple of small *pensões* in the city, if you need a room.

*The intricate design of a Spanish street*

## Torres Vedras to Alcobaca: 67 kilometers

From Torres Vedras, follow the winding **Road 8 north** toward
**Bombarral.** Light traffic, gently rolling terrain, and a rough road surface will mark your first 24 km as you cycle through eucalyptus forest
and quiet vineyards. The road improves after Bombarral. Continue on
for **Caldas da Rainha** and **Obidos.** Watch for stout windmills on the
hillsides as you ride.

Swing **left** off the main road to visit **Obidos,** an enchanting city
surrounded by well-kept walls. Spend an hour wandering the narrow
streets stacked with brightly painted houses, and peek into the countless shops where plates, sweaters, and cotton tablecloths tumble out
the doors. From Obidos, **rejoin Road 8** and follow signs for **Caldas
da Rainha.** Ride through rolling hills toward the busy city. You'll pick
up more traffic 2 km before town when another road joins Road 8.

Follow **signs for Leiria** as you wind through Caldas, a city with
handsome buildings and interesting streets. There's a campground in
Caldas, if you decide to stay and explore. Leave Caldas on **Road 8** for
**Leiria** and ride with steady traffic for the 25 km to **Alcobaca.** The
terrain is rolling for the first 11 km.

Climb a **long, steep hill** to gain a ridge, then descend and follow a
winding river valley into Alcobaca. The massive form of the twelfth-
century **Santa Maria Monastery** dominates the city. Alcobaca's
**tourist office** is just across the square from the church. Get recommendations on rooms there. Or stay at the convenient municipal
campground while you're in the city.

Spend an hour exploring the monastery complex at Alcobaca. Begin
with the vast church, where soaring pillars will mesmerize you. Marvel at the intricately carved tombs of Dom Pedro and Iñes de Castro,
then continue on to the beautiful Cloister of Silence, where hundreds
of Cistercian monks once prayed. Alcobaca's streets are a delight as
well. If you can escape the city without investigating at least one
hand-painted souvenir shop, you have more willpower that we do!

## Alcobaca to Tomar: 76 kilometers

You'll have two more monastery complexes to visit on this ride, and
you'll have an optional side trip to one of Portugal's most revered religious shrines as well. Begin by leaving Alcobaca on **Road 8** for **Leiria**
and **Batalha.** Climb a **long, steady hill** with heavy traffic and a narrow shoulder. Gain a long ridge and enjoy level riding to a junction
with **Road 1,** where you'll pick up more traffic and a wider shoulder.

Continue **straight** and sail down an **invigorating descent** to
**Batalha,** with the magnificent bulk of the Gothic monastery church
towering over the valley floor below. The luminous walls of elaborately
decorated stone and the pinnacles and buttresses that sprout from

every side of Batalha's church combine to make a majestic building. Walk to the rear of the church to explore the Unfinished Chapels. The decoration is overwhelming, made more powerful by the play of light and shadow through the open roof. The inside of Batalha's church holds treasures of its own, and the magnificent Royal Cloister is a poem in stone, rich in rhythm and rhyme.

From Batalha, endure **up-and-down riding** and steady traffic to **Leiria,** a large city ruled by a squat, square-towered castle. Take the **first exit off Road 1** for **Leiria** and climb a short hill to a **T.** Turn **right,** then go **left** as you follow **blue-and-white signs** for *Sanctuario Fátima.* Descend a short hill and continue straight toward **Tomar.** Follow Tomar signs up a **hill** and turn **right** (east) onto **Road 113.**

You'll have a roller-coaster ride on the roughly surfaced road to Tomar, but the light traffic and vine-covered hillsides are a welcome change from the congestion of Road 1. If you have time, consider making the short side trip to **Fátima,** a world-famous pilgrimage site where a large basilica was built in honor of Our Lady of Fátima. To reach the site, turn **right** on **Road 357** at **Q ta da Sardinha,** 15 km past Leiria. You'll add 12 km to the day's ride by cycling to Fátima. Rejoin **Road 113** via **Road 356.**

Continue on toward **Tomar,** passing through rustling eucalyptus groves and green valleys where women beat their laundry in the streams. Descend into **Tomar,** a small town on the **Nabão River.** Tomar huddles beneath the twelfth-century walls of its fortified Convent of Christ. There's a campground in the park on the river as you enter town.

Tomar's **tourist office** is near the **train station** on the southern edge of the city, and there are several inexpensive *pensões* in town. Climb the hill above the main square (Praça Republica) to reach the Convent of Christ. Stroll the parklike grounds to the beautifully decorated church, and go inside to see the Templars's Rotunda, an octagonal sanctuary styled after Jerusalem's Holy Sepulchre. Don't miss the elaborate Manueline window, immortalized by thousands of Portuguese tourist posters.

## Tomar to Castelo de Vide: 107 kilometers

The next two days of cycling are quite lengthy and may prove too strenuous for all but the fittest tourers. Unfortunately (or fortunately, depending on how you look at it) you'll be cycling through some lonely territory, and larger towns and accommodation options are few. If you need to shorten your riding days, be flexible and keep a sharp eye out for lodging opportunities.

Follow signs for **Lisbon south** on **Road 110** as you leave Tomar, and enjoy flat, easy cycling for about 6 km. Pass the turnoff for **Abrantes** and **Castelo de Bode,** and climb a hill before veering **left** for **S. ta Cita** and **Abrantes.** Pedal up a **steady hill** to a eucalyptus-covered ridge, then descend to the **Tagus** (Tejo) **River** to join **Road 3** for **Abrantes.** Traffic increases as you cycle beside the river through farmland dotted with olives.

**Climb steadily** from the river valley to Abrantes, a bustling city perched on a ridge above the Tagus. There's a fine view of the valley from the city's ruined fortress, and the fifteenth-century church has a lovely tile-covered interior. Descend steeply from Abrantes, following signs for **Portalegre** and **Castelo Branco.**

Cross to the **south bank** of the Tagus and go **left** onto **Road 118** toward **Castelo Branco.** You'll have up-and-down riding for the 15 km to **Alvega.** Then make the **long, steep climb** to Gavião. **Gavião** is the last town of any size until Castelo de Vide, 55 km farther on. If you're not camping, you should keep that in mind.

Climb through Gavião and angle **right** for **Portalegre** and **Castelo Branco.** Descend a **short hill** and veer **left** toward **Castelo Branco** and **Portalegre** at the **Y.** Climb again to a flat plateau and enjoy excellent road surfaces and easy pedaling for the next 20 km.

Stay **right** on the lightly trafficked **Road 118** toward Portalegre, and climb a **short, steep hill** into **Tolosa.** Continue on through **Gáfete** and **Alpalhão** past endless acres of cork. Road surfaces deteriorate in the towns, then improve again outside them. In **Alpalhão,** go **left** toward **Castelo Branco,** then turn **right** for **Castelo de Vide** and gain **Road 246** toward Spain.

Pedal through gently rolling farmland and climb a **long, steady hill** to Castelo de Vide, a pretty town flowing down a hillside ruled by a twelfth-century castle. Look for a room in the city, then go for an evening stroll in the picturesque streets of the Jewish Quarter and anticipate your return to Spain.

## Castelo de Vide to Aliseda: 96 kilometers

Rejoin **Road 246** toward **Spain** and continue climbing for a short distance. Reach the ridgetop and enjoy level or downhill riding to the **junction** for **Marvão,** a tiny town clinging to a hilltop north of the road. Decide for yourself whether the **punishing 7-km climb** to the amazingly situated city is worth the fantastic view from the top. If you're looking for a splurge, Marvão is a great place to do it. There's a fine *pensão* across from the city **tourist office** that provides stunning views of the surrounding countryside from its pleasant rooms. (You may need reservations in high season.) We celebrated the 10,000th mile of our first European bicycle journey here.

Continue east on **Road 246** toward **Spain** (Espanha), and climb gradually to the border. You'll note a marked improvement in road surface as you coast past customs and pedal gradually downhill (now on **Road N521**) to **Valencia de Alcántara.** Follow signs for **Cáceres** throughout the remainder of the day. From Valencia de Alcántara, you'll have mostly level riding with scattered hills as you enter a vast plateau of grassland, cork, and olive.

Pass through the small towns of **Salorino, Herreruela,** and **Aliseda.** Accommodation options are few along this lonely stretch of road. If you don't have a tent, Valencia de Alcántara is your last sure bet for a room until Cáceres, 93 km farther on. You can ask in the smaller towns and hope a hospitable local will take you in. **Aliseda** has a few small grocery stores, friendly townsfolk, and a pleasant olive grove just past town that makes a great spot to camp.

## Aliseda to Cáceres: 30 kilometers

From Aliseda, descend gradually to the **Salor River,** then climb gently toward **Cáceres.** The countryside is quiet, and you might spot a few long-bodied storks wading in the streams you cycle past. Enter the suburbs of Cáceres and join increasing traffic as you swing **right** onto **Road N630** and pedal into the city's busy core. Go past the turn-off for Madrid and Trujillo, then veer **left** at the **roundabout** in the **Plaza de América** onto the tree-lined **Avenue de España.**

Cáceres is rich in architecture and history, and you'll see mansions, medieval walls, and towers that give evidence of the city's illustrious past. One of the most entertaining things about Cáceres is its popularity with storks. The city's rooftops and towers are dotted with the nests of these ungainly creatures, and you'll hear their clacking calls as you explore the streets below.

From the Avenue de España, angle **right** onto **San Antón** and then onto **San Pedro** as you head into the oldest part of town. The **tourist office** is on the Plaza Mayor, just west of the medieval core. There's a busy youth hostel in the city, and there are lots of inexpensive accommodations in the streets outside the Star Arch (Arco de la Estrella).

## Cáceres to Trujillo: 49 kilometers

Return to the **Avenue de España** and **retrace** your route to the **junction** for **Trujillo** and **Madrid** to gain **N521 east.** The wide road has an excellent surface and heavy traffic. Turn back for a look at Cáceres's tower-studded profile as you enter a rolling plain of farmland and twisted cork. Stay on N521 for the entire ride to **Trujillo,** with gentle hills most of the way.

You'll spot Trujillo's striking silhouette ahead, its castle walls and towers following the crest of a low hill down into the city. Trujillo

*Storks rule the tower-studded skyline of Cáceres.*

claims an important place in Spanish history as the "cradle of the con-
quistadors." The most famous of its sons is Francisco Pizarro, con-
queror of Peru. The buildings that resulted from this glorious period of
Trujillo's past are clustered around the Plaza Mayor. Veer **left off
N521,** following signs for ***Centro Ciudad,*** and climb into the hillside
city to reach the plaza.

A handsome equestrian statue of Pizarro rules the square, and a
circular amphitheater of stairs and palaces surrounds it. Look for the
spike-topped Alfiler Tower, where Trujillo's storks hold court, and
climb the hill to the castle for a view of the city and the surrounding
countryside.

Trujillo's **tourist office** is on the **Plaza Mayor.** Ask for help with
your accommodation search there. Then devote an afternoon to exploring the city's twisted streets, wishing for all the world you had stayed
awake in freshman social studies.

*Spanish schoolgirls pose at a street market in Cáceres.*

## Trujillo to Oropesa: 106 kilometers

Another long day of cycling through lonely countryside and small towns awaits as you depart Trujillo. Return to the **main road** from the town center, turn **left,** then angle **left** on **Road E4** toward **Madrid** soon after. Stay on E4 for the rest of the day. There's an excellent shoulder but steady traffic as you follow signs for Madrid. The terrain is fairly level from Trujillo, with descents and climbs as you cross the Tozo and Almonte rivers.

Cycle through **Jaraicejo,** a small town with a big church, and coast downhill to cross the **Arroyo de la Vid.** Then climb a **long hill** (about 5 km) to reach a pass above the Tagus Valley. Enjoy the view before diving into a **long, winding descent.** The kilometers will fly by rapidly. Cross the **Tagus River** and climb a **short, steep hill** before gaining level riding again.

Ascend gently to **Navalmoral de la Mata,** a midsize town with several hotels and inns, and continue east on **E4** to enter vast grasslands sprinkled with cork. Traffic increases after Navalmoral. **La**

**Calzada de Oropesa,** 22 km beyond Navalmoral, has a large church inhabited by skinny storks, and **Lagartera** is famous for its embroidery craft. Swing off the main road to enter Lagartera, and watch for the townswomen busily working at their windows.

Continue on to **Oropesa,** an attractive town overshadowed by two large churches and a fourteenth-century castle (now a *parador*). There are a handful of rooms available here, or you can try to get permission to pitch your tent in a secluded spot in one of the surrounding fields.

## Oropesa to Toledo: 113 kilometers

From Oropesa, continue **east on E4** toward **Madrid.** Pedal through level countryside to **Talavera de la Reina,** a large town that thrives on the ceramic tile industry. Wind through the city core, following **E4** for **Madrid,** and enjoy the colorful ceramics shops that line the road. Stop on the far edge of town to explore the **Prado Virgin Hermitage** in a park to the right of the road. The interior of the church is almost completely covered in tilework dating from the fourteenth to the twentieth centuries.

Cross the **Alberche River** and angle **right** soon after, forsaking the traffic on E4 for a quiet **Road C502** toward **El Carpio de Tajo.** The first 10 km are flat, but hills increase as the road follows the winding course of the Tagus River toward Toledo. Stay on C502 with hilltop castles, olive groves, and vines to make your riding pleasant. Pass **El Carpio de Tajo** and cross a **creek.** Then climb a **long, steady hill** before descending to the **turnoff** for **La Puebla de Montalbán.**

Continue **straight** on C502 and **climb another hill,** then coast down to cross the **Tagus River** and follow its southern bank toward **Toledo.** Stop to admire the famous silhouette of Toledo springing from the valley floor, with pinnacles and turrets and church towers piercing the Castilian sky. Toledo's castle and cathedral rule a ridgeline over the tumbled city of brown stone.

There's a year-round campground on the left side of the road, 3 km from the city center, and there are two seasonal campgrounds closer in. Continue on **C502** and follow signs for the **center** to **recross the Tagus** and climb into town. Toledo's **tourist office** is just outside the **Bisagra Gate** (Puerta de Bisagra). Get a map of the city and help with lodgings here. There are scores of inexpensive rooms tucked in among Toledo's mazelike streets, and you shouldn't have any trouble finding a spot to call your own.

You'll quickly fall in love with this exquisite city of architecture, art, and history. Toledo's cathedral is overwhelming, a glowing white monument of soaring stone, and the treasures within its walls will occupy you for hours. Return to the city streets and join the strolling masses in the Plaza del Zocodover, or walk down to the banks of the Tagus to view the city from below. There are several churches in Toledo that deserve a look, and be sure to check out the Santa Cruz Museum as a warmup for your visit to the Prado in Madrid. If you're a fan of El Greco, Toledo will be a special treat.

## Toledo to Madrid: 70 kilometers

Despite the fact that it's Spain's largest city and has a population of more than 3 million, Madrid is surprisingly easy to cycle into, and it's a wonderful city to visit. Pick up a detailed Madrid street map in Toledo before you leave—it'll help make your arrival in the Spanish capital go more smoothly.

Leave **Toledo** via the **Bisagra Gate** and join **Road N401** for **Madrid.** We pedaled this main road the entire way, finding the steady traffic annoying but endurable and utilizing the wide shoulder and smooth surface to make excellent time. However, there are several good options for secondary routes if you're inclined to seek a more pleasant, if lengthier course to Madrid. Consider swinging east along the Tagus to visit the Royal Palace at **Aranjuez,** if you want to dawdle a bit.

**Road N401** climbs a **long, gradual hill** away from Toledo before entering rolling hill country dotted with farms and small towns. Truck traffic increases as you draw closer to Madrid, and the road gains extra lanes after **Getafe.** Pass a **large park** on the left as you enter Madrid. Continue on the **main road,** angling **right** and crossing the **Manzanares River** before climbing a **hill** deeper into the city.

Arrive at a **busy intersection** and turn **right,** then swing **left** on **Paseo de las Delicias** to climb a gentle hill. Reach the **Atocha train station,** and veer **left** on **Calle de Atocha.** This long boulevard leads into the heart of the city and to the majestic Plaza Mayor and Madrid's municipal **tourist office.** There are a host of affordable rooms in the city, as well as two youth hostels. Finding lodgings should be relatively easy.

Get a tourist map and English-language literature at the information office, and plan to spend a couple of days wearing the rubber off your shoes as you explore Madrid's streets. City life revolves around the Plaza Mayor and the Puerta del Sol, but you'll want to venture west to the Royal Palace (Palácio Real) and east to Retiro Park and the Prado Museum. Madrid's Prado Museum has one of the richest collections of paintings in the world, and it will take you hours to cover the place at anything short of a gallop.

If you're taking a train from Madrid to France or beyond, take your bicycle to Chamartin Station, north of the city center. Pedal the long boulevard that runs north from the Prado to get there. You'll have to send your bicycle a few days in advance, and it's important to remove all baggage, computer wiring, lights, and so forth for safe transport. There's a central train information office at Alcalá 44 where you can check on times and prices. Madrid's international airport is about 14 km northeast of the city at Barajas, if you're catching a plane for home from Spain.

# SUBJECT INDEX

# GEOGRAPHICAL INDEX

The MOUNTAINEERS, founded in 1906, is a non-profit outdoor activity and conservation club, whose mission is "to explore, study, preserve and enjoy the natural beauty of the outdoors..." Based in Seattle, Washington, the club is now the third largest such organization in the United States, with 12,000 members and four branches throughout Washington State.

The Mountaineers sponsors both classes and year-round outdoor activities in the Pacific Northwest, which include hiking, mountain climbing, ski-touring, snowshoeing, bicycling, camping, kayaking and canoeing, nature study, sailing, and adventure travel. The club's conservation division supports environmental causes through educational activities, sponsoring legislation, and presenting informational programs. All club activities are led by skilled, experienced volunteers, who are dedicated to promoting safe and responsible enjoyment and preservation of the outdoors.

The Mountaineers Books, an active, non-profit publishing program of the club, produces guidebooks, instructional texts, historical works, natural history guides, and works on environmental conservation. All books produced by The Mountaineers are aimed at fulfilling the club's mission.

If you would like to participate in these organized outdoor activities or the club's programs, consider a membership in The Mountaineers. For information and an application, write or call The Mountaineers, Club Headquarters, 300 Third Avenue West, Seattle, Washington 98119; (206) 284-6310.

*Send or call for our catalog of over 200 outdoor books:*
*The Mountaineers Books*
*1011 SW Klickitat Way, Suite 107*
*Seattle, WA 98134*
*1-800-553-4453*